ALSO BY LISA WELLS

The Fix

BELIEVERS

LISA WELLS

BELIEVERS

MAKING A LIFE

AT THE

END

OF THE WORLD

FARRAR, STRAUS AND GIROUX NEW YORK

Farrar, Straus and Giroux
120 Broadway, New York 10271

Title page photograph by Kardash / Shutterstock.com.

Owing to limitations of space, all acknowledgments for permission to
reprint previously published material can be found on pages 335–336.

Library of Congress Cataloging-in-Publication Data
Names: Wells, Lisa, 1982– author.
Title: Believers : making a life at the end of the world / Lisa Wells.
Description: First edition. | New York : Farrar, Straus and Giroux,
    2021. | Includes bibliographical references and index.
Identifiers: LCCN 2021006856 | ISBN 9780374110253 (hardcover)
Subjects: LCSH: Human ecology. | LCGFT: Essays.
Classification: LCC PS3623.E4755 B45 2021 | DDC 814/.6—dc23
LC record available at https://lccn.loc.gov/2021006856

Designed by Abby Kagan

Our books may be purchased in bulk for promotional, educational, or
business use. Please contact your local bookseller or the Macmillan
Corporate and Premium Sales Department at 1-800-221-7945, extension
5442, or by email at MacmillanSpecialMarkets@macmillan.com.

www.fsgbooks.com
www.twitter.com/fsgbooks • www.facebook.com/fsgbooks

1   3   5   7   9   10   8   6   4   2

FOR JMW, WHO BELIEVED

Before I received my calling, she said, I used to be a lot like you. I felt trapped. It was like I lived in a dark little corner of my own mind. She sighed. Ignatius, do you know what the opposite of love is?

Hate, I said.

Despair, Sister said. Despair is the opposite of love.

—CHARLES D'AMBROSIO, "The High Divide"

CONTENTS

BELIEVERS

This book began in a place called Sparta, a rug-ged swath of sparsely populated country near the Oregon-Idaho border. There I spent several days in the temporary encampment of a group of nomadic garden-ers, led by a woman named Finisia Medrano. For more than thirty years, Finisia had lived off the grid, trespassing her way through private and public lands, planting wildflowers with edible roots, and attracting the ire of the keepers of order. Finisia is trans, and she'd lived as an itinerant, self-anointed minister for a number of those years, preaching to flocks she described as "gay-hating" rural conservatives, and proclaiming her apocalyptic gospel to all who crossed her path. Those of us living in civilization were cast as "whores of Babylon" or "motherfuckers," because we rape Mother Earth with our industrial plows. Our Babylon would soon collapse, and Finisia was planting seeds for the world that would be born from its rubble. Suffice to say, it was an en-lightening few days.

I'd long been familiar with certain elements of the story Finisia was telling, mainly the notion that our civilization—characterized by a dependence on agriculture, colonization, and the building of permanent settlements—is inherently hierarchical, unsustainable, and doomed to collapse. In the mid-1990s, when I was a sophomore in high school, I read a couple of books that converted me to a version of this story and in response became a sort of secular teenage evangelist. I dropped out of school along with three of my closest friends. Together we enrolled in a wilderness survival program through which we hoped to acquire the skills necessary to form egalitarian villages on the post-apocalyptic frontier. Ideally, we'd spread the word and save the world. Barring that, we'd save ourselves.

In 2014, when I visited Sparta, it appeared the promised apocalypse was no longer an abstract future event but well under way. Biologists warned of a sixth mass extinction; dozens of species were going extinct every day, some of whom we'd never seen and now would never know. A massive hole opened in the earth that summer in Siberia, on a peninsula called Yamal, translated as "the end of the world," a name that took on special significance when scientists theorized the chasm was produced not by a meteor (or by extraterrestrials, as some internet sleuths believed), but by methane gas exploding out of thawing permafrost. Articles described nightmare climate change scenarios in which massive amounts of carbon and methane, previously trapped in the earth and ice, would surface. These releases could set off a warming feedback loop, thawing greater swaths of the Arctic, releasing greater amounts of carbon dioxide and methane and so on, superheating the atmosphere, until life on earth as we knew it was extinguished. If we managed to phase out fossil fuels in the near future, this "methane bomb" scenario could be avoided, but as one researcher put it, "There's a chance that some of these really big ecosystem feedbacks will take the fate of the climate out of our hands."[1]

Images of the Siberian chasm were disturbing and starkly beautiful. In some photos it appeared as if an oculus were punched in space-time, revealing an inky abyss devoid of stars—it seemed to encapsulate the anxiety so many of us were feeling: a fathomless hole torn into all that was supposed to be solid and immutable. Whether or not the "methane bomb" threat was imminent or overblown was a matter of debate, but the threat of reaching a point of no return was categorical. That point of no return is not the primary subject of this book, but it is the backdrop, the central prophecy.

Around a million plant and animal species are currently threatened with extinction.[2] There's more carbon dioxide in the atmosphere today than at any other point in human history.[3] The threats we face are overwhelming, way beyond the scope of our powers as individuals, or even as individual nations—and yet, as individuals, we must bear the grief of all that we know. This knowledge exacts a toll. A 2017 report by the American Psychological Association noted that "changes in climate can . . . surface a number of different emotions, including fear, anger, feelings of powerlessness, or exhaustion," and that "some people are deeply affected by feelings of loss, helplessness, and frustration due to their inability to feel like they are making a difference in stopping climate change." Others describe an "unrelenting day-by-day despair" and guilt in contemplating "the impact of their own behavior on future generations."[4]

We take it for granted that contemplation of climate change is happening on a scale large enough to merit a psychological study, but twenty-five years ago most people I knew hadn't given the issue much thought. Plenty of people were concerned about pollution and diminishing biodiversity, but those concerns weren't exactly mainstream. For those who were concerned, "global warming" was mostly an abstraction, an ascending line on a PowerPoint slide. One anxious afternoon in my sixteenth year, a fellow barista urged me not to worry: "If the ice caps melt, we'll just farm on Antarctica." Magical thinking of this sort still persists in some quarters, but at least it's migrating to the fringe.

These days, terms like "climate change" and "sixth mass extinction" are common, at home in most of our mouths. Recent years have seen a surge in films, popular-science books, and speculative fiction on climate change. There's discussion in the dominant culture about coordinated large-scale interventions, everything from a Green New Deal in the United States, to burying hundreds of gigatons of carbon underground, to planting two billion acres of trees. This increased awareness is undoubtedly progress, though toward what end remains unclear. A 2019 United Nations report on the subject of diminishing biodiversity noted: "Gains from societal and policy responses, while important, have not stopped massive losses."[5]

My friends and I didn't wind up saving the world, as you've no doubt noticed. Our idealism was slowly overwhelmed by feelings of fear, anger, powerlessness, and exhaustion. In time, I began to doubt my individual capacity for effecting even the most minor change. I drifted into adulthood and into this strange modern-day condition: that of an average, well-meaning person who daily participates—however grudgingly—in a system that is bringing the planet she loves to the brink of destruction.

My problem wasn't apathy: I didn't stop caring about life on earth; I just couldn't envision a plausible future, let alone what I might do to help it be born. One world was ending, but I had no image for what would come next, and the longer I knelt on the lip of that abyss looking in, the deeper and more cryptic its darkness.

One of the ways we humans organize and make sense of our experience is through the telling of stories. And the stories we tell, in turn, have profound effects on how we relate to ourselves and to those entities on which our lives depend. Many of us are learning that the stories we inherited are not only suspect but in large part responsible for the threats we now face and will visit upon our heirs: the story of infinite growth, of survival of the fittest; the story of human supremacy, and, incongruously, an innate human selfishness and propensity to destroy. Chiefly, the story that tells us that we are separate from the whole, at once alienated from the broader community of life and above its laws of ecological reciprocity.

New stories are in order, but often the dominant culture responds to the crises at hand by replicating old themes. Features about doomsday preppers, Silicon Valley tech bros with "go bags" and ATVs, million-dollar compounds in decommissioned missile silos in central Oklahoma (my particular vision of hell)—stories about life-support systems devised to keep self-interested individuals alive while the rest of us burn. Stories that are, of course, no deviation at all from the dominant narrative. Perhaps the fullest expression of this lack of imagination is the techno-utopian dream of colonizing other galaxies, as if colonization weren't at the root of our trouble but its solution: the ultimate geographic cure. Even if some eccentric but benevolent billionaire invented a machine to spirit the human race to outer space (big if), it's delusional to think we wouldn't take our problems with us.

It seems to me there is a surplus of terror and delusion in the ether, but spare few visions of how you and I, relatively ordinary people, might live otherwise. I believe the future of the world depends on those visions. If our descendants are alive and well in a hundred years, it will not be because we exported our unexamined lives to another planet; it will be because we were, in this era, able to articulate visions of life on earth that did not result in their destruction.

Ecologists have a term for species that first populate a landscape after a disaster. The term is "ruderal"; it comes from the Latin word *rudera*, translated to English as "rubble." I'm fond of the idea of being "of Rubble," the way those of high birth are "of Savoy" or "of Windsor." I like how "rubble" echoes "rabble," the disorderly mob of the ordinary. Indeed, ruderal species are known for rampancy, disparaged by some as ugly, or as weeds or invaders to be battled and subdued, though many perform critical functions like creating habitat, nourishing pollinators, and converting nitrogen to fertilize soil. The disasters that precede them could be natural or man-made—unlike us, ruderal species don't make the distinction. Ruderal plants can be native or foreign; they're defined not by where they're from, but by where they root and what they do. Some of the most virulently maligned weeds and invasives thrive in degraded landscapes, filtering heavy metals and industrial toxins, rendering harmful materials inert. Eventually, the plants die back, fertilizing the earth for the species that will succeed them.

I've become attached to this term "ruderal," and to the

idea of a ruderal legacy. Formerly, my idea of sustainability had been vague and of the leave-no-trace variety. But the story I heard in Sparta, and would continue to hear as I interviewed people for this book, was a revelation: ways of life are possible in which human beings not only thrive but also repair damage and even *increase* the biodiversity and beauty of the planet. It is a story predicated on leaving a trace, a legacy.

Finisia Medrano once said something that continues to ring in my ears: "I sit at a threshold." The threshold is neither the Babylon she was born to nor the gardens she dreams of. It is a territory between.

This book is a pilgrimage into that territory. It proceeds from a basic and, in many ways, impossible question: The world is burning; how, then, shall we live? It collects the stories of relatively ordinary people who came to believe that their inherited way of life was destructive and so pursued a different way, each by their own methods and according to their own beliefs. Like Finisia, many of them tell a story that begins in an Edenic "time before" and pivots on future cataclysm—events some optimists call "the great change"—but crucially, their stories don't end there.

One story is about a group of environmentalist Christians and their effort to live in cooperative communities while practicing "watershed discipleship." Another is about restoration radicals attempting to reverse desertification in former cradles of civilization around the world. In California, a North Fork Mono elder is using Traditional Ecological Knowledge to combat drought, prevent catastrophic wildfires, and repair ecosystems. An expert man-tracker known as "the Portuguese Sherlock Holmes" has devoted his life to passing on the skills future generations will need to learn the language of the land. One story is about my friend Peter and his alter ego, the Urban Scout, the protagonist in a divisive piece of performance art conceived to warn the public about the ills of industrial civilization. My story appears among theirs: a story about idealism, how it's lost, and what might take root in its absence, beyond cynicism or despair.

All my life I've been drawn to the difficult, wounded, and passionate outcasts among us, and you'll notice that demographic represented in these pages. Most of these folks have no formal training, very little funding, or much of an institutional shelter; they are people with addictions, traumas, stains on their consciences—ordinary mortals like me. The courage to step outside the dominant narrative and imagine a different way to live is what makes these mere mortals extraordinary. They are all ardent believers, though their belief systems and approaches to the problem differ. I suspect it's that belief—or, rather, the sense of purpose and narrative meaning that belief supplies—that emboldens them to act where many of us only point our fingers or wring our hands. Which is not to imply that having a vision precludes distortions, blind spots, or flaws. On the contrary, it virtually ensures them.

These are not stories of perfect approaches or uncomplicated virtue. They include all the petty obstacles, all the mess of human relationship. Nor are they meant to be representative of all that's being done to redress the complex social and environmental threats we face. If anything, they remind us that there is no single solution to the problems we face. Restoration has to happen on every level—ecological, cultural, interpersonal, psychological—however imperfect the execution. And while it's crucial to explore large-scale interventions while we still have the infrastructure to do so, I'll not be focusing on that scale here. You could say this book is interested in the level of the ruderal. It begins in collapse and ends in a garden, but its true subject is the territory between, the novel forms of life already springing up in the rubble.

We stand at a threshold. Extreme weather arrives every season; the coldest winters, the hottest summers, the longest droughts, the strongest hurricanes on record. Pandemics and famines and mass migrations. Wildfires haze the skies for days, occluding the sun and stars. The passage is dark, but our struggle to find the light isn't evidence of its absence. Another world is coming, one we can't yet see. This threshold asks that we imagine it anyway. It asks us to reconsider the purpose of our lives. What legacy will we choose to leave behind? What is a story worth living into?

I

—

ACROSS THE DESERT OUR BREAD IS BLOOMING!

I want to argue a paradox that the myth asserts: that the
origins, liveliness, and durability of cultures require that
there be space for figures whose function is to uncover and
disrupt the very things that cultures are based on. I hope
to give some sense of how this can be, how social life can
depend on treating antisocial characters as part of the sacred.
—LEWIS HYDE, *Trickster Makes This World*

But to live outside the law, you must be honest.
—BOB DYLAN

This is a story about an itinerant outlaw and her love
affair with creation. Specifically, her love affair with
a panoply of edible wildflowers belonging to the genera *Lomatium*, *Lewisia*, *Perideridia*, and *Camassia*. The
outlaw's name is Finisia Medrano. As a kid, witnessing the
destruction of the earth, she resolved to "go the other way"
and to "be all the world's outcast" if that's what it took to
fulfill her "obligation to God and the truth."

The truth, according to Finisia, was simple: our purpose on earth is to tend and keep the garden of God's
original planting. For centuries, earth-based cultures the
world over realized this purpose by cultivating more biodiversity than they harvested. And though she'd fallen in

love with the radical Jesus of the Bible many years before, this ethic—the ethic of sowing more life than you reap, of "planting back"—informed her worldview more than any other. She dreamed of many thousands of people returning to that way of life, all across the world, replanting the garden.

According to tribal historians and elders, ethnobiologists, and early settler accounts, edible gardens once blanketed the western United States, providing sustenance and freedom of movement to those who tended them. In the Great Basin, many of those gardens consisted of flowering tuber plants: camas and sego lilies, biscuitroot, bitterroot, yampahs. A hundred and fifty years of colonist ranching and farming destroyed most of the roots in the valleys, but throughout the basin were stony plateaus, unsuitable for grazing or plowing, and in those "abandonments" the roots survived.

For more than thirty years, Finisia Medrano traveled by foot, horse, and covered wagon through the backcountry of the United States in search of those abandonments, basing her moves on the seasonal availability of food, replanting as she traveled. Mostly she lived alone, but in her later years she sometimes traveled with a group of young queer folks whom she'd dubbed "the Prairie Faeries," in a caravan that included half-broke horses and a covered wagon painted with the slogan *Pulling for Wildflowers*.

I first heard about Finisia and the Prairie Faeries from my oldest friend, Peter Bauer. Peter was one of the three friends with whom I attended a wilderness survival school in rural Washington State in the late '90s. He'd continued to practice "ancestral skills" in the almost twenty-year interim, basic life skills his Celtic ancestors would have mastered in childhood—stuff like skinning and butchering animals, weaving baskets, and building natural shelters—and over those years he'd become acquainted with a number of unconventional characters living off the grid. He'd gone out to visit one of Finisia's camps and returned a convert. Not to Jesus, but to Finisia's land-tending philosophy.

I asked whether he might see her again and, if he did, could I come along?

It took six hours to travel from Portland to Sparta. Peter drove, I sat shotgun, and Peter's friend Jesse was crammed in the back seat with the gear. In my window, I watched the dense green of the Pacific Northwest rain forest gradually give way to farmland, then foothills, and finally to the high desert sage of northeastern Oregon: a semiarid country with big skies bounded by white-capped mountain ranges. In a few days, Finisia's crew would pack up their camp and ride off into Hells Canyon, and Jesse was going with them. Their pilgrimage would last forty-two days.

"Like Jesus," I said.

"Jesus wandered the desert for *forty* days," Jesse corrected. Finisia required a couple more.

Jesse, who uses gender-neutral pronouns, was in their early twenties and learned about Finisia and the Prairie Faeries the same way I did: first through Peter, then through Finisia's Facebook profile. In a previous season, Jesse and a friend had traveled out to one of her camps for the weekend "embarrassingly underprepared" in terms of gear. She'd lent them some silverware for digging. Finisia was "pretty attached to her silverware," Jesse told me; apparently she needed "just a few fancy items" in order to live "like a queen on horseback." Later in the weekend her wolf dog killed a fawn, and they butchered and ate it. It was a memorable trip. "The whole experience hooked me," Jesse said. "I knew I wanted to return."

It was hard earth in Baker County. The thaw hadn't yet come on, and I was feeling well excavated. Like a lot of people, I'd managed to live as though key aspects of my experience were separate: my physical health, my relationships, how I made my living, my emotional and mental stability, the news of the world. But there had been creep among the categories in recent months, and I was having trouble keeping them sorted. All that winter, I'd been experiencing spells of shitty health: unexplained fatigue, itchy skin, rolling panic, stabbing stomach pains. I'd been to doctors; none could land on a diagnosis. And though my symptoms felt real enough, neither the doctors nor I could tell if the source was in my body or in my mind. Such was my condition on arriving in Sparta in early 2014. I felt minced, tentative. I hugged my own arms and spoke from the neck, like a person recently choked.

Camping out in an unfamiliar place was a welcome distraction, and I looked forward to meeting the Prairie Faeries and to taking part in what I imagined would be a carnival of jubilant pagan nudism. But more than that, I was hoping to be reacquainted with an old part of myself, a more solid and vital part: the part that believed my life could serve a purpose greater than individual achievement in the marketplace.

We pulled into camp at dusk. In the far distance, the Wallowa Mountains reflected the last canted light, but the earth between was flat as a page, barren miles of dirt and scrub weed; no Prairie Faeries in sight, no covered wagon. A single tepee broke the line of the open range. Excepting a few horses, the camp looked to be vacant. Finisia appeared in the gravel road alone.

I'd seen photos, so I sort of knew what to expect, but Finisia's clothing was nonetheless impressive. She wore heavy, ankle-length skirts and a beaded leather tunic. Her skin was leathered. There were locks of hair (human hair, I'd later learn, cut from many different heads) sewn onto her tunic like fringe, and there were a dozen braids, cut from Finisia's own head, stitched into her hatband. The effect, in the glow of the magic hour, was at once regal and macabre—an otherworldly queen in an elaborate gown of hair and skin.

Two members of her crew were smoking cigarettes in the grainy dim of the tepee. Michael and Kelsey, or "the kids" as Finisia called them. They were both slender and blond, their skin unblemished and milky beneath the layer of dirt. I guessed they couldn't be any older than Jesse, maybe twenty-two. Kelsey, the young woman, wore an ankle-length skirt and handmade leather vest. The young man, Michael, had a bushy beard and chin-length hair and was bent intently with a pocketknife over a craft in the corner. Neither of them spoke.

We threw our sleeping bags off to the side and joined their

circle around an old woodstove. Empty tin cans, sauce bottles, and dirty dishes were strewn nearby. Jesse later told me that before moving to Sparta, the kids had been living on the streets of Spokane, a long-depressed former mining and mill city in eastern Washington, of which the writer Jess Walter once remarked: "On any given day in Spokane, Washington, there are more adult men per capita riding children's BMX bikes than in any other city in the world."

Despite being homeless, the kids had somehow managed full-time work and saved enough money to gear up for the season. Boots, horse feed, a full-tang blade—in the final tally, achieving freedom isn't all that cheap.

The drama in camp that evening was the abrupt departure of a group member, one of Finisia's longtime devotees, a boy I'll call Kevin. He'd packed up and left camp after a disagreement a few days earlier, but not before infecting everyone with a cold.

"His parting gift," Finisia scoffed.

They all lit cigarettes and Michael finally spoke. He told us that Kevin premeditated his departure, probably back in October, but chose to pass the winter in their camp, feeding his horses on the hay they'd scrimped to buy.

To complicate matters, they'd been receiving phone calls from journalists and TV people since some photos of the Prairie Faeries were posted on *Vice*'s website the month before. Someone, a producer, maybe, was supposed to come out in a few weeks and shoot a pilot for a reality show, and now they'd lost a cast member. Not that they were champing at the bit of fame.

"We're not signing with anyone," Finisia said. "They can go talk to Kevin."

Both Finisia and Michael had cell phones that they kept

charged with a small solar panel, and they were able to keep up with Kevin's movements on "Facefuck." Michael read Kevin's latest status update aloud to the group: "Riding out, on my way back to my old cabin to do some spring work for Cain. I'm willing to give to Caesar a little of what is Caesar's so I can get by the rest of the year giving to God what is God's."

Biblical allegory formed the basis of their shared vernacular. Caesar was invoked as the prototypical dictator, enslaver, and destroyer of Gallic tribes. Cain, the crop farmer, represented agriculturalists, a people who rape the mother with a plow. Abel, the pastoralist, whom Cain killed and God loved, represented nomadic hunter-gatherer-gardeners. Thus, those of us who took from the earth without planting back (i.e., those living in the empire) were referred to, variously, as "children of Cain," "whores of Babylon," or simply "motherfuckers."

Finisia's crew, on the other hand, called themselves "Landtenders," "Hoopsters," or "Terraists." A favorite Terraist activity was planting a kind of hillside graffiti in flowering tubers. One recent tag read THIS IS FOOD in ten-foot letters. It would take three years to blossom.

Kevin's Facebook page indicated that he would be leading his own pilgrimage that spring with three other people, and I sensed morale had been damaged by this slight. An angry sadness seeped into the darkening cone.

"Everyone wants to come out here and steal a piece of me," Finisia said. "Then they leave and I never see them again." She turned her attention on me. In the faint glow of the woodstove, her expression was grave. "I fucking hate you people."

She took a drag on her cigarette. The ember expanded and I felt the oxygen leach from the air.

"I don't love a motherfucker," she drawled, spilling her smoke. "I'm not doing this thing out of love. I'm doing it to get revenge."

Finisia's backstory is stranger than you might imagine, Homeric in scope, and impossible to corroborate. Most of the minor players were highway phantoms, and many of the key figures are dead.

Here's how she told it: She was born in California in 1956 and halfway raised in Las Vegas. Her father was a member of the radical right of his day, a John Bircher survivalist. He fled Las Vegas in the mid-1960s to escape the communist takeover he feared was already underway, moving his family to the Coeur d'Alene Reservation in Idaho, where Finisia's stepmother had family. Her father taught her basic survival skills and how to shoot a gun. They were formative days. She was twelve, going on thirteen, and it was around that time that an older boy began climbing in her bed, night after night, to abuse her. She calls him "Roy d'Raper."

She started using drugs and getting in trouble with the law. Her father fostered her out. And in the midst of it all, she felt increasingly confused about her gender. "I thought my insides and outsides ought to match up," she later wrote, "they just didn't."[1] Finisia's father was an atheist, but she tried out praying to the Christian God: "I asked Him to change me, inside or outside, I didn't care. Just match me up again."

But God didn't answer. A few years later, she left her father's house for good and hitchhiked west. Her hair grew long. Early on in her travels, she was picked up by a squirrelly guy who asked if she was a girl. She hedged, told him no. "Now you're in trouble," he said. "You're too pretty not to fuck." The man raped her.

She washed up on the Southern California coast in the mid-1970s, on Pirate's Cove, a nudie beach in Malibu. There she dug a cave into a sheer cliff, twenty feet above the sand, using nothing but a three-pound slap hammer and her bare hands and feet. After a day of digging, she'd scramble down and eat seaweed and mussels off the rocks. The cave was three car lengths deep by the time she finished, and upholstered with soft rugs, like "a great big pussy." Hippies and beach bums moved into the cave, and soon a little LSD-loving cult assembled around her. Naked bodies piled, slumbering on the rugs. Finisia told everyone she'd been born from the cave, a child of the earth and sea.

Many of these details come from Finisia's book *Growing Up in Occupied America*, a collection of allegorical personal stories, poems, and open letters of protest, written in an eccentric patois of high-biblical rhetoric and colloquial vulgarity (e.g., "God made my ass a javelin mitt so he could play catch with His sons of Cain"). It was assembled and published in 2010 by one of the Prairie Faeries who'd traveled with Finisia, a Landtender named Seda.

Growing Up in Occupied America includes pretty much every swearword and offensive epithet you can imagine—most frequently those hurled at gay and trans people, slurs no doubt thrown at Finisia at an early age, reprocessed through her idiosyncratic cosmology, and then thrown back at the reader, whom she convicts of every mortal sin by book's end, toggling between raw rage and elegy.

Chapter 2, titled "Fuck you," opens with the line "Just because you can't stand to be seen, doesn't mean it's my business to go blind!" Chapter 3, "Fuck me," turns the interrogator's lamp inward: "I fear I have taken the mark and image of the beast, condemning my soul to hell to bring you this message. I speak as one descending, not ascending."

The book includes photos taken at Pirate's Cove before Finisia's transition, a nineteen-year-old kid with a surfer's mop of sun-streaked hair. That was the kid who met Max Miller, a wealthy, much older man (born in 1910—"You do the math," she tells us). Max was "a social engineer" who "had interesting pictures of himself with presidents." He helped her financially with her transition in 1976. She said she selected the name Finisia because it means "the end," and long before the word "Anthropocene" existed, she knew she was living in it.

After two years in the cave, she packed up and moved in with Max full-time. They were married in the "tawdry" living room of a discount minister who'd strung paper bells above the television set.

Otherwise, she doesn't say much about the years of her marriage. She took some classes at Pierce College in the San Fernando Valley, tended to Max's pet macaw, grew pot and opium flowers in his yard, and more or less settled into domestic bliss. But like many young brides, she hadn't quite solidified and her world was about to be upended. She'd been smoking close to two packs of Kools a day and was coughing up gunk. A friend turned her on to a twelve-step program to help her quit, but she struggled with the second step, the one that requires relinquishing one's will to a higher power. Hoping to discover if she believed in God once and for all, she grabbed a sleeping bag and a borrowed Bible and went into the Santa Monica Mountains on a kind of impromptu monastic retreat.

On the third day, the tobacco "spell" was broken, and she was given a vision of the twelve Apostles. "I heard a voice," she wrote. "Whether in my head or in my ear I could not tell. The voice asked me, 'Who would I send?'"

She fell weeping to the ground and answered: "Send me!"

Like Finisia's father, Max Miller was an atheist, and upon hearing of this conversion he gave her an ultimatum: it was him or Yashua. But she'd already fallen in love with the Living Bread. She signed his divorce papers and, at twenty-seven, left their house with nothing but the clothes on her back. She walked out of Los Angeles in a baggy shirt, with her hair tucked up under a hat, because being a girl on the road was dangerous. After all that "work to be a woman," she wrote, she walked with Christ "in drag as a man."

That first night in Sparta, high winds whipped up through the basin, snapping the canvas against the poles. Finisia didn't love a motherfucker, and she frequently reminded us of the fact. I woke a dozen times in the night, wired with each snap, fearing she'd cut my gluttonous throat in my sleep.

Around seven, I was jarred awake by her hand palming my face and a falsetto coo. "Are you sweeeeeping?"

She made coffee for everyone in a metal press, suddenly cheerful, nearly a different person from the one who'd professed to hate our guts the night before.

The Landtenders had planted a small experimental garden about a klick from camp some weeks before, and Finisia asked Michael to take us out to see it. It was a postcard high-desert morning, clear blue and frigid. We trailed Michael into the range, wending through sagebrush and combat-crawling under wire fences, until we'd crossed onto private property. Or maybe it belonged to the Bureau of Land Management (BLM); I couldn't really tell the difference. BLM land often abuts private ranchland or national forest in the West, but it all looked the same to me: a scrubby sea of sage and cheatgrass. I scanned the ground for signs of life, for any of the wildflowers they cultivated, but didn't see anything.

Eventually, we came on a flat expanse with twenty or so circles of disturbed soil, each about two feet in diameter. A few tiny sprays of ferny leaves dotted the ground. These were biscuitroot, Michael told us, or biscuit-cous, a species of the genus *Lomatium*. In the spring, *Lomatium cous* is identified by lacy clusters of bright yellow flowers and parsley-like leaves. Underground, their tuberous taproots assume a variety of shapes. Some grow as fat and stubby as radishes; others grow in slender fingers like their carrot cousins. They can grow short or stringy or as big as sweet potatoes. Depending on how they're prepared, their flavor is compared to that of parsnips, spicy carrots, or stale biscuits.

Each root species has its own harvest protocol, but in general the Landtenders loosened the soil surrounding the plant with a digging rod, harvesting the larger tubers, then dropping the seeds and smaller root segments back into the freshly aerated earth—replanting as they harvested. Finisia called this practice "the reach-around," named for the sex act in which one lover "reaches around" to manually stimulate the partner they are penetrating—an act perhaps better summarized in this context as "reciprocal care."

In an addendum to *Growing Up in Occupied America*,

Finisia's former student Seda gives a simple definition: "The reach-around is a way to give life back to that which gives you life."[2] But there's more nuance to the process than simply dropping seeds in the dirt. Successful planting-back requires intimate knowledge of the plants and a good sense of timing. One must first learn what helps a particular plant to grow and thrive. Seda gives examples: "When gathering roots, wait until the seeds have ripened so they can fall into the cracks you make. When you gather and eat berries, remember to defecate the seeds in places where they will grow."

Finisia frames the approach more poetically: "The lomatium and lily would be in their joy. They would be full of seed when we dug . . . If one eats berries, and plants those seeds back in one's defecations, then that planting is occurring. If one collects the seeds of the plants one eats, and plants them back, then that one is working to make things more abundant."

The genus *Lomatium* is a member of the family Apiaceae, also known as the Umbelliferae—so named for their umbrella-like umbels. The flower clusters are described as little parasols, or as a circular spray resembling a spoked wheel.[3] But to my eye their displays are far less mannered: they look more like exploded fireworks or like textbook illustrations of complex molecules. Either way, it's a big family under that umbrella, including many members of a common spice cabinet: anise, caraway, coriander, cumin, dill, fennel. And though in the company of such ubiquitous and indispensable relatives *Lomatium* tends to get short shrift, it is a truly miraculous genus. Taken together, its more than eighty species form a kind of nutritional and medicinal panacea. Indigenous nations of the Northwest have used *Lomatium* species as antivirals, analgesics, and expectorants to treat asthma, colds, and other respiratory issues. The seeds of *Lomatium nudicaule* have been used to treat a number of ailments, including headaches, itchiness, and colds.[4] Seeds could be mashed into poultices and applied for stomachache and carbuncles, sucked to soothe a sore throat, eaten as a laxative, or made into an infusion for pregnant women "to ensure easy delivery."[5] James Selam, a John Day River elder and author, remembered that fishermen would mash a handful of *Lomatium dissectum* inside a sack and set it in a slow-moving part of a stream. The fish would become temporarily unconscious, as if "drunk" or "knocked out," and float to the surface, where the larger fish would be harvested.[6]

In the early 1920s, Ernst T. Krebs, a notorious physician-cum-snake-oil salesman, tried to capitalize on *Lomatium* in the wake of the 1918 flu pandemic by peddling a miracle remedy on the streets of San Francisco. His Syrup Leptinol, distilled from *Lomatium dissectum*, was purported to combat bronchitis and influenza, and to be "five times as efficacious as any other treatment in pneumonia." Krebs told customers there had not been a single death among the Washoe People from the flu pandemic or its pneumonia complications thanks to the miracle herb.

The U.S. Food and Drug Administration (FDA) wound up seizing Krebs's product in 1922, finding his claims fraudulent, with the potential to cause more harm than good—a common enough outcome when con artists appropriate Indigenous medicine. And if we look at his recipe, it's no wonder. According to Krebs's testimony in the FDA's investigation, here's how the concoction was prepared:

The alcoholic extract 'Leptinol' is glycerinated in a machine, using one part of the alcoholic concentration to

four parts glycerin. This is then added to eleven parts of a
heavy syrup, containing 7½ pounds of sugar to the gallon
of syrup, and thoroughly mixed in an agitating machine.[7]

Surely consuming what amounted to liquid treacle wouldn't
kill people suffering from the flu, but neither would it cure
them.

To this day, tinctures of *Lomatium dissectum* are adver-
tised to treat everything from hepatitis to the human papilloma
virus (HPV) to the Epstein-Barr virus—many of their sellers recycling old tropes of frontier doctors stumbling on miracle "Indian cures." This is not to detract from the real healing power
of *Lomatium*, only to underscore a broader problem, one that
would-be herbalists, like some who came out to Finisia's camp,
often fall prey to: the problem of outsiders extracting resources
from the land while giving nothing back and imposing a romantic story on a way of life they do not understand.

The *Lomatium cous* plants that Michael showed us were not
yet "in their joy" and were far too tiny to give us a sense of
their full potential. Even so, they gifted me a sort of second
sight. I had a case of what the mushroom hunters call the
now-you-see-'ems: where once there was only dirt, my eyes
found new life and color.

Michael called us over to a rocky mound, and we stooped
to check out a little green plant with glossy tendrils that sort
of looked like a sea anemone. It was bitterroot, an ancient
staple of the Great Basin and the state flower of Montana.
This particular bitterroot was prime for harvest, before the
emergence of the broad, lotus-like bloom, for which it was
nicknamed "rock rose."

Bitterroot was given the Latin name *Lewisia rediviva* after Meriwether Lewis, who "discovered" the plant in the late summer of 1805, in territory now known as Lemhi County, Idaho. In truth, Lewis discovered nothing— western tribes were intimately connected with bitterroot for millennia—but he did document quite a few plants. Lewis dried and pressed several bitterroot specimens and sent them back to Philadelphia—more than two thousand miles by horse, boat, and stagecoach. They were inherited by a young German-born botanist named Frederick Pursh, who planted them. Much to Pursh's astonishment, the specimens, which had appeared lifeless for more than a year, bloomed. Thus the plant earned its second name, *rediviva*, a Latin word meaning "brought back to life." Indeed, all of the species Finisia loved possessed powers of resurrection. They are extremely hardy and drought resistant, sometimes sleeping through several growth cycles in wait of favorable conditions.

The roots are survivors, but in order to thrive they rely on low-level soil disturbances. Digging around a root recycles nutrients, aerates the earth, increases its moisture-holding ability, and creates better growing conditions for seeds.[8] Some of the Landtenders said these plants evolved symbiotically with humans, that they needed human hands to proliferate. In this light, so-called wildflowers were not wild at all, but members of a cocultivating relationship between plants and human beings that deepened over the course of millennia. Others suggested that the first symbiotic relationship developed between the root foods and the megafauna of the late Pleistocene, when giant ground sloths may have subsisted on starchy bulbs and corms, violently rooting them out of the earth.[9]

This rooting is one theory for the existence of bulblets and cormlets, the little rice-grain-sized bulbs and corms that adhere to the base of their "parent." These bulblets detach only when the parent bulb is unearthed, falling into the fresh till, where they live to see another day. As with people, the growth of cormlets and bulblets is limited so long as they're attached to their parent, but once they individuate they're able to reach maturation. After megafauna populations dwindled, humans, grizzly bears, and other species who eat roots filled this ecological niche.

Any species that survives a shift-change in epoch must possess an adaptive genius, but no matter their admirable self-sufficiency, the root foods don't live in a vacuum any more than the rest of us do. They require disturbed soil to flourish, just as blackberries flourish when they are scarred by digestive enzymes and planted in the nifty self-fertilizing seed package animals deliver to the earth in their excrement. This world of interrelationships is a far cry from the conservationist credo that begs us to "leave no trace."

In an online audio presentation for Gaya University, Seda described this interaction between humans and plants, noting that some of the most prolific populations of edible roots exist on roadsides, or in campgrounds where people are sleeping right on top of them. "The people in these campgrounds don't know or care, but the ground is just thick with food," he observed. "In the roadless areas they're far more scattered. I've come to think these plants want to be touched by people. Even if it's a neglectful relationship, they keep showing up."

Another writer who has noted this irony is Tao Orion. Orion is an expert in the field of permaculture, a portmanteau of "permanent" and "agriculture," whose practitioners seek to create self-sustaining ecosystems by integrating human activity and nature. Orion used to work in the field of wildland restoration, and she frequently sourced native plants like camas, biscuitroot, and wapato tubers in construction zones, on roadsides, and on the edges of landfills.

The root foods are threshold beings. In fact, the etymological root of *Lomatium*, *loma*, derives from the Greek for "fringe" or "border." Maybe this ability to survive between worlds, this stubborn display of color in harsh conditions, was part of what drew Finisia and the Prairie Faeries to the roots in the first place.

When Finisia walked out of L.A. in 1984, she kept walking for two years, ministering to people she met along the road. Those who picked her up could hardly believe she was real, they told her. It was as if she'd stepped out of a dream.

"I could see plainly, after a year of walking that most of humanity was the living dead," she wrote.

We were alone for a moment in camp when I asked her how she found out about the roots.

"My dad taught me all he knew about how to live as a survivalist," she said. "He taught me the white-man military ways, but I didn't know how to fucking really eat." She prayed to Jesus for guidance. "He said he was a Living Bread, and I said, 'I need some fucking help, man.'"

Soon after this prayer, she was picked up while hitchhiking. The driver listened as she preached, and he decided to take her home with him, to the Fort Hall Reservation of the Shoshone-Bannock, to meet his devoutly Christian grandmother. At Fort Hall, Finisia made some friends who showed her how to dig the roots with a *kup'n*, a digging stick about three feet in length, with a crossbar handle on one end and a hook on the other.

Like the fireboard and the basket, the digging stick is one of those cross-cultural implements found among subsistence-based cultures the world over. In pre-Hispanic Mesoamerica, the Aztecs used fire-hardened digging staffs called *uitzoctli*. Staffs of similar design were used throughout Central and South America. Ethiopia has the *ankassay*, and the Noongar of Australia have the *wanna borna* for harvesting flowering roots and bulbs. The ancient Greeks had the rhizotomists, root-digging herbalists who performed ceremonial dances and spoke to the plants before they harvested them.

The rhizotomists are generally derided in the old botany literature for their tendency to "attribute magical virtues to roots and herbs" and for their "superstitious" gathering practices: "Some plants were to be gathered by night, some by day, some with the body anointed, some while fasting, others while eating garlic and drinking strong wine."[10] The rhizotomists were said to use their digging sticks to draw a circle three times around a plant before uprooting it, a practice resembling other Indo-European pagan rituals. Finisia's book includes an open letter, penned by the Prairie Faeries, asserting that pagan witches were the "Indo-European Natives who walked in beauty and harmony with the earth" and that the symbol of the magic wand had been decoupled from its original purpose as a digging stick, used to plant back herbs and roots in ancient Europe.

In 1909, the American botanist Edward Lee Greene wrote: "The occupation of the root gatherers is by no means peculiar to Greek antiquity. In every part of the world it may be as old as, or older than, the beginnings of civilization.

Nor is it probable that in Europe there was any interruption or cessation of the occupation during the two thousand years intervening between the time of Homer and Hesiod and that of the Renaissance."[11]

In many cultures, the digging stick was crafted from fire-hardened wood, a good tool for tending softer soil. In the Great Basin, after colonization, the valleys had been largely plowed under or "cowed out" and since many of the surviving roots lived on stony plateaus, Finisia used a rod made of titanium. She'd lined her rod with skateboard grip-tape to provide traction for her boot.

"I was asking Jesus to guide me to a Living Bread," she said, "and by God, he did. I ended up right in the middle of it."

A donation from a sympathetic acquaintance arrived in camp, and since no one else had a car, we would drive a couple of the Landtenders twenty miles into Baker City, to the bank, to cash the check, and to the Feed and Seed to pick up some last-minute supplies for their pilgrimage.

Michael stayed behind with the horses while the rest of us crammed into Peter's Toyota Tercel. It was cold outside and the air was thin, but something heavy had settled in the atmosphere. As we sped through open range toward Baker City, the sun was high and white, and the blue of the sky had darkened to cobalt. White-toothed mountains cut sharply against the horizon, but we never appeared to get any closer to them or farther away. I had a strange feeling in my body, like a pre-migraine aura or déjà vu—not dreamlike so much as like climbing out of a deep, stupefying sleep.

Coming into the farmlands on the edge of Baker City, we

passed a field of rusted plows, and Finisia announced, "The machines of wrath!"

No opportunity to critique Babylon was let pass. Baker City's historic Main Street had lately been restored, and as we pulled into town, for some reason I chose to say, "This is cute."

"Yeah," she shot back. "They got it all cuted up for the end of the world."

Finisia went on to say that the town was gutted and that what I'd found so "cute" was actually a facade. It was true that the closer I looked, I could see that, in the windows of many of the restored storefronts, painted murals hung where wares might have been displayed. The businesses were vacant. That's the way it was with Finisia: all things taken to an extreme, and yet at that extreme one was faced with what should have been an obvious truth.

The townies rubbernecked and smiled as the Land-tenders did their business at the bank and the supply store. When they were done, we drove out the other side of town into some hills. Finisia's knees were bothering her, so she stayed behind with the car while the rest of us hiked toward a distant patch of alien green that lay on the hilltop like a cap of AstroTurf. We walked for a while, losing and regaining sight of it. A crude track was dug in the mud by a rogue 4x4, and evidence of a makeshift shooting range—shells, sheets of plastic riddled with holes—lay scattered in the ruts. Cresting the hill, I finally understood what I'd been seeing: the alien green was a sea of camas lilies, not yet in bloom, maybe five hundred square yards of them.

When that sea of lilies blossomed, it would be blue and purple. As I came to the edge of it, their vision became real to me for the first time. Imagine standing between two football fields filled with brilliant blue lilies, knowing that each one contained what Meriwether Lewis called "a nutricious" and "agreeable food," and this was just a tiny fraction of the camas prairie that once blanketed the region. The idea that a human community could sustain itself while increasing ecological abundance and beauty wasn't at all pie-in-the-sky in that moment—it was obvious.

In 1804, when Lewis and Clark moved west across the continent, the gardens of the Great Basin remained largely intact. Because the landscapes they'd left behind in Europe had been so domesticated, successive waves of colonizers viewed North America as a Garden of Eden, with its abundant game, rivers so thick with wild salmon it was tricky to set a boat in the water, and migrating flocks of passenger pigeons—billions strong—that darkened the sky for days. The convenient and deadly misperception of that time, one that many continue to harbor, is that the gardens of North America evolved outside the reach of human hands, when in fact they had benefited from deliberate land management practices for generations.

Prairies and meadows and wide valleys filled with blossoming *Camassia quamash* were common in the West. The Corps of Discovery and other early visitors to the region describe coming upon camas prairies so vast and vibrant that on first sight they appeared to be great lakes. Lewis describes this trick of the eye in a June 1806 diary: "The quamash is now in blume and from the colour of its bloom . . . it resembles lakes of fine clear water." Then, repeating himself, he wrote, "So complete is this deseption that on first site I could have swoarn it was water."

David G. Lewis, an anthropologist and a member of the Grand Ronde tribe, has observed that a common misperception about Indigenous hunting and gathering practices in the region is that people largely depended on animal flesh to survive. But seasonal calendars collected in the late 1800s from Grand Ronde "focused almost exclusively on the cycle of the Camas and Wapato plants . . . They appear to have really devoted their whole seasonal round to the cycles of these plants."[12]

Camas is typically harvested in summer and autumn, once the plant begins to die back and go to seed. There are at least two reasons for this: seeds can be easily dispersed and replanted as the bulbs are harvested, and the harvested bulbs are more mature and higher in carbohydrates than they are earlier in the season. Both bulblets and older bulbs are left behind to propagate future lilies. Older bulbs are left behind because they produce more seed and, also important, because they are not as tasty.

The camas bulbs are superfoods, high in carbs and protein and rich in inulin, a powerful prebiotic starch that becomes a digestible fructose when steamed or roasted at low temperatures. Freshly harvested bulbs have a dark outer layer that is peeled back to expose an opaque white inner bulb. It's tradition to cook the bulbs in earthen steam ovens at low temperatures for a day and a half or more. The cooked bulbs caramelize and become brown and translucent, like a sweet onion. Low-temperature cooking preserves the bulbs' nutrition, and the longer you cook them, the sweeter they become.[13] Their flavor is commonly compared to that of a baked sweet potato, though I've also read comparisons to baked pears and figs.

Lewis and Clark had their lives saved more than once by

gifts of camas, and though it made them ill at first, they grew quite fond of the plant and even took some for the journey home. Lewis undertook an exhaustive, if occasionally inaccurate, botanical description of the plant, noting, "It delights in a black rich moist soil, and even grows most luxuriantly where the land remains from 6 to nine inches under water untill the seed are nearly perfect."[14]

As to their harvest, Lewis remarked of both camas and *Lomatium cous*: "To it's present inhabitants nature seems to have dealt with a liberal hand, for she has distributed a great variety of esculent plants over the face of the country which furnish them a plentifull store of provision; these are acquired with but little toil."[15]

Alas, in spite of his appreciation of camas and those who furnished him with it, Lewis could not see that it was the "present inhabitants" themselves—not some disembodied "nature"—who had dealt their own abundant hand.

The prairie we were standing in had been gardened by generations of Nimiipuu land-tenders, better known to some readers by the French exonym "Nez Perce" (pierced nose). Nimiipuu territory once stretched over seventeen million acres from Montana to Washington and Oregon. An 1863 treaty dispossessed the Nimiipuu of their ancestral lands, and in the years that followed, tribal members were forcibly removed to reservations in Idaho, Washington, and Oklahoma.

Like the "barbarian" of Europe, the figure of the "savage" wandering the landscape aimlessly in search of food was manufactured to facilitate the theft of tribal lands. It was one of the oldest colonizing tactics in the book: "How can the land belong to them if they aren't even using it?"

The most expedient way to achieve control over a people is to control their food supply, and for a long time this was unofficial U.S. military policy. Lieutenant General John M. Schofield summed up the genocidal zeal of the time in his 1897 memoirs: "I wanted no other occupation in life than to ward off the savage and kill off his food until there should no longer be an Indian frontier in our beautiful country."[16] The destruction of the gardens and the slaughter of the great herds made it easier to force Indigenous peoples onto reservations, often hundreds of miles away from their ancestral homelands, in foreign bioregions.

By 1914, the colonizers were fully entrenched in the Great Basin. Martha, the last extant passenger pigeon, died inside a cage in the Cincinnati Zoo, and in a couple of generations many of the ancient gardens were effectively destroyed. The prophet Joel's vision had come to pass: "The land is like the Garden of Eden before them / But a desolate wilderness behind them, / And nothing at all escapes them."

The first time Peter visited Finisia, she was living with the Prairie Faeries in a run-down trailer outside the tiny south-central Oregon town of Beatty. They were working a sixteen-acre expanse of biscuitroot in Klamath territory. The former occupant of their trailer had kept around a hundred cats. They'd pulled out all the carpet, but it still reeked of cat piss, so everybody chain-smoked in the place to mask the smell.

"They took me out to the tablelands the next day," Peter said, "and it blew my mind. It was literally food for as far as I could see . . . You get to someplace like those tablelands in Beatty, you can see the garden and feel the intention and effort of a people who lived there for thousands of years, fiercely maintaining it for future generations . . ." He grasped for words. "You just . . . feel it."

As teenagers, Peter and I searched for examples of how to live without destroying everything. We'd encountered plenty of theoretical possibilities over the years, but in Beatty he'd had a sixteen-acre glimpse of a lived reality. He'd stood in the manifestation of a dream planted long ago, the dream of a line of caretakers that spanned countless generations. A people who'd imagined the lives of their descendants and acted in their interests, hundreds of years before any of them were born. And he'd no doubt felt the shadow of that revelation: the systematic devastation of that way of life, of those caretakers; the desertification of the land, of which they were an extension; and the dispossession of their descendants continuous to that very moment.

Seda was with Finisia and the Prairie Faeries in the tablelands outside Beatty one spring when he spotted several trucks coming down the road to camp. He walked out to greet them, believing they were friends.

"I'm coming down from the hillside toward them," he said, "and then all these police in bulletproof vests and helmets are jumping out of these trucks and they're all pointing machine guns at me."

The county sheriff had come with a convoy of state troopers and a few guys who presented like military. They grabbed Seda and frisked him.

"I tried to explain the situation. How we were just, like, avid botanists—and we'd gotten permission from this guy to plant on his land." But property lines beyond the city limits aren't always clearly delineated, and it turned out they'd accidentally crossed onto another private property, a vacation rental owned by a man who lived in the resort city of Bend. The man had driven all the way down to Beatty to ride along for the bust. He stood sheepishly with the officers, in a bulletproof vest.

"The property owner came over, and he was kind of feeling guilty, I think," said Seda, "because he was trying to appeal to us, which I thought was really weird. One of the people with us is Shoshone, and he started trying to tell her that he protects the land and all the artifacts. He was like, 'Oh yeah, I'm part Cherokee,' or something. And we're like, 'This is occupied land; it's a sacred place for Native people and we're doing work with the native food and you're arresting us?'"

Finisia said she'd received more than six hundred police visits over the years. They came when she was digging, when she was gathering seed, when she was long-hauling with her wagon. She'd driven the wagon back and forth across the country, stopping in such locales as "Whorelando," "Los Angesleaze," "Lost Wages Nevada," and "Poke It to Ya, Idaho." Finisia was not cowed by cops, or anyone else as far as I could tell. In fact, you might say she relished the "puckering of anuses," be they attached to law enforcement, the Bureau of Land Management, or the armed ranchers on whose land she often trespassed.

Back when she had the wagon, she'd drive it right through urban centers, and the spectacle drew a lot of heat. But she was clever, and in thirty years she'd rarely failed to talk an officer out of hauling her in. She always offered to teach the officers, or anyone else who was interested, about the plants.

"I'm a political atheist," she told me in Sparta. "I don't care if they're ranchers, BLM, cops, or meth heads."

Getting people interested in the work, by education or by spectacle, is a savvy move in country where trespassing on private land is liable to get you shot.

She'd draped her horse with a wide belt of buckskin studded with a line of police patches, like the merit-badge sash worn by a Boy Scout. The patches, typically sewn onto an officer's sleeve, read *City of Roses* or *Denver Police* and were bedazzled with plastic gemstones at their edges. Whenever Finisia was stopped, she asked for one of these patches. Sometimes an obliging officer would drive to the station and grab her an extra. Every once in a while, they'd cut one right off their own shoulder.

Mostly, she'd been able to skirt or seduce or baffle the authorities. But she did wind up getting arrested once, in Lemhi County, for planting on National Forest land. Authorities received a call from a concerned citizen who'd spotted "a crazy lady" digging holes on protected land. When they arrived on the scene, they discovered Finisia pushing her digging rod into the earth and dropping seeds in the holes it made. They ordered her to stop, but she ignored them, behaving as if they weren't there, and went on about her work.

She waited in jail for weeks while the powers-that-be tried to figure out what to do with her. She'd ignored the responding officer's orders, but she hadn't physically resisted arrest, and the laws about planting on National Forest land are ambiguous.

After two months, they found her guilty of obstructing an officer and released her, time served.

I asked Seda why, after hundreds of similar encounters with no arrest, Finisia was unable to subdue the officers in Lemhi County.

It turns out the "concerned citizen" was Finisia. She'd called the police on herself.

"They'd been threatening to arrest her for a long time," he explained. "We're not supposed to plant or gather on public land, but it's also kind of a gray area because we're not bringing in foreign species and planting them where they don't belong."

Finisia wanted to see if they could make the charges stick, but she also wanted a platform. In her letter to the Lemhi County Court, she framed her activities as civil disobedience. "Now only 2% of God's aboriginal planting is left on earth . . . All of nature is in travail crying out to us . . . to do the work of restoration and re-creation. If I cannot have this, my life is worthless to me and a forfeiture."

Needless to say, not everyone can get away with—and by that I mean survive—illegally planting on private land, let alone asking a cop to cut a keepsake from his uniform. The point was not lost on her. She claimed she wanted to see if the white whores of Babylon would murder their own children as readily. The white kids "with the pretty blue eyes" were conceived as a kind of first-wave infantry, and that plot of land in Sparta, a site to convene her very own Agoge— grounds for training in militant asceticism, for sorting the strong from the weak and malformed of spirit.

"I understand that the reason I'm crying is because I suffered great loss," she told me. "And really the only thing that would heal that fucking pain would be some campaign of revenge whereby I'm going to turn their goddamned children into what they took from me. Maybe I'll turn the little devils, little fucking minions, into something worthwhile."

In the mid-1990s, a paper in central Texas, the *Abilene Reporter-News*, ran a profile on Finisia as she moved through town with her horse-drawn wagon. The article was titled "Wagonmaster 'Pulling for Christ.'"[17]

"She walked for several years," the paper reported, "until some 'rednecks' in Alabama built the wagon." Who these mysterious covered-wagon-building rednecks were is unclear. She'd passed through Wyoming, Colorado, and Oklahoma on her way to Texas—averaging about a hundred miles per week.

"Somebody once asked who I witness to," she is quoted as saying. "I told them largely newspaper reporters and cops."

This was during the era when she lived as an itinerant preacher. One of her pickup lines was "Damn the children of Cain!" And just when all the righteous believers were nodding in agreement, she'd inform them that *they* were the seed of Cain and headed straight for hell. At first, they were angry to be called bad seed; then they were hooked. It's like Finisia says: some people love to have their asshole puckered.

"I would say to them, 'If you don't agree with homosexuality and don't want it in your church, start your own church.'"

She claimed to have founded seven different community-based churches over the years. "I'd start them with Bible studies, and I'd preach to them a little bit, and that was genuine, you know? It still is," she told me. "Later, I came out . . .

and so they all freaked out. Because it was a transsexual that helped them start their fucking gay-hating church."

I asked if any of them had seen the light.

"I think they all pretty much feel betrayed," she shrugged. "It's like everything else: love looks like revenge to me; revenge looks like love. I felt an obligation to the truth to do it. To show these Christians how to love thy enemy."

In Sparta, she was out to everyone, and she encouraged her camp to follow suit. Over the phone, I asked Seda if he feared being out in rural areas, if he was afraid of violence from the locals.

"The thing that Finisia always taught us," he said, "because she moved around for all those years—every time somebody new comes into her camp, she always says, 'I'm a [t-word], blah blah,' and she goes off about all her sexual stuff, because she wants to see how they're going to react."

The strategy made some sense, I guess, but I couldn't help feeling alarmed for their safety.

"I'm surprised I'm not dead yet," Finisia told me, matter-of-factly.

"Me too," I said.

Finisia and her wagon were in the news again a decade later, in a 2007 issue of the *Nevada Appeal*, only this time her message was far more blunt.

"I'm living in a world full of monsters," she told the reporter. "I look around and see I'm all alone in a good thing."[18]

Certainly she didn't begin as an aw-shucks optimist, but the person interviewed in Abilene twenty years earlier wasn't merely younger but also far less bitter. In Sparta, she was often sad or furious—possessed with pain, forsaken by her God.

"If God loved me, maybe I'd have been born a hawk and had a good life," she said tearfully. "But no, I'm born this rotten two-legged that's going to be responsible for an ecocide, and just to live this life they've given me I'll go to hell."

Her vision demanded hundreds, or even thousands, of people in the Great Basin working in small groups, coming together to trade. At the time, her crew totaled four, plus a passel of the half-broke horses.

"Everybody is polishing and handing each other lies," she said, "and I'm supposed to believe all these beautiful fucking stories, but when it comes down to real energy spent in the deliberate saving of these things, well, everybody's got something better to do."

"People don't understand Finisia," Seda told me. "They get pissed off, like, 'Why isn't she love and light?' But she's a warrior. She had to be that extreme and that intense to be able to face what she has faced."

Volatility was probably her fatal flaw; it repelled the community she so obviously desired, the family denied her since her family of origin, but it also enabled her, against all odds, to stay alive and out of jail as an itinerant trans woman trespassing through the rural United States. Seda told me that Finisia loved the truth above all else. She had little tolerance for those who'd evade responsibility for their share of the disaster. If we refused to give up our whoring in Babylon, the least we could do was own up to our sins.

If anything about her was unguarded, it was her love of the plants. Pretty much the only time her anger abated was while we were out on the land. In *Growing Up in Occupied America*, her devotion to the plants is expressed in sudden, passionate exclamations. One of these exuberances so wooed me that I copied it in large script to a piece of notebook paper and tacked it to my wall: "Everywhere across the desert our bread is blooming!"

Driving back to camp from the camas prairie, we pulled the Tercel to the side of the road, where biscuitroots were plentiful. Watching us dig them up, peel back the bark, and taste them, their surprising sweetness, Finisia appeared quite pleased. We were children in the garden, and she was gentle there. But that didn't change the fact that her main concern, beyond that of our safety or even survival, was for the roots. She'd sacrificed her life for them and wouldn't hesitate to offer ours should the occasion arise.

She loved the plants—that much was true. I wasn't sure what to make of the rest. Following Finisia presented challenges in excess of physical hardship and verbal rebuke. One made certain adjustments in response to her "political atheism." Beyond the biting irony of the tableau—a half dozen white people critiquing settler colonialism inside a tepee— her behavior could be, as they say, problematic. It was both how she drew you in and pushed you out. Sometimes her riffs were achingly beautiful, not in spite of but on account of their obscenity—suffused with brutal and numinous truths. But by other turns, the stuff she said was pointlessly offensive and, at times, blatantly appropriative of Native cultures. In addition to whatever else you might call those appropriations— destructive, reckless—her refusal to reckon with the issue when it was raised seemed to me uncharacteristically dishonest, and it didn't help her cause. Which is not to suggest that her way of life was put-on—there was nothing plastic about the way Finisia lived—or that there was consensus opinion about her among the Native people who knew her. I'd heard her described both as an important teacher and as someone setting a dangerous example. One person spoke vaguely, saying Finisia had done some things that were "not so good." No one I asked wanted to be quoted on the record, though this may have more to do with my inexperience as an investigator than the subject of my inquiry.

More generally, I couldn't tell if Finisia always meant what she said. It was hard to tell if what came out of her mouth was deliberate, or the spontaneous expression of the cultural shadow, or the product of instability, or of divine inspiration. Some viewed her cruder eruptions as aspects of her trickster nature, devised to provoke and discomfort the children of Cain, like Loki sowing discord at the banquet of the gods, fucking up other people's day, poking at their pretensions—these were sacred duties.

One night, she mentioned to the group that she was glad she wasn't "raised a girl" because girls learn to develop a kind of manipulative, indirect power over others. It was clear to me that this remark was less a statement of personal preference than it was a comment on my own pathological deference and choked-out voice. Just as, several years later, she'd seem to channel a subset of the culture in telling me, "I want that white woman's entitlement. I want your entitlement, bitch, while you claim to be a victim. It's the highest entitlement in America. *Crrryyy*, because that ecocide ain't giving you enough?"

In short, she seemed to feel entitled to say whatever she wanted because, unlike those of us who just talked pretty, she was out there leading "the only real resistance left in this bitch," a campaign of "wild food freedom." Of course, it didn't take but a shift of the light to behold a chilling resemblance to certain other entitlements assumed by certain other "servants of God's will," the bleak destiny manifested by the ancestors she hated.

All of this raised, for me, a related question: By what shall we be judged? Several generations in the future, should any of our descendants survive, and should they happen across one of these gardens, will they care if it was tended by a drug addict, or a cop, or a libertarian ideologue, or a democratic socialist? Will they care what we believed if the force of that belief did not translate to a habitable planet? And on the other hand, what is their survival worth to them if their human relationships are distorted, if the empire falls but its ethos remains?

On the morning we left Sparta, the kids stripped the camp to its bones. They'd sleep out the next few nights before hitting the road for Hells Canyon.

Breaking down camp seemed to trigger a sense of reality regarding their impending endeavor.

"I can already see the first wall you'll come up against," Finisia was telling Kelsey, the young woman from Spokane. "It's all inspiration until you're on that horse heading out. Then it's like, 'Oh, shit, I'm actually doing this.'"

Kelsey nodded, apparently having already arrived at the oh-shit stage.

Finisia was wrapped in her bedroll near the morning fire. We'd gathered around to drink coffee and say goodbye.

"Before you go," she said, "we have to draw cards about the journey."

She produced a tarot pack and told us she'd pull a card for each of us. The card would represent what we meant to the future of the Hoop. Peter appeared to be unnerved by this plan. Finisia had been hammering him all morning for being a "corporate slave" and "whore of Babylon" (his job, as it happened, was serving bone broth out of a family-owned food cart called The Cultured Caveman). She'd finally simmered down but would no doubt ramp back up if she pulled the Death card or something.

"For Jesse," she said, fanning the deck, "we have . . ." She slipped her fingers into the center and plucked a card. "The Devil."

She read the meaning of the card from her guidebook. The Devil, it said, represents our shadow: all the repressed desires that lurk beneath.

I don't remember what Michael and Kelsey were given, but Peter got the World, a card about giving back what we've learned or gained in life.

I'd asked Finisia if I could write about her. So when she pulled the Star card for me, she quipped, "We already knew she came out here to elevate her star."

She shuffled the deck. "That was the bullshit round, let's go again."

Next, I was given the Queen of Cups and the others received auspicious cards. Michael got the Fool, which was fitting: a spirit who walks without worldly possessions in search of experience.

Finisia pulled the Knight of Swords for herself and read aloud: "'The Knight of Swords shows a man in his armor riding a horse into the midst of battle . . . He does not see, nor care about, any risks or dangers, and instead moves forward with his intent to succeed. He is self-sacrificing in pursuit of his goal and is often alone . . . He is opinionated, hasty . . .'

"Yadda yadda yadda. Blah blah blah. You know what?" she said, shutting the book. "Sometimes you peel an onion, and you get to the center, and there ain't nothing there."

But once conversation drifted to the tasks of the day, she revisited the theme: "I have this problem of credibility versus accessibility. In order for me to be credible, I need to be out there full-time doing this work. But if I'm out there, I'm inaccessible and I can't teach anyone these ways." She jerked a thumb over her shoulder. "The world I'm talking about isn't here, it's behind me. I sit at a threshold."

My eyes lifted from her body across the desert to the far mountains, and in that moment, she looked acutely small. We all did.

I returned home and mostly lost track of Finisia and her crew. I'd hear things every once in a while, usually anecdotes involving her showing up somewhere uninvited and pissing people off.

A year after their pilgrimage, I caught up with Jesse, who was living back in Portland, trying to pay down old school debt. They told me forty-two days had become eighty-two as the group rode, walked, and crawled through Hells Canyon, digging and planting all the way. Jesse couldn't say how many acres they'd planted, but they'd sown roughly 150 pounds of seed. Once or twice a week, the police came by to reprimand them and, on one occasion, to warn them of a death threat. The threat was painted on a raccoon skull and posted up the road from their camp. Jesse didn't know who made it.

"Could've been annoyed ranchers, or kids dicking around," Jesse said. "It could've been the cops for all I know."

What had they learned out there, beyond the basics of survival?

Jesse said they'd learned about the expense of human life, how much effort it takes to be truly symbiotic. "I think one thing that is very difficult to convey is that these gardens are ancient, they're older than recorded history. They could be four or six times as old as recorded history, I don't know. This sacredness doesn't really register."

That particular group eventually disbanded. Kelsey settled down and started a family. Michael split off from Finisia but has lived nomadically ever since, continuing to replant and subsist on flowering tubers. Last I saw, he was camped out in Idaho. Jesse had been all over the place. They'd herded sheep for a time in western Arizona, and studied European silviculture through a "social forestry" program in southern Oregon. Their longtime partner purchased a small parcel of land on the eastern slopes of Mount Hood, where together they practice Landtending and host an annual acorn camp.

In 2017, I was forwarded an online fund-raiser for Finisia. After decades of rough riding, her joints and back finally gave out and she'd had to cede care of her horses. Her body was giving her too much pain; she'd have no choice but to move into town, or at least to somewhere reachable by road. The fundraiser money would be used to purchase a 1987 Mazda 4x4 with a camper shell, a slightly more advanced iteration of the covered wagon.

This put me in mind of an exchange in Sparta. I'd given

her a chapbook of poems, and she'd hobbled to the car as Peter and I were pulling out.

I rolled my window down.

"In that poem you wrote, 'You should never trust what comes to you limping,'" she said.

I nodded. I did write that, though I was referring to a dog, and I'd meant it as a metaphor.

We looked at each other.

"I have a limp," she said finally.

Eventually, Finisia moved in with a friend in Lucerne, California, a lakeside place of chaparral hills about a hundred miles northwest of Sacramento. Her friend's name was Mary, and Mary had a brother named Joseph who lived either with them or somewhere nearby. "So Mary and Joseph invited Jesus to stay," she explained.

I'd called to find out how things were going. Moving into town had been a difficult transition, a defeat really, but what else could she do?

"I spent fucking decades with guns on my hips, riding horses, setting up camps in the cold, bending over, digging roots . . . That's what fucked me up, a lifetime of that shit."

Our initial exchange was cordial, but soon she slipped into the acidic rasp she favored for haranguing Babylonians like me: the voice with which, over the course of the hour, she would call me a "piece of shit," a "bitch," a "motherfucker," and in a characteristic burst of scathing improvisation, a "deliberate, hateful goddamn thing that wants to give poison to the natural world and call it love."

In this respect, talking with Finisia felt less like talking with another person and more like conversing with one's own fragmented psyche, how shadow aspects of the self sometimes show up in a dream, condensed in the form of a single persecutor. I'd learned not to take these insults personally. They weren't, as far as I could tell, personal. Nor were they, in every case, untrue.

"I'm walking through this flood of people stepping onto the freeway with their backs turned to traffic," she said, revving up. "Sometimes my wake will spin one of those motherfuckers around and they'll see what's happening, what their choices are, and they'll be mad at me, like I made those choices for them. Just traveling through your world in the opposite direction, giving life to what you'd kill."

Toward the end of the hour, her harangue reached a peak.

"I'm holding you accountable for your choice, Lisa Wells, because ain't nobody else will. They ain't gonna hold you accountable for things they're not holding themselves accountable for. You've got a mandate to fix this shit. You got a mandate to answer climate change. That's why I'm the only one going to tell you the truth. You're a piece of shit, girl."

An even more corrosive voice was taking over. It was the growl of an injured animal, seething with rust and razor blades and ash.

"This place eats fucking souls and spirits. How healthy you think you are? You probably look as poisoned as that landscape around you. You're probably as devastated as those woods in Oregon. You're probably as polluted as Fukushima. If you could see the inside of yourself, cooperating with this cunt . . ." She gnashed as the voice torqued through her, and in that moment it felt to me that this new voice belonged to the earth itself, a distillation of all the poison, all the Superfund sites and malignant tumors, all the blasted mountaintops and dead fish and catastrophic fire. "One of these days people will wake up in a near-dead world, and they will look around them and they will look inside and see that same devastation. They'll reach for some lie, for some comfort, and they ain't gonna find none. They're going to reach for absolutions and find none. And they will hunt for excuses and they will find none."

Her mouth was a channel, an articulate wound, and though she could not have known how sick I'd been, she'd twigged to it all the same and I was shaken. It was a curse she spoke, or some kind of intuition, or else the meaningless coincidence of a well-worn rant striking too close to home. Did it matter which? I was sick, and I suspected she knew why.

2

ON THE RISE AND FALL OF A TEENAGE IDEALIST

Clearly, apocalyptic thinking is nostalgia at its very worst.
—ADAM PHILLIPS

The events that precipitated the end of my idealism were many, none of them very novel. There was disillusionment, naturally; then somebody died, and some people went to jail. It didn't end all at once, and in some respects, I continue to live with the ghosts of my former ideals. For example, I didn't change my mind about the viability of industrial civilization in the long run; I only stopped believing myself capable of living outside it. On the one hand, I had a philosophy problem. My choice to drop out of high school and radically alter my life—and the course of my future—was based on certain premises about which I'd come to feel uncertain. On the other hand, my problem was practical. After having spent eight months at the wilderness survival school in rural Washington, I'd mastered few survival skills. Most of my time there had been spent shivering on the edge of a slough in a cotton hoodie, mildly hypothermic, listening to birds I couldn't identify.

After those months of freezing in the woods, I gave up and moved back home to Portland, Oregon, in a state of low-grade shell shock. It was then that I met Tre Arrow, the local celebrity activist who, on July 7, 2000, had spontaneously free-climbed the side of the U.S. Forest Service building downtown during a protest against cutting near Eagle Creek. Tree sitters in Eagle Creek had been forcibly removed from their camp that morning, and the demonstration was held in solidarity, but Tre felt protest alone wasn't accomplishing enough, so he climbed. For eleven days he camped out on a nine-inch ledge, lecturing onlookers below via bullhorn, while crowds gathered and dispersed on the ground. Media had been blocked from entering the timber sale site, but Tre's "criminal" ledge-sit was visible to the public and covered by every local news outlet. As one alt-weekly reporter noted, presciently, "His act of civil disobedience should teach enviros an important lesson: If a hippie falls in the wood, no one hears it. Public, high-visibility crime pays."[1]

In the newspaper photos his bare feet dangle, he flashes a peace sign. He's baby-faced and doe-eyed—barely recognizable as the same prison-ravaged visage we'd come to know. His actual identity, however, matters less than the personae he accommodates. Was he an "insolent tree hugger" or a "revolutionary hero"? I was inclined to view him as the latter.

My two best friends, Peter and Nick, had both attended the wilderness survival school with me, and both had defected back to the city. It was a new millennium, and one by one that spring we reached legal voting age. We'd been campaigning for Ralph Nader's presidency when the Green Party tapped Tre Arrow to run for Congress. His stint on the side of the Forest Service building had garnered him a little fame around town, and it wasn't beyond the realm of imagination in those days to think the city might elect a barefooted freegan to public office.

As for my friends and me, we had no faith in government, but we had to concede the point: some leaders were better than others, and we thought Tre might become one of the better ones. On several occasions, we aided his campaign by handing out leaflets on the side of the road. Our group was pitifully small: me, Nick, Peter, Tre, and a mother-daughter activist duo who wore their long blond hair identically parted down the middle. A kid our age named Jake showed up right around the time we began to tire of the scene. He was like Tre but on steroids: intense, prone to moral scolds, sanctimonious (descriptors any number of people might have applied to me in that era). We thought Tre was a good guy, but he was self-righteous to a humorless degree and not all that fun to spend time with. He just wouldn't clock out. Even after we failed to elect him to public office, he kept on lecturing everyone around him like a politician. One afternoon, we were approached by a homeless woman in Pioneer Courthouse Square who asked if we could spare two dollars.

"What are you going to buy with it?" he asked.

"I'm going to buy some Chinese food," she said, cautiously. "Which has all the vegetables and vitamins I need."

Tre explained that she could walk a few blocks to the vegan grocery and obtain a box of bruised organic fruit for free, a healthier choice. He then gave her detailed walking directions to the store and sketched the detrimental effects of MSG.

She stormed away, understandably pissed.

Some months later, the news came down that Tre Arrow had fallen from a hemlock during a tree-sit in Gods Valley. I don't know how long he'd been up in the trees before the Forest

Service and police sent climbers after him, but I know he evaded them for hours, leaping from branch to branch. They began to narrow his escape routes—cutting the branches below him, then all the surrounding trees—until he had nowhere left to go. When that failed to bring him to earth, they used sleep deprivation tactics: floodlights, deafening sirens. After forty-five hours he finally lost his grip, falling sixty feet to the forest floor, puncturing his lung, cracking several ribs, and breaking his pelvis.

A few months after that, another tree sitter—a twenty-two-year-old woman named Beth O'Brien—fell from a platform at Eagle Creek, plunging 150 feet to her death.

At the time, Peter and I had jobs at the same downtown coffee shop. It was on the street where the buses ran, downstairs from a methadone clinic. Overdoses were common in the cafe, no matter your shift. An officer from Downtown Portland Clean & Safe would be summoned, arriving in a sci-fi uniform of lime green hashed with reflective tape. We'd point to the table where a customer nodded off, and the officer would slam his hand again and again on its surface until they came to, or didn't.

One day, one of our regulars—a guy we called Elvis on account of his massive muttonchops and the gold aviators he wore indoors—was sipping his coffee when he abruptly vomited a bright spray of blood, jerked to the floor, and died. The paramedics said it was an alcoholic seizure. The mucosal lining of his throat ruptured.

Twice a year or so in the shoulder seasons, someone would leap off the roof of the adjacent parking garage. I heard the sound of something heavy hitting the pavement one morning and rushed outside to find a man folded in half the wrong way. Paramedics drew a blue plastic sheet over him, and soon a line began to form again at the register.

"How terrible . . ." The customers shook their heads. "Can I get a large mocha with whip?"

These deaths felt, to me, illustrative of a larger motif: average days, punctuated with terrific violence—terrific violence that could, in all its gore and spectacle, only briefly stall the gears of commerce. You'd steam the milk, grind the beans, or whatever, while bodies rained from the sky.

I met Peter Bauer in 1997, on the first day of my sophomore year of high school. He was new, a transfer from one of the big-city schools. He dressed in button-down shirts of shiny, space-age material and those wide-legged jeans some kids wore in imitation of anime characters. His spiky hair was dyed maroon, and it looked like a splotch of it had stained his ear and the side of his face. From where I sat, across the classroom, the stain resembled a head wound, as if his dermis were partly exposed.

We hung out most nights at a Lyon's diner in Beaverton, Oregon, draining dollar cups of bottomless coffee. Our usual waitress had teased blond bangs and a gummy, nicotine-stained smile. She didn't card for the smoking section, and unlike most of the adults we knew, she didn't appear to resent our very existence—which we understood as an implicit invitation to convert her section into our living room.

Peter started bringing a new friend around the diner, a freshman named Matt. He was a year younger than us but already reading and absorbing material way above our heads:

Marxist theory, continental philosophy, *Guns, Germs, and Steel*. Matt had a deadpan humor and dark gaze that worked like helium on the girls. He wore his body resentfully, an ill-fitting garment. And this cellular discomfort—combined with the unruly eyebrows and ashen complexion—was like a fable in which a tortured Russian intellectual wakes to find himself confined in the body of an American teenager.

I brought Nick into the group, a skinny stoner kid from the city with shaggy black hair who liked to belt his pants mid-buttock. He'd quit school the year before and spent those truant hours in his parents' basement composing twelve-verse revolutionary anthems on an acoustic guitar. I found his disaffection convincing. It seemed to be the direction my life was going.

I'd just discovered Daniel Quinn's novel *Ishmael*, a 250-page Socratic dialogue between a middle-aged man and a telepathic gorilla. Most of the novel unfolds in a sparsely furnished room smelling of menagerie inside a "very ordinary sort of office building." Ishmael, the gorilla, sits in repose behind a wall of glass and soberly unpacks the history of civilization and the decimation of hunter-gatherer peoples by beaming his questions directly into the human's brain. In the final pages, the gorilla is sold into a carnival sideshow, where he dies of pneumonia.

It would be difficult to overstate the influence this story had on me; everything that followed was, as the poet W. S. Merwin had it, "stitched with its color"—a true conversion experience.

Like most teenagers, alongside my negative assessment of my elders and the poison I felt they'd sown in place of my future, I harbored the optimistic belief that the world could change for the better, if only people understood the problem. The problem, as *Ishmael* helped me to understand it, was this: What we call civilization is not, as most of us have been trained to believe, an evolutionary pinnacle at the tip of a human-advancement graph with our club-wielding anteced-ents at one end and machine-human hybridism at the other. Nor was it a synonym for civil society—art, philosophy, science, and so on. Rather, it was an unsustainable expan-sionist system that in ten thousand years had metastasized over the planet, erasing and oppressing other forms of life in its path. Finally, this slavery-dependent, earth-destroying civilization was doomed to collapse, and soon.

The others read *Ishmael* and were similarly affected. In a booth jaundiced by a faux chandelier, a group of teenagers with no curfew and little cash could pass hours unmolested, discussing the collapse of civilization, while rain sheeted against the window and gathered in pools on the blacktop outside. It was the only kind of weather, or so it felt to me at the time. We lived in a purgatory state, manifest in themes of taupe and slate and neo-eclectic nods to the Tuscan villa. A compromise between city and country in which one is denied the benefits of both.

As former doomsday cult members attest, when one fervently believes the end of the world is nigh, it becomes difficult to justify doing the basic things that are expected of you: going to school, working a job, planning for a nonexistent future, being courteous to people simply because they share your DNA.

I stopped showing up at school toward the end of my

sophomore year. Peter followed in the fall, on Halloween. He'd gone to school dressed as Jesus at the Crucifixion. There'd been a complaint about his costume, and after a heated argument in the principal's office he slipped the security guard who'd been escorting him from the premises and leapt from a window, leaving behind his cardboard crucifix.

The stain on Peter's face, it turned out, was a birthmark. The stain of his birth, he said, could be traced etymologically. *Bauer* is German for "farmer." The Bauers had been in the Portland area for six generations, and you could still see their surname inscribed on some of the sidewalks in the city. *Ishmael* divided humanity into two neat camps: there were the Leavers (hunter-gatherer peoples), and the Takers (civilized plunderers of the world). Totalitarian Agriculture, as the author called it, was a Taker invention and responsible for the rise of civilization—the tiller shared a continuum with the concrete mixer, and there was a message in that circuit embedded in the Bauer name. Peter decided his fate was to atone for that legacy. Wherever a Bauer had poured a concrete scab, he would dig it up and plant something living.

Matt dropped out of school on his sixteenth birthday, and after that our days were mostly unconstrained. Peter bagged groceries for a few months at the hippie market, but the boys were otherwise unemployed. I had a half-time job at a strip-mall coffee shop near our former high school where I served mochas and milkshakes to my ex-classmates. We spent my days off downtown, leafing through punk records and collecting pamphlets on vivisection at a place called the Liberation Collective, a drafty activist space in an abandoned Salvation Army Building. A bald guy with the pallor and affect of a mushroom was the only other person ever there. He lurked nearby as we studied images of exposed monkey brains and depressed beagles forced to chain-smoke by Big Tobacco.

Late at night we convened in a motorboat parked in Matt's parents' garage, smoking cigarettes and stacking empties of Milwaukee's Best Ice, discussing how to spread the word about the "Taker" problem. Days we'd walk the streets of our suburb with oracular intensity, surveying the future ruins of strip malls and car lots and wondering if anyone else in the multitudes foresaw what was coming.

As Peter, Matt, Nick, and I discovered that the world was not as we'd been told, we felt less outraged than chosen. There was power and responsibility in that feeling, an electric sense of importance that amplified when we were together—so we were always together. Every few weeks there would be an animal rights protest or an anti-police-state protest, or a protest against NAFTA. Or the tree sitters, redolent of camp smoke and pinesap, would come to town to protest, and we'd join in, promiscuous in our disapproval.

One of Daniel Quinn's more chilling assertions, this one from his autobiography, *Providence*, is that civilization's assault on the natural world "makes the Nazi holocaust look like a limbering up exercise." Our grandchildren, if any survived, would look back in horror at the monsters that allowed it to happen. It's ill-advised to analogize anything to the Holocaust, a display of what Quinn himself might have called ethnocentric solecism, but I suppose his point was to take the very worst thing one could imagine, a situation in

which one identifies with the victims by default, and super-
impose it on an unimaginable future. If we could not feel
for the species going extinct each day as we did for Anne
Frank, perhaps we could feel for the specter of our hypothetical grandchildren, their hypothetical starvation bellies and
radiation burns. Sure, most of us didn't feel like monsters;
we just sort of bumbled along in the received world, but that
didn't absolve us from our complicity. We were sixteen. The
specter did its work on me.

We started pooling change in an empty vase, labeled with
a strip of notebook paper *The Opening Minds Fund*, and
soon collected enough money to purchase a case of *Ishmael*,
bulk. If people would just read this book, we reasoned, they'd
learn the Truth and the world would change—though we
weren't sure how. Daniel Quinn imagined a renaissance in
which the newly enlightened would abandon civilization and
form egalitarian communities of mutual aid. That sounded
good enough to us. Matt had the idea to rent a gorilla suit.
He'd put it on and stand in the public square handing out
copies from his huge vinyl paws.

We gave the books away to friends in the end but failed
to attract new converts. Mainly I recall the satisfaction of
opening the box, handling the smooth spines in duplicate—
the thrill of having done something so real you could hold its
material dimension and weight in your hands. That we were
essentially teenage evangelists, no less annoying than the
Mormons and Jehovah's Witnesses who plagued our mothers door-to-door, was lost on us. Like all believers, we had
the actual Truth.

❧❧❧

A daily surplus of novel experience is one of the pleasures of youth, a pleasure that can be fully appreciated only in retrospect. This must be why early life feels so much longer: novelty elongates the moment, the day, whether that novelty produces joy or agony. The dulling of one's pain receptors through repetition is one consolation of adulthood. The price of adulthood is the curtailment of possibility, of newness, the exponential dying of time. We realize that what we believed about ourselves in youth—our possibility, our potential power—was in fact overdetermined by larger forces from the outset. We begin to see ourselves in the context of our particular subject positions. We begin to see ourselves in the context of a whole generation: of historical, sociopolitical, and geographic forces beyond our control. We realize we are not so special after all.

In time, I came to see that I was the product of a particular microclimate. I came to see that growing up in the Pacific Northwest in the 1990s—a high school dropout with a trauma history and an ax to grind, the daughter of a white, liberal, working-poor single mother who'd relinquished her authority over my life basically the instant I refused it— virtually ensured I'd have at least passing contact with activist movements. Not to say that there wasn't altruism and genuine feeling for others at the root of my activism, just that the primary animating emotion (rage) was far more personal than I understood at the time. I was primed to reject received authority, but I also happened to be coming of age in an epicenter of radical environmental and animal rights movements.

Plenty of aboveboard environmental organizations and advocacy groups were active in the Pacific Northwest throughout the 1970s, '80s, and '90s, but it was also a hotbed of covert action. In 1995, activists affiliated with the Earth Liberation Army (ELA) burned down a hunting lodge in British Columbia, Canada, the first recorded "earth liberation" action in North America. The first such recorded action in the United States happened the following year, on Columbus Day. Activists from the Earth Liberation Front (ELF) spraypainted the phrase "504 years of genocide" on the walls of a PR firm, a gas station, and several McDonald's restaurants in Oregon. Over the next thirteen years, Oregon would become a locus of ELF activity. During that period, more than twenty-five ELF actions, ranging from graffiti to arson, were committed in Washington and Oregon alone.

My friends and I were dimly aware of this underground, but our participation in direct activism waned as we became obsessed with a series of memoirs by the naturalist and tracker Tom Brown, Jr., whose stories included descriptions of a childhood apprenticeship to an elder shaman known as Stalking Wolf. (With adult eyes, this premise strikes me as obviously dubious, but the books were gospel to us then.) Brown mourned the destruction of the natural world and predicted the collapse of civilization with the fire-and-brimstone prosody of a pastor. He deplored "the mindless grey masses" that destroyed the earth and warned the reader to wake from civilization's stupor before the final signs came to pass. One day soon the skies would bleed and great white serpents would traverse the air. He'd seen it in a vision.

But in the same vision, Brown had seen small groups of people turning their backs on the destruction, dressed in the tattered remnants of modern clothing and wielding handmade tools. These groups would disappear into what remained of the wilderness and build a new, sustainable future for humanity. If we hoped to join their ranks, we'd need to shift our energies from public to personal liberation. Sadly, but necessarily, in this version of the future most of humanity would die.

Peter found out that Brown's Tracker School would run an inaugural youth camp in New Jersey that summer. If we liked the camp, we could enroll full-time in its sister school in Washington State. And so, a month after my seventeenth birthday, the four of us boarded a Greyhound bus bound for the New Jersey Pine Barrens, the setting of Brown's 1978 Bildungsroman, a place that had become, in our imaginations, a mythic wilderness.

Taking the Greyhound cross-country saved us about $90 a head on airfare and tacked on around 150 hours of travel. I don't know whose idea this was, but it turned out to be a bad one. Perhaps we believed we would shut down in a kind of cryogenic freeze, like space travelers in the movies we liked, for we failed to consider what those 150 hours might actually entail—stuff like eating out of gas stations, pooping in a tiny room five feet from a fellow passenger, and regularly fearing for our lives.

We tried to sleep, but I found it difficult. Though we were seated close and buddied up, I felt the leer of men on me like bugs and was afraid to drop my guard lest I wake from an etherized stupor, bound in some backwater, the mangled bodies of my friends littering the ground. Years later, I read a news story about a middle-aged Canadian man who boarded a Greyhound bus and cut the throat of the twenty-two-year-old stranger asleep in the seat next to him.

The other passengers fled the bus and barred the door so the killer could not exit. For a long while they stood helpless on the side of the road, awaiting the authorities, while the man carved scraps from the boy's body and ate them performatively in the blood-smeared window. And though that's not exactly what I imagined would happen, the vibe on Greyhound was "Anything's possible!"

On the first evening of the Tracker School's Coyote Camp, we were blindfolded and deposited in the woods. One of the ways the instructors taught you to feel was by taking away your sight. Most people were sight-addicted, they said. The eye was hideously overbuilt: a flexed, steroidal organ that bulges with veins while the remaining senses atrophy. They told us that certain elderly country folk had sensitized their ears so exquisitely they could pick up movements in the forest up to a mile away. Our grandparents were broken-down cyborgs by comparison, with pacemakers and dentures and Beltones dialed up to screaming. According to the Tom Brown oeuvre, their decay was not the inevitable progression of natural processes, but the outcome of a life lived in pursuit of "safety, security, and comfort," which were merely "euphemisms for death."

Before the blindfolding, we were taught a new style of walking in which you use your bare feet as eyes, padding around with one foot for a clear spot before transferring your weight from the other. This "fox walking" enabled you to keep your eyes trained on the forest, tuned to the slightest movement of an enemy. If you didn't have use of your eyes, this method helped you avoid hurting your foot or giving away your position by snapping a twig or something.

Supposedly, it took ten of those steps to enter an "Alpha brain state."

After reviewing the findings of a Harvard study on brain patterns, Brown got his hands on a biofeedback machine and was using it to conduct his own tests—or so we were told. As expected, many of the skills he taught triggered higher brain states. It was hypothesized that Brown's childhood mentor lived in the superior Theta state most of the time, whereas "the mindless grey masses" mostly lived in Beta. People in the Beta brain state are not very aware at all. It takes them a long time to learn things; even their wounds take longer to heal. But with just ten measly steps using a fox walk, you could be liberated from inferiority.

In the dark of my blindfold, I heard a far-off drum begin beating. We were supposed to use our newly acquired fox walk to feel our way back to camp until we reached it. I'd had the hang of it in the field, but the woods were a different story. It was summer in New Jersey and sweaty-hot, even with the sun almost down. My feet were weft in a stringy plant. I hoped it was not blackberry. I especially hoped it was not poison ivy. As soon as I extracted my foot, I unleashed a cloud of insects—gnats maybe—and nearly tipped over, reflexively ducking their clipped whines. My sweaty arms were glue strips, and the bugs adhered to my skin wherever I swatted. I set my foot back down and breathed. Soon the papery mayhem of some-one stumbling through the underbrush moved past me. I felt pity at first, wondering if it was one of the younger students, running out of there in a panic. My next thought was, *What if that little fucker beats me to the finish line?*

Some psychotherapeutic traditions suggest that the search for God is a search for the Father. I didn't use that word, "God," but I heeded a distant and disapproving figure all the same. The god I'd made of whoever was observing us out there in the woods was fatherly in the Lacanian sense: the one who guards the passage back to the Mother, the voice that interjects his thunderous *No*. And he was fatherly in the way of my earthly father, in that I became a kind of anxious weathergirl, locating patterns within the caprice of his moods. There's a scene in James Agee's *The Morning Watch*, where the twelve-year-old protagonist takes up an early-morning vigil on Good Friday but cannot keep his mind focused on prayer. He is thwarted by vile or petty thoughts, desires to be seen as self-sacrificing, then quickly castigates himself for desiring. That was the tug-of-war convened in my consciousness, moment to moment. I wanted to be seen as good—an Alpha brain, a Leaver in the making—I punished myself for wanting, felt cleansed for rebuking myself, and then felt guilty again for having thought myself clean. *Lord, make my mind not to wander!*

Back at camp, once I finally reached the drum, I was told to sit down and remove my blindfold. Our instructors stood before us in the dusky field. They told us we were now part of the new generation, the prophesied children of the earth. Then they sang a song about the bravery of "walking on the edge." For my friends and me this was a complete arrival, a promise realized. Reduced to its essence, it was a story about mattering. We were desperate to believe.

Our instructors observed that human beings are not especially strong or fast or graceful—about the only edge the human animal has is the ability to emulate—and so we started each day by practicing "animal forms," a physical warm-up based in mimicry. "Owl eyes" was an expansive, soft-focus way of seeing, useful for detecting movement in the periphery and less threatening to other creatures than tunnel vision, our usual way of looking. As an experiment, we looked at birds both ways. If you used owl eyes, the bird would go about her business like you weren't even there, but if you stared at her in tunnel vision, she'd become agitated and fly away. Later we'd examine a series of skulls and notice the placement of the eye sockets. Prey animals—deer, rabbits, rodents—had sockets positioned on the sides of their heads. Predators tended to have sockets near the fronts of their faces, just above the nose: tunnel vision. The birds went nuts when we glared at them because they felt they were being hunted.

We practiced the fox walk and owl eyes and the "deer run," a high-stepping trot through the tall grass. One animal form required that we press our legs tightly together and undulate our hips like a dashboard hula dancer—a motion meant to mimic, inexplicably, the river otter.

A portion of each day was spent practicing the "sacred order of survival": shelter, water, fire, food. A person could live for several days without water and weeks without food, but without shelter, even in mild conditions, you'd be lucky to survive the night. We made survival shelters from tree limbs and leaf litter. We created basic solar-stills to gather water; we made fire by rubbing wood together. We constructed traps from big heavy rocks propped up by a precarious arrangement of sticks. We twisted the inner fibers of milkweed and stinging nettle into cord.

———

The other primary component of camp was "scout training," learning to move silently and invisibly through the woods. Scout skills were important for tracking and hunting animals, but they'd also be useful for evading roving gangs of homicidal children in the apocalypse (another of Tom Brown's visions). We donned neutral-hued bathing suits and streaked our bodies, toes to scalp, with ash and mud. Then we practiced hiding from one another in the leaf litter.

At the beginning of the week, we were told there would be highly trained scouts hiding in the woods, camouflaged men and women watching our every move. One afternoon, the instructors scolded us for our lack of awareness. There had been scouts under our noses all day, they said. "You guys are so distracted out there." Some of the scouts weren't particularly well hidden. Some of them weren't even camouflaged. Some of them, they said, were wearing their bright blue instructor shirts.

What the fuck? I thought. I'd been scanning the woods with the vigilant paranoia of a former combatant and I didn't see shit.

The next day, the four of us were on our way to the lodge to practice making friction fires, when we came on a bespectacled middle-aged stranger frantically trying to conceal himself at the base of a tree. We stopped in our tracks and watched him work. There were wide streaks of mud across his naked torso. He kept pressing a handful of leaves to his head, but they wouldn't stick. He took us in with wide-eyed horror and, without a word, burrowed into the leaf litter. Then he just stopped moving, though he remained plainly visible to anyone who passed. We waited for something to happen, and after a while, when nothing did, we shrugged and moved on.

It was years before it dawned on me. There were no scouts in those woods, save for that single shirtless man. It was just another one of the camp leaders' "coyote stories," as they called them, stories they told to raise your awareness, your sense of being watched by an unseen evaluator. I guess they reasoned their fibs were in service to a greater purpose, but the effect, on me at least, was a feeling of futility. I could have looked until my eyeballs fell out of my head and would not have seen what plainly was not there.

When a projection fails, most people do not make immediate peace with their new reality; instead, they attempt to salvage the projection, to re-up their investment, and so did we. When our week at Coyote Camp ended, we took the Greyhound back across the country. Then Nick, Peter, and I moved to rural Washington and enrolled in a year-round program at the sister school. Matt elected to stay behind in our hometown, eventually moving into a motor home in his parents' driveway, out of which he ran a small but prosperous weed-dealing operation.

Nick's dad agreed to pay his rent, so I moved in with him. In order to pay bills and school tuition, we both got jobs in the same shopping center in an emerging exurb of Seattle. And in quintessential Seattle fashion, I was hired at Starbucks and Nick was hired at a Starbucks inside the Barnes & Noble next door. Peter rented a room in the house of an instructor, way out in the sticks, and worked five days a week at a rural hardware store to cover his tuition and bills. In retrospect, our situation bore the whiff of a pyramid scheme, in that we found ourselves working menial jobs full-time in order to learn how to live for free.

We imagined we'd acquire the skills necessary to form self-sufficient egalitarian villages on the frontier of the post-apocalypse. But in real life, the wilderness school had a sort of *Lord of the Flies* vibe. It was the kind of place where teenage boys, covered head to toe in camouflage, leapt from hiding to drag red Sharpies across one another's throats.

There were six or ten other students, depending on the day. The demographic was unique but fairly uniform: most of the students were white, lower middle class, and rural. The boys had long hair, the girls had fuzzy legs. They wore wool sweaters and shorts in cold weather, and went barefoot over all terrain. Many of them played acoustic instruments, and they frequently convened impromptu bluegrass jam sessions.

Our instructors told us that a significant portion of their student body had grown up on the edges of suburban developments, at the dead ends of streets bordered by woods. What mobilized people—or radicalized them, depending on your view—was seeing their childhood haunts cut down and cleared for asphalt, for by then the forest had become a friend. And it was true that something like that had happened to me. The hills bounding the river where I'd camped each summer with my family had been clear-cut, rutted, and piled with debris. The fields where I'd wandered were paved over, as Joni Mitchell sang, to put up a parking lot for a Blockbuster video.

It was at the wilderness survival school that I first heard the adage linking knowledge to love and love to care: "You can't love what you don't know, and you won't fight for what you don't love." The lumberjacks who drove the dozers didn't know what they were killing—they saw a green smear, a tangle of sameness. Contrary to the idiom, it was only in the detail of the trees that the forest would be revealed.

As a kind of initiation, our instructors administered something they called the Alien Test, a battery of 133 questions pertaining to the local environment. The object of the test, in our case, was not to gauge our knowledge so much as to prove a point. Very few people could correctly answer more than a few questions. For example: *Which wind in your area is the harbinger of heavy rains? Describe the odor of red fox urine. Where would one most likely encounter a network of vole trails (describe the environment especially concerning the relative height and species makeup of the vegetation)?* Several pages were devoted to drawings of animal tracks, followed by questions like *Increase or decrease in speed? If head turn, which way?*

Aside from proving what aliens we all were, the test was aspirational. By the end of our training, we were supposed to be able to answer most of the questions correctly and thereby find ourselves at home on earth. To graduate from alien status was to become fully human, a human who could thrive in their own habitat without the assistance of utility companies and grocery stores or even a bunch of high-tech synthetic gear.

In our efforts to become human, we gathered berries, wild greens, and dandelions. We practiced tracking animals. We picked up roadkill, then racked, skinned, and butchered it. We made fires every morning, then sat for hours in the woods trying to quiet our minds.

The other students were all younger than my friends and me, and they were all exceptionally skilled. But in spite of their hippie trappings, the vibe was pretty uptight, and our more or less constant sarcasm was not appreciated. It was as if we'd crashed on an island inhabited by a small tribe of teenagers genetically similar to us but culturally foreign. Where was their angst? Their laziness and distrust of adults? Where were the pop culture references? I admired their abilities, but I internalized their purity as evidence of my own defilement. My mind began to concoct some bad news about it all. At seventeen years old, I was already ruined. While they were out in the ferns mind-melding with forest carnivores, I'd hemorrhaged my teen years submitting to bad acid trips and quarterly STD checks.

Each day provided new challenges and new opportunities to shine, but I wasn't shining. I felt betrayed by my body at every turn. When everyone else made friction fires, I could only summon smoke and blisters on the palms of my hands. Because my veganism prohibited the wearing of wool, I wore cotton and got soaked to the bone when it rained. My ass sopped the dewy groundcover. I was frequently distracted, shivering cold. All the while, like the boy in *The Morning Watch*, my mind engaged in a volley of self-congratulation (*How nobly you endure your discomfort!*) and self-castigation (*Stop. Fucking. Thinking*).

The height of this betrayal arrived on Peter's last day of school. After about two months, he'd decided he'd had enough and would move home. We held an impromptu ceremony to mark his departure, out on the sandbar where we went tracking once a week. I'd started my period that morning but had neglected to bring supplies. My periods were so painful back then, I'd swallow four ibuprofen and draw a bath the moment I felt the first cramp come on. Years later, I'd vary my diet of soy cheese and vegan bologna, and the cramps would more or less vanish, but on this particular day they were as bad as they'd ever been.

One of the younger students cut me a stalk of red willow and explained that I should chew the bark for its pain-relieving properties. I chewed voraciously, hoping to stem the aching tide. Meanwhile, I'd shoved my hat—a hideous pouch fashioned from purple fleece—into my underwear as a makeshift pad and was waddling behind the others when all at once I felt my guts surge. I had not yet learned how to properly shit in the wild, and there was no way I was going to ask now. This spiraled me into a panic that intensified the surging.

I managed to hang on until we reached the woods, where many had already gathered around the fire ring. I waddled away from them quickly, just out of sight, then dropped my pants and exploded on the ground. The smell was immediate and expansive, the pain nauseating. I squatted over the mess shakily, bleeding clots. There wasn't much debris on the ground, so I pulled a few waxy leaves from a nearby bush and wiped up as best I could, then returned the bloody hat to my underwear and pulled up my pants.

The scene was an abomination. Desperate to conceal the evidence, I took a stick to the earth and tried to excavate a little hole that I would—I don't know what I thought, that I'd sort of squeegee it in there? But the stick snapped. I frantically swept all the moss and pine needles I could find onto the pile, leaving a large circle of conspicuously clean earth around it, like a bull's-eye.

Back at the fire, they were taking turns wishing Peter well in his future endeavors. I squatted on the outside edge of the circle, doubled over in pain. Intermittently, I caught a whiff of my own shit and checked the waffling of my shoes. I couldn't tell if it was the breeze bringing it over or if I'd messed myself. Meanwhile, a little melon baller scalloped sharply through my pelvis.

By the time one of the instructors drove me to town, I was in a very bad way. We pulled over twice so I could throw up into a ditch. When we finally arrived at the café/general store in the nearby town of Sultan, I bought a bottle of painkillers and swallowed a handful. My face was pale in the bathroom mirror, my pupils were blown, and I was trembling. I bent over the sink and rinsed my mouth with cool water and splashed the sweat from my skin, patting it dry with paper towels. Then I extracted my hat from my pants and wrung pink water into the sink until it ran clear. I didn't know what to do with it then. If I carried it wet to the table, the instructor would know where it had been, but I couldn't bear to put it back on my head, and I couldn't afford another if I trashed it. In the end, I carried it half-heartedly concealed under an arm. Icy water swabbed up from the hat into my armpit. As usual, I was freezing.

I said that I felt betrayed by my body at every turn, and this is true. But it's also true that I didn't have much of a relationship to my body. My body was the location where the proverbial rubber met the road, the vehicle of uncompromising idealism making contact with the corporeal real. My ideals were disembodied reactions to a world that I did not so much encounter as project from my own inner life. A world divided into neat dyads: the destroyed and the destroyers, Leavers and Takers, children of the earth and mindless gray masses, and, embedded in them all, good and evil. But consummating the ideal required bodily confrontation with the actual world, exertion, exposure to the elements, and frustration at having little aptitude for the task.

My feeling of failure and my inability to integrate these parts of myself ignited the old sanctimony, and soon I began to judge the other students as self-interested separatists. While Nick and I skipped class to go get gassed at the World Trade Organization protests, our classmates traipsed around the forest communing with birds and practicing capoeira in their rustic dojo. Meanwhile, Weyerhaeuser's chainsaws buzzed day and night on an adjoining parcel. At a minimum, they might have used their extreme stealth and legal status as minors to spike a couple of trees. I lectured them on politics and animal cruelty, and did not mind the dissonance of doing so while kneading a deer hide soaked in watery brains.

Every animal contains enough brains to tan its own hide. That's one lesson I don't forget.

Once we'd all returned home to Portland, each of us interpreted our failure to graduate from alien status differently. Nick harbored no hard feelings; he'd just lost interest in the project. Instead of being a wilderness nomad, he thought he might like to be a folk musician or a movie star or maybe a famous rapper.

Peter felt it was a flaw with the program. In his words: "I realized I was working five days a week at a minimum-wage job in order to pay people to babysit me in the woods."

I wound up locating the flaw within myself. I'd met the chosen children of the earth, and they weren't me; I lacked the grit. I started reading outside our little canon. The

Quinnian ideal of voluntary transformation—in which hordes of the awakened would abandon civilization—had come to sound pathetically naïve. Violent dismantlement was looking like a far more realistic and satisfying option, the thrill of doing something so real you could touch its material impact with your own hands. Turns out, I was not alone in this thinking.

Before dawn on April 15, 2001, three trucks were torched at Ross Island Sand and Gravel with a homemade incendiary device. The Earth Liberation Front claimed responsibility for the arson in a communiqué:

> For many years Ross Island Sand and Gravel has been guilty of stealing soil from the Earth, specifically the lagoon on Ross Island. Further, the recent acknowledgment of the [dredging] of toxic disposal cells has drawn our attention to the exploitation that Ross Island Sand and Gravel commits against our Earth. In their Easter basket we decided to leave four containers of gasoline and a time delayed fuse packed under two of their cement trucks.[2]

About a month later, someone blew up a couple of logging trucks and a front loader at Eagle Creek using similar materials: gasoline-filled milk jugs and a MacGyver-like fuse fashioned from a stick of incense.

Tre Arrow's friend Jake was repeatedly arrested and interrogated. Eventually, he "snitched"—in the idiom of activist-watch sites that keep track of these things—implicating Tre and two other conspirators. The other two took plea deals. Tre ran.

In May 2001, a different ELF cell, calling themselves "the family," firebombed the University of Washington's Center for Urban Horticulture, targeting the office of a researcher named Toby Bradshaw, whom they believed to be responsible for genetically engineering trees at the behest of industry bad guys. Bradshaw denied this, stating that his lab was researching the cultivation of poplar trees for wood pulp as an alternative to logging natural forests. The ELF communiqué describes him as a driving force in the research of genetically engineered trees:

> After breaking into Bradshaw's office at the Center for Urban Horticulture, we inspected the building for occupants and set up incendiary devices with a modest amount of accelerant. Although we placed these devices specifically to target his office, a large portion of the building was damaged.

The fire spread from the office to surrounding labs, resulting in millions of dollars in damage, the extent of which the communiqué attributed to "a surprisingly slow and poorly coordinated response from the fire department."

Reading these communiqués in the local paper, in all their verve and goading, you got the sense of someone kicking a hornet's nest: reckless but not necessarily lethal. That was the early summer of 2001. Reading them now—knowing that a few months later the planes would hit the towers—the timing seems so extraordinarily bad as to be predestined by a cynical god.

It was in 2001 that a young man named Jeffrey Luers, who went by the nickname "Free," was sentenced to twenty-two years in prison—one year longer than his years on earth at the time—for setting fire to three SUVs one night at a Chevy dealership in Eugene, Oregon. He'd torched the trucks, he said, to protest gas-guzzlers in a warming world, an action that resulted in no injuries but caused around $28,000 in damage.[3]

We'd known, in theory, that the dominant culture valued property over people—and trees, polar bears, watersheds, and so on—but we were shocked to see some kid's life effectively end, while rapists were going up for three years at a pop. Of course, this was nothing new. For Wobblies, Panthers, even the Suffragettes, imprisonment and state-sanctioned murder were par for the course. Older activists in the scene, people who'd been active in the 1960s, feared these primarily middle-class kids didn't have the mettle to withstand the opposition. They worried they'd roll on each other after the first interrogation—and for the most part, those fears came true.

The world in which the Ross Island trucks were torched was far different from the world that tried and convicted those who lit the fuses. Activities once bearing the whimsical label of "monkey-wrenching" were now "domestic terrorism." Anyone with their ear to the rail could see that Tre Arrow had been right to run. The FBI's campaign to search out "ecoterrorists" was well under way before 9/11, but 9/11 would bring the Department of Homeland Security, the Patriot Act, and increased resources for hunting down activists—not to mention a deluge of Orwellian rhetoric, including the preposterously vague "If you see something, say something."

In late 2002, Tre Arrow was added to the FBI's

most-wanted list. His charges included "interference with commerce by violence."

His given name, the reporters would tell us, was Michael Scarpitti, a detail seized upon, no doubt, for its intimation of corruption. An alias implies criminality, never mind if its origin lies in some totally mundane rite of hippiedom, some vegan-potluck naming ceremony at the co-op. Presumably, Scarpitti was what Tre Arrow hoped to conceal—with its hint of the Italian mafia, its evocation of "scar." You understand how these decisions are made. When the only photos of "America's most wanted ecoterrorist" show some kid in purple cutoffs with a peony tucked behind an ear and a bright, childish smile, consistency demands you edit the image: make it black-and-white, zoom in on the lazy eye.

In 2002, Peter and I organized a reading and interview for our new favorite author. Derrick Jensen had released a book called *The Culture of Make Believe*. Ostensibly on the subject of hate crimes, the book quickly goes wide to connect the objectification, oppression, and murder of individuals to the systematic destruction of the planet. Civilization has a death drive, Jensen said. It will not stop until every living thing on earth is dead. There will be no voluntary societal transformation. If we want a world with any bears or birds or trees left inside it, we have to bring a stop to civilization.

The interview tape is lost, but in it, Jensen essentially warned us: *The only reason I'm alive right now is because they don't perceive me as a threat. The minute they consider us a threat—me, you, everyone in this room is dead.*

I did not think to ask who "they" was, but I remember

peering through a blind to the street, with tweaker-intensity, at a white utility van parked in front of my house. Had it been the same van tailing Peter's car that week? We hadn't blown anything up ourselves, but we'd associated with those who had, and now we'd brought an author to town who'd said in print, in person, and in no uncertain terms: we have to put a halt to civilization by any means necessary.

Years later, Derrick Jensen would be called out for transphobia (a claim he denies), precipitating a falling-out between him and Peter and others in his community—and shifting his fight, in the immediate aftermath, toward some of the people who'd admired him most.

Paranoia, antipathy, and defensive aggression are all predictable responses to a zero-sum world divided into "us" and "them." As for me, my paranoia was probably unfounded, the distorted reflection of an overblown sense of importance, the shadow of the narrative I'd relinquished, the one that told me I mattered.

Then again, maybe they *were* watching.

One night in 2003, my old friend Matt happened into the coffee shop while I was working and we decided to meet up for a drink after my shift. I hadn't seen him in a couple of years. He looked good. That sort of pallid, haunted vibe was gone. He'd quit smoking cigarettes, and his band, the Exploding Hearts, was getting pretty popular. Lookout Records—a label we'd worshipped in high school—was interested in signing them. I was surprised by how much he'd grown up, and I wondered if I had, too. I searched my face in the bar's bathroom mirror for signs of maturation, but I didn't see much. And after that night, I didn't see him again.

He was driving the band home from San Francisco a few months later, when the tour van rolled, ejecting him and two of our other friends from the vehicle. The other two died in the road. Matt died at the hospital.

This event acted as a kind of psychic fulcrum. The death of the dream, the anxiety and paranoia of those months, and the realization of mortality collided, flinging me into a de-personalized state of inarticulate grief. The word I had for what happened to Matt was "wrong." I started time travel-ing. It's two days before the crash: What do you do to save them? *Fly to San Francisco, show up at the club, demand to drive along.* It's ten minutes before the crash. *Call highway patrol, report a reckless vehicle with their make and model.* It's two minutes before. But I couldn't solve that one.

From the outside, these events probably appear unre-lated, but in my nervous system it all wired up together. We couldn't save the world. We couldn't save one another. We couldn't even save ourselves.

Tre Arrow was picked up in 2004, in Victoria, Canada, steal-ing bolt cutters to open the locked dumpsters he depended on for food. He fought extradition for several years. In the meantime, the FBI executed a national dragnet called Oper-ation Backfire, and thirteen people, most of them based two hours south of us in Eugene, were charged with ecoterrorist crimes, including arson, conspiracy, and the use of destruc-tive devices. A former activist-turned-informant wore a wire for over a year, flying all over the country on the FBI's dime, collecting confessions from his friends.

In 2005, an activist named Bill Rodgers, a member of the Eugene-based ELF group that called themselves "the Family," was busted in Arizona. He killed himself inside his jail cell a few weeks later, leaving behind a note:

> Certain human cultures have been waging war against the Earth for millennia. I chose to fight on the side of bears, mountain lions, skunks, bats, saguaros, cliff rose, and all things wild. I am just the most recent casualty in that war. But tonight I have made a jail break—I am returning home, to the Earth, to the place of my origins.[4]

Whatever your feelings about the ELF's actions, whether you view them as misguided or reprehensible or heroic, there was a major disconnect between their actual effects and the hysteria they ignited among certain lawmakers and FBI administrators. Over the course of a 2005 Senate hearing on ecoterrorism, the ELF and the Animal Liberation Front (ALF) were repeatedly compared to Hamas and al-Qaeda, though their ethos was explicitly nonviolent toward living beings and their actions had not resulted in the loss of a single human life.[5] Several testimonies feverishly laid out the case that extremism of the ALF and ELF was intensifying and speculated that it was only a matter of time until people were killed.

In a written statement to the committee, then Illinois senator Barack Obama pointed out that a far more substantial threat to public safety was posed by hate crimes and far-right extremist groups—not to mention the lead in children's drinking water.

When Deputy Assistant Director John E. Lewis was asked how the FBI came to the conclusion that the ALF and

ELF were the "No. 1 domestic terrorist organizations," he replied:

> There is no question, as you look over the past several years, at the amount of damage and the amount of criminal activity that has been racked up by these various groups, that animal rights extremists and eco-terrorism, also known as ALF/ ELF predominantly are way out in front, in terms of the damage that they are causing here in the United States.[6]

Considering that anti-abortion activists and white supremacist fringe groups actually have murdered people, one can only conclude from this statement that Lewis's definition of "damage" was limited to monetary losses and did not include damage to and loss of human life.

I suspect the radical environmental movement gained traction in the western United States because we were connected to vast tracts of forestland that didn't exist in many other places. The "environment" wasn't an abstraction; it was where we lived. We knew what we stood to lose, intimately, and what we were actively losing. The losses included places where I'd played as a kid, living places I talked to, depended on, loved. Over the course of my relatively brief lifetime, I'd seen many of those landscapes reduced to slag heaps, bald hills littered with stumps. The only way to face that abomination was to feel you might act against it, that you might apply your life in some way to the preservation of what remained.

The aim of Operation Backfire, and other "countermeasures" like it, was to crush something—the violent element,

I guess—but its shock wave put down more than that. Anxiety, paranoia, and fear pervaded the ether. To the tree-hugging addressee came a scoffing promise: There would be no recourse to power. One could spend every waking moment of life filing petitions, thrusting picket signs impotently into the sky, and possibly postpone the destruction by some negligible measure, but one could never stop it. Nothing would. Even Kirk Engdall, one of the architects of Operation Backfire and the lead prosecutor on the case, was quoted as saying, "My heart's with these people . . . They were desperate, because they felt that their cause wasn't being addressed appropriately."[7]

"Disillusionment" implies abandonment by illusion, or else freedom from delusion: from a fixed belief deranging the mind. We'd been looking for someone who could extract a unified and stable theory of "how to live" from the increasingly complicated field of the present, propping up idols and knocking them off their pedestals. Daniel Quinn had articulated the problem, but his idea about how to solve it was a pipe dream on a par with "Be the change you hope to see in the world." Tom Brown, Jr., offered a more feasible alternative: run away to the woods and wait for the sky to fall. But aside from the questionable ethics of such a stance, I lacked both the ability and, frankly, the will to pull it off.

As for the prospect of burning the system to the ground, I couldn't get my head around the logistics, let alone the probably substantial collateral damage. To "bring down" or "dismantle" civilization would require manpower and resources on an unimaginable level. I just didn't see how it could be done without the voluntary societal transformation we were sure would not be coming. Abandonment and dismantlement came to resemble the two faces of Janus, stalled out between one world and the next. What was left to us, then, if we couldn't work within the system, we couldn't walk away, and we couldn't take it down? Maybe that's cowardice talking, or the limit of a middling IQ, but my primary feeling at the time was despair. I couldn't see any feasible way to proceed, and out of that paralysis bloomed a deeper terror: that I was powerless to keep anything or anyone I loved alive.

3

PROMISED LANDS

To be rooted is perhaps the most important and least recognized need of the human soul.

—SIMONE WEIL

After the 2008 market collapse—before the Wall Street sleep-ins and the calls for America to commence "its own Tahrir"—I spent a couple of unemployed weeks camping around rural Oregon with a friend. Many of the small towns we passed through were boarded up. These were towns I remembered vaguely from childhood drives, former mill towns for the most part, places you'd stop for an ice cream cone and postcard but likely not for the night. One afternoon, on an almost empty tank, we pulled into the only gas station for miles and found it shuttered. We stopped at the single open grocery store for supplies, but its shelves were nearly bare.

At the time, I'd been reading a blog by a guy named Jason Godesky and had become interested in one of his theories about peak oil and the collapse of industrial civilization. Passing those boarded-up buildings, town after town, seemed to confirm Godesky's theory of an emerging frontier. Oil was once available at an energy return of 100 to 1, he wrote, "a geological savings account of solar energy accumulated over hundreds of millions of years . . . Civilization used that energy to close the map."

By "the map," he meant anywhere the land had been carved up and claimed, anywhere the land could be accessed, serviced, and exploited by empire. This notion derived in part from the work of the anarchist-philosopher Hakim Bey, who'd published a series of communiqués in the 1980s on pirate utopias and other enclaves of self-governing persons, collected in the book *T.A.Z.: The Temporary Autonomous Zone, Ontological Anarchy, Poetic Terrorism*. "Ours is the first century without *terra incognita*, without a frontier . . ." Bey wrote. "Not one speck of rock in the South Seas can be left open, not one remote valley, not even the Moon and planets."[1]

Godesky theorized: "In decline, we will see a new phenomenon: the *opening of the map*."

Practices like fracking and tar sands extraction are not only dirty and dangerous, their energy returns are low, a mean of 4 to 1 in the case of tar sands. There is no viable substitute for pure crude, and if there isn't enough crude in the ground to support a network of shipping and commerce extending to the edges of the map, the map will roll back.[2] This was more or less how Godesky and other like-minded writers imagined the collapse of industrial civilization playing out: Resources will dwindle in rural areas. People will flee to the cities. The empire will contract and implode.

The newly liberated frontier, he suggested, might be the silver lining in the shitstorm, a fringe where autonomous zones could be established: enclaves of peaceful self-governance where the refugees of empire could rewild themselves as free people.

Generally speaking, "rewilding" references a process of "undoing domestication" and restoring natural systems. To conservation biologists, this means returning a landscape to a "wild state" by, say, removing dams and reintroducing native plants and animals—but the official definition makes no mention of that most divisive species, *Homo sapiens*. Fitting human beings into that vision is of special interest to those who call themselves rewilders. My friend Peter is a prolific writer on the subject and has devised his own comprehensive, if unwieldy, definition:

> Rewild, *verb*: to foster and maintain a sustainable way of life through hunter-gatherer-gardener social and economic systems; including, but not limited to, the encouragement of social, physical, spiritual, mental and environmental biodiversity and the prevention and undoing of social, physical, spiritual, mental and environmental domestication and enslavement.[3]

When it comes to humans, many rewilders view domestication as a form of learned helplessness. To be "wild" in their view does not mean to be "uncultivated," it means to be autonomous. One can't be free and simultaneously dependent on the empire and its industrial infrastructure for meeting basic survival needs. The empire has intentionally fostered this dependence by criminalizing self-determination through the privatization of property. In a nutshell: control the resources, control the people. Terra incognita was a kind of Promised Land, but its promise depended on the loss of that control and the consolidation of the empire in its urban centers.

If you'll permit a bit more digression on nomenclature: The *Oxford English Dictionary*'s definition of civilization, the meaning many of us have absorbed, is "the stage of human social and cultural development and organization that is considered most advanced."

Daniel Quinn's definition—one that resembles the definition held by rewilders and other "anti-civ" groups—notably does not refer to civil society, but rather to a system of life dependent on what he called "Totalitarian Agriculture." So dubbed, he wrote, "in order to stress the way it subordinates all life-forms to the relentless, single-minded production of human food."[4]

Totalitarian agriculture, according to Quinn, demands complete sedentism. When a people become fully sedentary, their ecosystems are stressed because they're afforded no rest to replenish. Stockpiled grain and domesticated animals (whose living bodies are used as a store of meat) explode the human population, further stressing their ecosystems. Forests are continuously cleared for agriculture and firewood; the soil's fertility is depleted through monocropping, or is denuded and compacted by overgrazing. Irrigation canals—and later, cities and their dams—drain and salinize the watershed, further depleting the soil. This is how a living land is desertified in a relatively short period of time. Having outstripped their own resources, the people then colonize and displace other cultures in order to seize theirs. Eventually, the system becomes so pervasive that those born into it believe it was inevitable. This was Quinn's history of the Holocene, in a gist.

Recently, I encountered a critique of the anti-civ narrative as propagating a false binary between civilization and wilderness, and thus dehumanizing tropes of "civilized" conquerors and "primitive" peoples. "Rewilding" is a false premise, this critic said, because the land was not "wild" to begin with. Indigenous societies supported large human populations with sophisticated knowledge of ecology, science, psychology, languages, art, social systems—the list goes on—all while increasing the biodiversity of their ecosystems through horticulture and other methods of extensive land management. In this light, according to the *OED*'s definition, the most advanced "stage of human social and cultural development and organization" was exemplified by Indigenous nations.

This may be why still others prefer to use the term "Empire" ("an extensive group of states or countries under a single supreme authority") to describe a system that relies on colonization and totalitarian exploitation of the landbase.

No doubt, the language used to discuss these issues, and how that language is understood, will continue to be challenged and to change. In any case, it may be helpful for the reader to know: when the people in this book say "civilization," by and large, they are referring to a concept along the lines of what Quinn described.

What does it mean to "go back to the land" in a country that was never yours? Perhaps that's an obvious question to ask, but it's not one I'd often heard considered in naturalist circles until recently. It's difficult to recall precisely what I believed as a sixteen-year-old with a desire to live off the grid, but vaguely, I suppose I believed that connecting to the natural world was the divine right of all, and that land could not, a priori, belong to anyone. It turns out the latter way of thinking was only one or two removes from some interpretations of the Promised Land scripture, which says that all lands belong exclusively to God, and if a people by force occupy a land, then that is proof of God's will. Put another way: possession is nine-tenths of the law.

In later translations, the scripture grew more militant. Reading the New International Version of Deuteronomy 20:10–14 is like reading an instruction manual for the pioneers of Manifest Destiny:

> When you march up to attack a city, make its people an offer of peace. If they accept and open their gates, all the people in it shall be subject to forced labor and shall work for you. If they refuse to make peace and they engage you in battle, lay siege to that city. When the LORD your God delivers it into your hand, put to the sword all the men in it. As for the women, the children, the livestock and everything else in the city, you may take these as plunder for yourselves.

Whether or not land cannot be owned by a people, a people can certainly belong to the land. The distinction is fairly blunt—akin to the difference between a consensual relationship of equals and that of a master to a slave—but it can be tricky to discern in practice. By necessity, most folks who hope to "go back to the land" begin by first buying a few acres of it.

In a 1942 essay, Simone Weil attributes the condition of uprootedness to military conquest, an evil that persists in the descendants of conquerors who remain strangers in the land their ancestors occupied. That those descendants could relinquish oppressive control of a place, atone for their ancestral sins, and maybe even put down roots themselves is an idea taking hold in some Christian communities, where congregations of "radical disciples" are attempting to "rewild" their religion. Not all of them use that word, but the gist is similar: the notion that Christianity had been severed from its roots as a love- and earth-based religion, distorted, and made to serve as an accomplice to an evil empire.

Each community of radical disciples has its own method for reconnecting to those roots. In Philadelphia, a group called The Simple Way subscribes to the New Monasticism, a set of twelve tenets, including "relocation to the abandoned places of Empire," sharing resources in common, and caring for their corner of "God's earth." In Portland, Oregon, a faith-based leadership development effort called EcoFaith Recovery draws on twelve-step principles to restore "sanity in the midst of an addictive culture and economy." And another Portland community, called The Wilderness Way, lists as part of its mission the creation of "'wilderness' spaces within the context of empire in which to resist its domesticating and death-dealing influence." In Chicago, a group called Faith in Place hosts conversations on race and the environment, and helps local congregations organize around environmental activism and the planting of urban organic gardens. A Burning Man–esque traveling Christian eco-village called the Carnival de Resistance lists such highlights as "cooking for the community without using fossil fuels or electricity" and "receiving the grace of farm produce" and "righteous dumpster catches."

Maybe it's because I wasn't raised Christian that I find all of this so exotic and improbable. Like many alterna-kids growing up in the 1990s, I held Christians in lazy contempt based on sound bites from evangelical conservatives and half-remembered social studies units on the Salem witch trials. My image of a modern Christian was a pasty homophobe in pleated khakis beseeching his "Father." I hadn't heard of Christian socialists, Diggers, Quaker abolitionists, or Catholic Workers. I hadn't heard about the Berrigan brothers burning draft cards with homemade napalm. I suppose Finisia Medrano was the first to introduce me to a radical Christianity, but her dogma was so idiosyncratic her Bible recitations felt more like a rhetorical tactic than testimony on a deity.

Christians were not the only followers of Abrahamic religions rising to the occasion of social and ecological collapse. Both Islamic eco-theology and Jewish environmentalism have read their respective scriptures in conservationist terms. Islamic eco-theology emphasizes the tenets of *fitra*—harmony in the "natural state"—and *zohd*—asceticism, interpreted in this context to mean "living lightly on the earth." In 2015, Muslim leaders and scholars from thirty countries gathered in Istanbul for a symposium to launch the *Islamic Declaration on Global Climate Change*. The declaration names a dozen instances in the Qur'an in which the Prophet Muhammad acted in the interest of the environment. As outlined in the declaration, Muhammad "forbade the felling of trees in the desert," "established inviolable zones (*harams*) around Makkah and Al-Madinah, within which native plants may not be felled or cut and wild animals may not be hunted or disturbed," "renewed and recycled his meagre possessions by repairing or giving them away," and "took delight in the created world."[5] In essence, the Prophet articulated rules of conduct that would enable his people to live sustainably in a particular place, and though it's easy to glance past the last item in that litany, taking delight in the world was no less an instruction.

In the fall of 2015, more than four hundred rabbis signed *The Rabbinic Letter on the Climate Crisis*, writing, "As Jews, we ask the question whether the sources of traditional Jewish wisdom can offer guidance to our political efforts to prevent disaster and heal our relationship with the Earth." They cite Leviticus 26, in which "the Torah warns us that if we refuse to let the Earth rest, it will 'rest' anyway, despite us and upon us—through drought and famine and exile that turn an entire people into refugees."[6]

In Judaism, the concept of *tikkun olam*, or "world repair," is broadly understood as activity for the betterment of society. It stems from the notion that people should not wait for God to heal the world but participate actively in its repair. To the Orthodox, *tikkun olam* might be achieved through the study of Torah and strict observation of Jewish law. In liberal Jewish activist circles, the term is primarily understood as a prod to social and environmental action—though conservatives critique their reading as loose.

"A brand-new liberal-oriented idiom," writes one conservative columnist in the ignominious *Daily Caller*, "*tikkun olam* as understood in recent decades is not only alien to Jewish traditions, it undermines them."[7]

Many progressive Rabbis have dismissed these critics, including Rabbi Nicole Roberts, who writes that "calls for justice [are] rampant and *emphatic*" in the Torah, "in its *36 calls* for treating the stranger, the widow, and the orphan with dignity and not oppressing them; in the Torah's commandment to feed the needy from the corners of our fields; in the Torah's call to be stewards of the earth and to give our animals a day of rest."[8]

Suffice to say, holy texts lend themselves to contested readings. This is the beauty and tragedy of poetry, its possibility and its limit, and is to some extent inevitable. I was particularly interested in the radical Christians' reading of the Bible, because so much blood has been shed in the shadow of the cross. I wanted to know how Christians today made sense of that history. Christianity was one of the driving forces of colonization the world over, yet the radical Christians I encountered read the Bible as an argument against empire. Jesus and his Apostles were ascetic nomads on a crusade for liberation from oppressive systems and for direct connection to God through nature.

"A human being has roots," writes Simone Weil, "by virtue of his real, active and natural participation in the life of a community which preserves in living shape certain particular treasures of the past and certain particular expectations for the future." By this definition, the radical disciples were on the path to becoming rooted. They believed elements of their inherited version of Christianity were toxic, but rather than reject and dispose of their faith, or steal someone else's tradition, they told a different version in the spirit of rehabilitation.

It was early 2017, and stories of rehabilitation and reconciliation were in short supply, at least in my news cycle. I knew firsthand how seductive and convincing rage could be, how cleansing its fires. But time had complicated my understanding of the others I once viewed as enemies. Now doubt and caveat shadowed my every perception, and I could find no place for myself in the world of unforgiving certainty. I was clear on what most people were *against*, but I had very little sense of what anyone was *for*. If it was true that the radical disciples had managed to construct at least a provisional blueprint for a better world, I wanted to see how it was working out in practice.

Taos, New Mexico, was a long day's drive from Tucson, Arizona, where I was living at the time. I made the trip in the first warm week of spring. Billboards along the highway shoulder marked a sort of strandline, dividing the urban islands from the vast rural sea. Amid the ads for personal injury attorneys and 800 numbers for the gambling addicted (*How much are you prepared to lose?*) came the intermittent reminder that *Jesus Is Lord*. Silhouettes of chimpanzees rising to the stature of a man were circled in red and negated, for *In the beginning GOD CREATED*. Then came the jagged line of a heart monitor gone flat, and the promise that after we die *We will meet Him and be judged*. But that punitive Lord of the highway shoulder was not the God of the land where I was headed, though the two were known by the same book and called by the same name. I was headed to the land of an "earth-honoring" Jesus people: the Taos Initiative for Life Together (TiLT).

TiLT members describe themselves as a "parallel society existing within the dominant consumer culture of North America." Todd Wynward and his wife, Peg Bartlett, founded the community in 2015. For many years, they'd lived without plumbing in a rustic yurt in the mountains of northern New Mexico, raising their young son and running an outdoor-based public school called Roots and Wings. Once their son reached high school age, they decided to move to downtown Taos, into a dilapidated, seventy-five-year-old adobe hacienda with seven fireplaces and twelve rooms. They'd since improved much of the house, planted a garden, and taken on a few live-in interns.

The ground thawed out just days before my arrival, and the TiLT members had finished putting seed in the dirt that very afternoon. It was the intern Tyler's turn to make dinner and it was pizza night, but this pizza would not be arriving in a cardboard box: it would be assembled on homemade crust and topped with vegetables he'd grown himself in the backyard, in service to the ideal of "right relationship" between man and creation.

Tyler was twenty-three years old, the youngest of the interns, and had lived in the house the longest—nearly a year. He was clean-cut, articulate, cheerful. He'd moved from his home Mennonite community in Harrisonburg, Virginia, where he'd completed a degree in sustainable agriculture and peace and justice issues at Eastern Mennonite University. The darker, shaggier interns, Tony and Mike, had arrived just four weeks before, and were still getting the lay of the land. They were twenty-six and twenty-seven, respectively, which cast their decision to move into a communal house in a different light than Tyler's. This wasn't a gap year kind of thing; they'd left other lives behind.

Tony's previous life had consisted of working the supplements section of a Mother's Market in Huntington Beach, California. He hoped to one day have a communal farm of his own. "Do a CSA, but with herbs, tinctures, different things like that." Planning to serve as the resident apothecary at TiLT, he kept a shelf in his bedroom lined with empty glass bottles, a kind of altar to this intention. I couldn't figure out if he was a Christian or a hippie in need of a place to crash and grow plants. Maybe both. He had a dreamy way of smiling at you, softly and for unnerving durations, seeming to feel no impulse to fill up the lull with talk or look away, his finger in the socket of a higher vibration.

Mike grew up in Maryland but came to Taos by way of Tucson, where he'd worked for a nonprofit providing emergency home repairs for poor people. He said he'd been looking for a change when he was introduced to Todd at the Tucson Mennonite church. Mike wore a beat-up black leather jacket, blue jeans, and sneakers, and had the melancholic-contemplative mien of guys I grew up around, the kind of guys who sobered up before they reached legal drinking age, prematurely sloughing all the grasping and striving of the young, and winnowing their expectations to basic and mortal concerns.

Then again, he was a quiet dude. I was probably just inventing.

TiLT is not a Mennonite organization explicitly, but most of its residents are. Todd Wynward is a licensed Mennonite Minister for Environmental Justice, and TiLT sees itself as part of the broader Peace Church tradition, practiced by

Mennonites, Quakers, and the Amish. According to TiLT materials, they "seek to live community-centered lives of active reconciliation, mutual aid, simplicity, and justice making."

The stipulations of their life together are loose but many. There are shared meals, cyclical liturgies, and wilderness treks. Interns agree to a host of weekly commitments like house meetings, chores, volunteer work, gardening, and construction projects. On Wednesdays they open the house to the larger community for Food Lab, where they practice traditional cooking and food-storage techniques like drying and canning. They organize in the community for racial and environmental justice, and work with Tewa Women's United and the Poor People's campaign. But they are also asked to undertake personal transformations of the spirit and of their political consciousness: recovering from internet addiction, for example, or distributing personal wealth to those in need.

The interns cook at a men's shelter a couple of times a month and fellowship with the men. Sometimes men who've fallen on hard times will stop by the house to see if there is work to be done, and Todd employs them when he can afford to. Other times they want to volunteer.

"Speaking of men's shelters," I asked the interns, "is this going to be co-ed?"

A wave of shy laughter rolled through the group.

"Yeah, that's a great question," Tyler said.

There were problems with their application process. The year before, applications were sent only to those who requested them, and all the requests were made by white men.

"That's part of why I'm excited about the fall and the

people who are coming," Tyler went on. "Because they are females. I mean, just some diversity."

All TiLT residents have part-time jobs in the community, working at shelters or at the Roots and Wings School. And they devote three days a week to their own acre of land, tending to plants or earth-building projects. Their acre includes a small permaculture farm, a few greenhouses, a solar shower, a composting toilet, and a hut-like structure that they loan out to visitors for solo retreats. When I visited, they were in the process of renovating the outermost wing of the hacienda to serve as a bunkroom for future community members, making adobe bricks from earth hacked out of the backyard, just as those who'd built the house had done nearly a century before.

Todd was researching the life of Udell, the man who'd built the house. Udell was a Renaissance man: a doctor, an amateur painter, and a writer who'd helped his fellow man, despised consumerism, could garden and build, and delivered more than three thousand babies in the region before retiring in 1965.

Unlike Udell, TiLT had use of a cement mixer for combining earth and water. They poured the sludge into a mold that resembled a stepladder, and once the sludge hardened to a stiff jelly, they'd lift off the mold and leave the bricks in the sun to dry. Todd and I were sitting near a pile of these adobe bricks, on a grassy knob in the backyard, overlooking the garden. Afternoon was giving way to evening, all the yellow light soft-edged and slanted, the year's first warm rays.

"The guy who built this house," Todd told me, "he

basically said, 'Man in Taos has been transported by the earth, and has been the transporter of.' We cycle back."

When we say that someone lives close to the earth, "the earth" is generally understood as a metonym for nature. I preferred this more literal version: intimacy with actual dirt.

But the TiLT members hadn't had a heap of luck growing food in that resident dirt, so Tyler built a greenhouse and dumped seven cubic yards of topsoil in it.

"The ground is super tough to grow food in," Todd said. It was 70 degrees Fahrenheit that afternoon, but the night before it had dropped to 30. "In the winter, it's negative twenty at the coldest, and then it warms up to fifty-five, and it totally messes with the growing season . . . That's the almost impossible task that we're faced with in northern New Mexico. But people have been doing it for a thousand years."

I could see why the young men were drawn to Todd. Between the black-rimmed glasses and graying goatee, the farmer tan and blunt hands and mild indignation, he cut a kind of Whitman-Trotsky figure—which, come to think of it, is a decent likeness of his vision of Jesus Christ. He is an intense, charismatic guy. No matter what question I asked, he'd listen intently and become very still—as if he were waiting to be inhabited by the answer—then, after a beat or two, he'd unleash a rapid-fire riff.

I asked him if starting a communal house had always been his dream.

After some silence he commenced: "I've had a yearning to help rewild and transform Christianity back to the subversive, earth-honoring, empire-resisting, hope-engendering kind of thing, for a long, long time. But I didn't find it in the Church . . . and I didn't want to go and join some club or bourgeois self-affirmation team, or any of those kinds of options." He paused to ponder this conundrum.

Planting a greenhouse garden and building a structure as permanent as a house wouldn't qualify as rewilding in many people's minds. There are those who believe the seminomadic hunter-gatherer-gardener model is the only truly sustainable lifestyle for human beings. Others, more extreme, believe that the only sustainable lifestyle is nomadic, immediate-return hunting and gathering, meaning you don't store food or manipulate its production. These folks believe that all forms of sedentism and intensive land management—no matter who's at the helm—contributed to the advent of the Anthropocene. I suppose you could make the argument that any anthropogenic alteration of the landscape (layman's terms: changes made by humans) is linked to the Anthropocene by default. But failing to make a distinction between human activity that resulted in increased biodiversity and human activity that resulted in ecological catastrophe seems odd, and not a little cynical.

For those willing to strike a compromise, some land management might provide a transitional middle ground. Todd was in this camp, interested in winding the clock back a couple hundred years as opposed to, say, ten thousand. For folks like Todd, preparing to transition from the fossil fuel economy—growing your own food, sourcing your own water, bartering services within the community—is a more pragmatic approach to the crises of our current moment.

TiLT's philosophical orientation toward the land, what its members call the Watershed Way, came down to "*inhabiting a particular place*—experiencing its characteristics and being molded by its constraints, its bounty and its boundaries."[9]

"Given the fact that there are so many Christians in this country," I said, "the prospect of these ideas catching on is kind of exciting. Imagine if all that Tammy Faye prosperity gospel were transformed into the gospel of bioregional stewardship."

"Christianity has the weird wild card of God behind it," Todd said. "If it's just up to us, I think we're fucked. We're addicted to what we've done, and we're destroying the planet, and we know it, but we still keep saying, 'Can I have another cappuccino?'"

Behind the Watershed Way is the concept of Watershed Discipleship, popularized by a man named Ched Myers. Myers and his partner, Elaine Enns, run Bartimaeus Cooperative Ministries, a nonprofit based in Oak View, California, that is focused on church renewal, social and environmental justice, and restorative justice. Myers first became known among leftist Christians with the 1988 publication of *Binding the Strongman: A Political Reading of Mark's Story of Jesus*.

Over thirty years, his work had grown quite a following, thanks lately in no small part to disenfranchised Christian millennials looking for a way to reconcile their faith with their politics. One of the ways Myers understood the recent surge of interest in his work was through a cyclical theory of history. In the 1970s, he told me, there was "an exodus toward intentional communities, away from Cold War–era religion." In the early 2000s, he noticed a similar disillusionment among the millennial generation. And in between those two rebellions, evangelicalism had emerged as the institutional church in the United States.

Even if their parents' church promoted hateful distortions,

these young Christians didn't want to give up the gathering and the singing, the ritual of it, and they didn't want to give up on their God. This would require either a makeover on his part or an excavation, depending on your view.

Several of the young Christians I spoke to used the word "reconcile" explicitly. The secular world doesn't tend to think of Christianity as a gateway to radical left politics, but for these folks it was. People like Jesse, Peter's friend who'd traveled with Finisia Medrano. Jesse was raised in a charismatic Christian community that they describe as "dysfunctional but super tightly knit." It was at a 2009 conference hosted by The Simple Way in Philadelphia that Jesse was first introduced to the concept of rewilding. Ched Myers was the keynote speaker.

"I became politically aware during the Bush era, the Iraq war, 9/11, Katrina," Jesse wrote in an email, "and I saw a huge discrepancy between the theology and politics of my community, and what the bible had to offer . . . It was at that conference that I first heard anyone challenge the myths of progress and seek a more earth-based spirituality."

Many U.S. denominations, according to Myers, had been deformed by a shared heresy: "A functional docetism has numbed Christians to the escalating horrors of both social and ecological violence."[10] Docetism is technically the belief that Jesus was not actually human, but a phantom that only appeared to be flesh—hence the qualifier "functional." Functionally, it's the notion that the kingdom of God is otherworldly, exclusively spectral, death the single path to the Promised Land. No need to concern oneself with the affairs of the world if the kingdom is still coming. In fact, investment in the world might even distract you from your ultimate destination.

In a basic sense, Watershed Discipleship is a reading of Christian scripture through an animist lens, a call to re-invest in the phenomenal world. Its tenets, which TiLT calls marks, are many, but it's essentially a form of bioregionalism wherein the faithful come to know, defend, and rehabilitate their particular watersheds. Some marks focus on limiting consumption, eating seasonally and locally, and using renewable energy. Others call for the seeking of "Truth & Reconciliation of past abuse, extraction & colonization of your place and its people."[11]

Among nonreligious environmentalists and rewilders, it is common to view animism and paganism as the primary alternatives to empire and its orientation toward nonhumans as objects. Both are forms of earth-based spirituality that avow the subjectivity of animals, plants, and other natural phenomena. For example, most of us who speak English are taught to refer to a plant, an animal, or a river as an "it," whereas animists refer to a world of relations, in the grammar of "Thou." Our worldviews are built into our languages, and our languages determine, by some measure, our behavior. Killing an "it" is a far less loaded proposition than killing a "him," a "her," or a "them." In an essay exploring the power of language and its influence on worldview, the Potawatomi author and biologist Robin Wall Kimmerer writes, "Grammar, especially our use of pronouns, is the way we chart relationships in language and, as it happens, how we relate to each other and to the natural world."[12]

Animist traditions teach human cultures how to relate sustainably with their environment indefinitely, but the stories are situated in the specific egalitarian, biodiverse contexts that bore them—contexts that are foreign to many of us. The Abrahamic traditions, on the other hand, developed alongside and in reaction to empire, and so their stories may prove uniquely relevant to the situation at hand. In the book of Exodus, the Israelite slaves are freed in reaction to a series of plagues (thought by some scholars to be a record of actual interrelated events subsequent to a period of climatic warming).[13] But once their freedom in the "wilderness" on the edge of empire was upon them, many longed for their former comforts, complaining: "Would that we had died at the Lord's hand in the land of Egypt, as we sat by our flesh-pots and ate our fill of bread, but you have led us into this desert to die of famine."[14]

According to the word's various roots and definitions, "wilderness," a cousin of the word "bewilder," refers to an uninhabited place, a place of disorder and neglect. Put another way, a wilderness is a form of frontier, "the limit of knowledge," the unknown place: terra incognita. In the Exodus story, the wilderness is the vast unknown territory of freedom: freedom to worship, freedom from the restraints of forced labor, but also the freedom to starve. In their wandering, the Israelites were forbidden by God to stockpile food; they survived upon their daily manna and were purified through the relinquishing of their will (the empire's pathology of control and domination).

You could read it as a recovery narrative: the subjugated escape captivity, admit powerlessness, and purge their addictions and dependencies in order to live again in "right relationship" with creation (i.e., within the limits imposed by their ecosystem). Achieving freedom from an external oppressor is only the beginning of the story. The far murkier and more difficult second act involves the conversion of exploitation and dependency to interdependency. It takes more than one generation. The Promised Land would be realized only if the Israelites upheld their covenant with God, a set of instructions for living sustainably in a particular place. It was promised, "If you listen carefully to the LORD your God and do what is right in his eyes, if you pay attention to his commands and keep all his decrees, I will not bring on you any of the diseases I brought on the Egyptians, for I am the LORD, who heals you."[15]

In other words: *Here is a method for belonging to this place. Here's a way to live without destroying everything, including yourselves.*

And yet, even in the Promised Land, even within the container of the covenant, creation would ultimately belong to herself. As the Rabbi Jeremy Schwartz has written, "We're living on borrowed land. That's the astounding claim of the Biblical tradition . . . Leviticus 25:35 instructs, 'the land shall not be sold in perpetuity, for the land/earth is Mine, for you are sojourners or temporary residents with Me.'"[16]

As for my own selective reading of Exodus, it's worth noting that the Promised Land was not terra incognita. As the writer Naomi Dann observed:

> The liberation of the Jews from oppression in Egypt did not come without a violent cost, and the Promised Land they reached was not empty . . . Telling the Exodus story without acknowledging the violence against the Canaanites is similar to repeating the Zionist myth that Israel was a "land without a people for a people without land."[17]

I'll not wade into a lengthy disquisition on Middle East history and politics, about which I know pathetically little, except to note that using scripture to justify the occupation of other people's lives and lands is common, and I needn't reach far to find examples.

In the Americas, Christianity had served as empire's primary collaborator. Todd Wynward and Ched Myers trace the sinful condition of Christendom to two pivotal historical events. The first was the adoption of Christianity by the Roman emperor Constantine in A.D. 312—an unholy marriage of church and state that effectively expunged Christianity's origin as a subversive force of resistance to empire. The second event was the adoption of *Dum Diversas*, the fifteenth-century papal bull that decreed the king of Portugal could, by divine right, "invade, search out, capture, and subjugate" any non-Christian lands and "reduce their persons into perpetual servitude." Church-sanctioned murder and enslavement would be renewed and extended to the king of Spain through the *Inter Caetera* of 1493.

The impact of these geographically unlimited decrees cannot be overstated. In the "New World," they paved the way for the Middle Passage and Manifest Destiny, and then reservations, boarding schools, forced sterilization, tribal termination, chattel slavery.

In the American Southwest, the Doctrine of Discovery played out in the Pueblos, a group of related but distinct tribal communities spanning a territory that includes New Mexico, and large swaths of Colorado and Arizona.

Taos Pueblo is located one mile north of the TiLT House. It is the ancestral home of the Red Willow People and, since 1992, a UNESCO World Heritage Site. I drove to Taos Pueblo one warm and cloudless afternoon; the sky over the mountains was blue as a swimming pool. The main adobe complex is said to be the oldest continually inhabited site in the United States—built between A.D. 1000 and 1450. The north face of the complex is famous, widely reproduced in paintings and photographs, including a few by Georgia O'Keeffe and Ansel Adams. Rough-hewn rafters and skinny ladders cast dramatic shadows over the earth and over the face of the adobe, breaking the seam between them, a lattice weaving light and shade.

A small group had gathered outside the little adobe church for the official tour: a diverse assembly of genders, nationalities, ethnicities, and ages, frozen in the universal bent-neck pose of cell-phone worship. I am not ordinarily a joiner of groups or tours, and have an uneasy relationship to sightseeing generally. My discomfort increases an order of magnitude when the visit is to someone else's home or place of worship. Normally, I'd be inclined to wander on my own, but in this case it seemed a greater trespass not to join.

Our guide arrived and we filed after her into the dim cool of the church and took seats in the pews. As she described the building's history, and later the effects of the Church on the Pueblo more broadly, I was struck by the ubiquity of Catholic symbols, the persistent influence of the Church, but also by the reminders from our guide that "Catholicism was forced on us." Many community members are practicing Catholics, but the truth of what happened is remembered and spoken of honestly.

In the year 1660, the people of Taos Pueblo dispatched their resident priest and destroyed his church. The Spanish built a new church, and in 1680, the people of Taos Pueblo destroyed it, too, this time killing a pair of priests. That summer, a co-ordinated alliance of Pueblos rose up against their occupiers and drove them out of the territory entirely—an act of resistance that some have called the most significant challenge to occupation in the history of European colonization in the Americas. The man who planned the revolt, a Tewa religious leader by the name of Po'pay (who five years earlier had been jailed and sentenced to die for the crime of "sorcery"), encouraged the Pueblos to destroy all evidence of the occupiers. Warriors across the Pueblo World killed their resident priests and destroyed their missions.[18]

"Now the god of the Spaniards is dead," Po'pay famously said. "He was made of rotten wood."

The Spanish returned a year later and were once again repelled. In 1692, Diego de Vargas commenced a campaign to take the territory in what history has called "bloodless reconquest"—though plenty of blood was spilled.

In 1696, fourteen Pueblos rose up once more against the Spanish, but they failed to drive them out. In the common narrative, 1696 represents the end of resistance, inaugurating a century of Christianization and the attendant underground transmission of traditional rites and ceremonies. Other narratives emphasize the Pueblo World's assertion of sovereignty throughout history continuous to today.

Our tour moved on to an old cemetery, overgrown with long grasses. Many wooden crosses stood askew in the earth. In the center stood the crumbled ruin of another adobe church—destroyed by the Americans in 1847 as retribution for the execution of the territorial governor, Charles Bent. When the Pueblo warriors pulled Bent from the chimney where he was hiding and scalped him, they'd spared the lives of the women and children in the house. Days later,

Pueblo women, children, and elders were sheltering inside the church when the Americans arrived to exact their vengeance, taking pains to spare no one. This was the story of "discovery" playing out all across the Americas.

One of the trickiest problems with "living wild" or "going back to the land" is the immediate invocation of oppositional categories that are not easily defined: "domesticated living" or "living separated from the land." Domestication may be distilled as dependence on the empire, but what way of life is not fundamentally dependent on one system or another? Those who would "live wild" remain dependent on the plant, animal, and elemental entities that sustain them; and while this may be preferable, dependence it remains. It is not possible to live separate from "the land" or from "nature." It is only possible to imagine that you do. And therein lies a crucial difference between city dwellers and back-to-the-landers: one way of life forces daily reckoning with that essential dependence, while the other supports its denial through abstractions like money, utility companies, and grocery stores.

Still, it can be difficult to disentangle yourself from these categories, so endemic are they to the ideologies of industrial civilization. The binary between the wilderness and the city raises the specter of other false binaries: dependence and independence, wildness and refinement, purity and filth, heaven and hell.

Other creatures don't appear to have this problem. The cormorant who alights on the dumpster and later touches down on the wetland is not plagued by contradiction or by accusations of hypocrisy from his fellow cormorants. The rain precipitates and falls on us all. To collapse the categories is to acknowledge our fundamental interdependence with all other beings, an interdependence that both comforts and terrifies. To know this inextricability is to dispel the illusion that we have total control over our lives—and to accept that we are in relationship with the world, at the mercy of others who are at our mercy, too.

The foundational myth of the American West relies on the idea of a wild emptiness. The colonizers saw the land as un-utilized frontier, predestined by God for their control and cultivation. The journals of Meriwether Lewis are filled with the usual composite of beauty and peril ascribed to the "wild" by colonist eyes. Lewis toggles between endless "scenes of visionary enchantment" and merciless torment by foul weather, sickness, bears, and mosquitoes that "invade and obstruct us on all occasions."[19]

This view of the non-agrarian landscape as simultaneously alien, dangerous, and untouchably beautiful unfortunately persists today among many well-meaning conservationists. A view that holds us apart from true intimacy—and thus the capacity to coexist—with our own ecosystems. Lewis's part-ner on the expedition, William Clark, pretty much summed it up in commenting on the death of one of their party: "Thus a man had like to have starved to death in a land of plenty."

My home state of Oregon was widely considered frontier, though it had been inhabited by dozens of tribes for time immemorial. I'm reminded of a remark made by the anthro-pologist and historian David G. Lewis, in a talk on Oregon's

Indigenous history: "Somebody introduced themselves in a meeting as having been here five generations," he said. "I was thinking, huh, how many generations have *we* been here. A generation is about every twenty years? So, probably, a good five hundred generations or so?"

Five hundred generations born and raised and buried in the same homeland, and the Europeans called it "wilderness."

I was the first in my family to be born in the state of Oregon. It is the only place that has ever felt like home to me, though given my remedial knowledge of its watersheds, its native plants and animals, its birds—"home" is a bit of a reach. My people have been in the western United States for less than forty years. From there, I track my ancestry east, through the Midwest and the Northeast, to Western Europe, Scandinavia, and the Middle East. I know that one ancestor migrated for reasons of religious persecution, that two fled a civil war, and that for some there were occupations and internal displacements—but most of that history is lost to assimilation. I don't know when they were last truly rooted in a place or what Promised Land they envisioned. I don't know who they were before they began their migrations, how they felt upon leaving home, or where the bodies are buried. To me, the frontier is a tundra of intergenerational amnesia.

For those, like me, who are effectively rootless, it is difficult to fathom what rootedness means, or how it might feel to have roots five hundred generations deep, and to maintain those roots in spite of continuous incursion by an occupying force. It is difficult to fathom but worth a shot, and if you are able to imagine it, you might ask: *What wouldn't I do to defend my home?*

Stories of Indigenous resistance were making mainstream news in 2017. In North Dakota, at Standing Rock, the site of the Dakota Access Pipeline resistance, a shadowy private security firm called TigerSwan had used "counterterrorism" measures against the "pipeline insurgencies." Leaked internal documents referred to the Oceti Sakowin Camp as "the battlefield" and likened activists to religious extremists. Helicopters were meanwhile buzzing the Unist'ot'en Camp in British Columbia, Canada. And back in Arizona, the Apache Stronghold was entering its third year of resistance to Resolution Copper, a joint venture formed to sink a seven-thousand-foot mine in Oak Flat, an Apache sacred site.

It's tempting to interpret these incursions through the theory of cyclical history. But a cycle implies periods of dormancy, and in this case the violence ebbs only from the consciousness of the dominant culture, which is always at war with Indigenous life. The breaking of treaties is not a past-tense event. Lands promised by treaty to tribes have been stolen and stolen again, their boundaries redrawn whenever it suits the needs of corporations or their representatives in the government.

To live "the illusion of history," as Ched Myers has written, is to live in a state of sin. To dispel the illusion, to "turn history around," is "the meaning of the biblical discourse of repentance." The word "repentance," in this context, does not refer to performative self-reproach or sheepish apology, but to an inner alteration. To repent is to be changed.

Whether or not the exodus *off the map* ever comes to pass, I've since grown suspicious of my attraction to the premise. I've come to think that terra incognita was, and is, no less a fiction than the map itself. And it's easy to project whatever you like into the gap: danger, adventure, self-determination, and, most problematically, vacancy. A frontier can exist only in the minds of those who do not call it home, for not one remote valley or speck of rock has gone uncounted by the inhabitants of that place. Any pursuit of rootedness depends on this understanding, on the simultaneous "undoing" of the "social, spiritual, and mental" structures that train us to perceive a vacuum where others make their homes—a "terra" that will not be recovered in our geography but within our own imaginations.

James Agee once wrote that each of our "incommunicably tender" lives is "almost as hardly killed as easily wounded." I sometimes repeated those words to myself at my sickest, when in absence of a diagnosis my mind substituted worst-case scenarios. *You're unwell*, I'd tell myself, *but difficult to kill*. On my worst days, possessed by acute panic, I skipped past moderation and worst-case scenarios and instead recited, *You are already dead*. When you are already dead, there is nothing to resist, to stave off, or to fear.

Both of these ideas return to me when I think about empires, past and current, and their remarkable capacity to withstand wars, coups, plagues, famines, storms, and droughts—often shifting shape, bearing limps and scars, but surviving, sometimes many hundreds of years past their peaks—almost as hardly killed as easily wounded. And I am lulled into thinking that the life I am used to will indefinitely go on.

But as a realist might note, we are almost as hardly killed as *inevitably* killed. The body is finite. Eventually and without exception, *every* body dies, and this is true of empires, too.

Our contemporary empire depends on the smooth functioning of intricate networks that are far more vulnerable than anyone who likes to sleep at night wants to know—shipping, agriculture, heat and shelter and water—but every once in a while some archaic force rears up and wakes us to their fragility. Extreme weather arrives, or pandemic, almost anything to interrupt the supply chain—and we are forced to reckon with our dependence, like tyrannical children who've made one too many demands on their beleaguered mother and find themselves suddenly cast out into the elements. This is old news to much of the world, where steady supplies of food and water and electricity and the uninterrupted functioning of governments have never been the norm. But even in the so-called overdeveloped world, we are feeling the tenuousness of all we take for granted. In the United States, Hurricanes Katrina and Sandy and Maria provided stark demonstrations of that tenuousness; and for many of the people who survived those storms, the collapse has already come, life will never return to what it was.

The supply chain breakdown I witnessed in rural Oregon in 2008 was by no means conclusive evidence of our empire's collapse—it was evidence of a wounding, not a mortal blow—but that wounding did reveal core vulnerabilities in the system. It is one thing to understand those vulnerabilities in the abstract, and it is another to experience them firsthand, on an empty stomach, with an empty gas tank.

In the winter of 2013, Todd Wynward and Peg Bartlett were still living in the mountains off the grid. Todd had driven into Taos to re-up on supplies, but when he reached the gas station he found a line stretching down the block, dozens of cars long. As he drove past them, he slowed and watched a physical altercation play out between two men at the pump. When he reached the grocery store, the lot was overflowing. Inside the store, forty to sixty carts waited in each lane. He wondered what the hell was going on. Someone explained that winter conditions had prevented trucks from delivering natural gas to the area, so people were without heat and had tried to rely on space heaters, which then collapsed the electric grid. One missed shipment had plunged a sizable town—known for its rugged and self-sufficient population—into chaos.

In light of this experience, Todd began to come to terms with the inevitable collapse of infrastructure and, as he puts it, "embrace the unraveling." If we imagine that our civilization is already in collapse, the question we are faced with is this: How, then, shall we live? The question is derived from Peter 3:11, used essentially as shorthand for one's response to certain inevitabilities. We know for certain we will one day die; how, then, shall we live? Knowing what we know—knowing, as Peter writes, that "the day of the Lord will come as a thief in the night, in which the heavens will pass away with a great noise, and the elements will melt with fervent heat." Knowing that the systems on which we have relied will likely fail, and that the earth may soon become uninhabitable—how, then, shall we live?

Now that you know "all these things shall be dissolved," Peter asks, "what manner of persons ought you to be?"

The chaos in Taos that Todd encountered in 2013 had inspired panic buying and hoarding, but it had also mobilized locals to band together to set up hot-meal stations, donate firewood and blankets, and go door-to-door checking on the elderly. There will always be predatory outliers, but when the chips are down, human beings demonstrate time and time again that they are wired for cooperation. Todd began to view the collapse of infrastructure as both a threat and an opportunity. He turned his attention toward the Transition Town movement and how he might help Taos and the surrounding area live as if the inevitable had already happened.

The Transition Town movement was born in Ireland in 2004 when a teacher named Rob Hopkins assigned his class the task of applying permaculture principles to the problem of peak oil. His students generated the "Energy Descent Action Plan," proposing how their town in West Cork could produce food locally, limit waste, and become energy independent. In 2006, Hopkins took this idea back to his hometown in Southwest England and formed Transition Town Totnes, a charity focused on resilience through peak oil and climate change. In essence, where the empire is most damaging and vulnerable, those in the movement propose transitioning to more resilient and sustainable alternatives. For example, if large-scale agriculture and shipping are vulnerable to peak oil and extreme weather, a community could transition to growing organic local food. It sounds simple, but it's hard to pull off in practice. Still, hundreds of communities all over the world are trying.

At the TiLT house and among those involved in the larger Taos community, this has meant setting goals to generate zero waste, growing food locally, applying green building practices, using renewable energy, and repairing the local ecosystem. One of TiLT's goals was to achieve energy independence throughout Taos County, and its members had developed a loose network of relationships in the area to that end, mostly with other organic and permaculture farms, where they also volunteered their labor.

Put bluntly, one of the greatest barriers to realizing energy independence is our addiction to stuff—to having what we want whenever we want it. It may be true, as Finisia and her crew sometimes said, that it's easier to jump off a structure that is standing than a structure that is collapsing, but so long as the structure stands, most people will—in ignorance or out of fear or habit—return to its eaves when the rain arrives. This is why some frustrated rewilders I've spoken to doubt very much that consciousness-raising will create lasting change. Change will come when the collapse of our current way of life demands it. Communal subsistence living inevitably results in periods of discomfort and strained relationships, and so long as warm beds and Netflix and grocery stores exist, most people will return to those comforts when the going gets tough.

That's why Peter believes social skills like cooperation and conflict management are far more crucial than the so-called hard skills of wilderness survival. And that's why Todd Wynward believes that if it's just up to us, we're fucked, that spiritual conviction is required to bridge the divide.

"Despite our professed values of love and peace and justice," Todd writes, "we compulsively make choices that are unfair, unjust, and unhealthy for our world. We need serious help, and cannot do it alone."

In 2015, a small Mennonite press published Todd's book *Rewilding the Way: Break Free to Follow an Untamed God,* and it includes several commentaries on addiction (e.g.,

"Christianity is captive to corporations. God calls us to break free of our addiction to ecocidal behaviors"). Todd was using the addiction-recovery model to describe how Christians in the global North might repent of their insatiable consumption habits. Todd calls this addictive illness "affluenza," which he defines as "extreme materialism and consumerism associated with the pursuit of wealth and success and resulting in a life of chronic dissatisfaction, debt, overwork, stress, and impaired relationships."

Christians are already familiar with the second of the twelve steps—surrender to a greater power—but their addictive illness, Todd felt, needed to be addressed with the fourth step: Conduct a searching and fearless moral inventory. "We are repulsed by the idea of raping nature, but our voracious standard of living demands that the raping continue," he writes, likening the circular logic of addiction to sin, to the Apostle Paul's lament, "For I do not do the good I want to do, but the evil I do not want to do—this I keep on doing."[20]

It occurred to me that the TiLT house was also a kind of halfway house: a place where a person might escape captivity, admit powerlessness, and purge dependencies in order to live again in "right relationship" with creation. In addition to the moral inventory and calls for selfless service, overcoming isolation through community is one of the core tenets of the twelve-step model. Studies have shown time and again that addictions thrive when people feel isolated—unlike shame or punitive exclusion, community can help the addict overcome.

Similar concepts have been employed in the secular world. For example, the environmental activist and author Joanna Macy created a workshop called The Work That Reconnects, which includes steps like "honoring our pain for the world" and "go forth," a call to service. The Good Grief Network, founded by LaUra Schmidt in Scottsbluff, Nebraska, lists ten steps to prevent burnout among activists. Their slogan: "Community is the cure for tragedy."

What are we doing when we conduct a searching and fearless moral inventory? We shine a light in the shadows, acknowledging what was denied, becoming acquainted with estranged parts of ourselves and our histories. We are, in other words, making a home in ourselves. And what is it we are doing when we turn to the community for support, when we offer the community our service in return? We are making a home in others. We are practicing interdependence.

To develop a relationship with the water we drink, the food we eat, the people on whom we depend, our own psyches—these activities are inherently revolutionary, in direct opposition to the isolation, distraction, and individualism on which the market economy thrives. Intimate relationship is a way of making a frontier a home. But it is less a form of homesteading than a shifting of perspective: these connections were always there; we just couldn't, or wouldn't, permit ourselves to feel them.

"I hope this is a place where people who've gone to high school or college can come," Todd said. "Like, you've been to school, but now you *really* need to go to school. In response to overpopulation, climate change, overconsumption, you know? *How, then, shall we live?*"

"You just asked the central question of my book," I told him.

"That's the central question of my life," he said.

❦❦❦

Of all that Moses brought down from the mountain, the commandment to remember the Sabbath day and keep it holy is, to me, the most instructive. In addition to a day of rest, Leviticus 25 provided for a sabbatical year—one year in every seven—in which agriculture was abandoned, and for a year of jubilee—one year in every fifty—in which debts were forgiven, slaves freed, and repossessed lands returned. This jubilee would zero out the accounts, level class stratification, and serve as a culturally imposed limit to growth.

Roughly twelve thousand years ago, at the dawn of the Holocene, the world began to warm and the primary environmental limits to human population growth were greatly diminished. The Ice Age ended, making both sedentism and agricultural dependence possible (thus, the formation of cities), and many species of megafauna died out, effectively ending predation on humans. This is where our trouble started, according to a lot of people. But if you look at cultures that remained relatively stable through that period and did not exceed their means, you'll find that most of them observed culturally imposed limits to growth.

Among tribes on the Northwest Coast of North America, this includes the potlatch tradition, in which the potlatch host affirms their social standing by giving gifts to the community. Limits to growth also include the ethic of using every part of a hunted animal and the practice of considering how any given decision will affect life seven generations into the future. These traditions, in addition to their spiritual and social import, are methods for delimiting consumption and surplus, and redistributing wealth.

Limits to growth aren't necessarily a moral proposition, but they certainly are pragmatic. As four hundred rabbis promised in 2015 in their open letter on the climate crisis, "If we refuse to let the Earth rest, it will 'rest' anyway, despite us and upon us—through drought and famine and exile that turn an entire people into refugees."

Rewilders have proposed different methods for living sustainably in the wilderness of the Anthropocene, for "undoing domestication" and "fostering biodiversity," but most of their methods come down to commitment. Committing to the health and well-being of a particular community and bioregion, and in so doing, overcoming their estrangement from the land and getting to know their home.

The Christians' word for this is "covenanting." I asked Ched Myers what it meant to "covenant" with the land.

"It's like a marriage," he said. When you form a covenant with a person or a place, you take a stand, and that person or place becomes the locus of all your work. "Making a covenant with another person is about committing to them," he explained, "not just until they're no longer useful, or attractive, or titillating or interesting, but committing to that person as an expression of limits. I'm going to focus my energy relationally in this covenant because life can flourish within it. The kind of life that sits at the dying person's bedside. The kind of life that endures the worst of the other."

Todd Wynward thinks that "sin" is one of the most poorly understood concepts in Christendom. He traces its roots to a Greek verb, *hamartanein*, an archer's term that means "to miss the mark." He told me that sin was originally understood as a lifestyle, as opposed to an isolated personal transgression. To live in sin was to live out of step with creation, in violation of God's command to "serve and keep" the Garden of Eden. The Bible, in its original language, makes no mention of hell, but it frequently mentions heaven's fiery inverse, a smoldering trash dump on the outskirts of Jerusalem called Gehenna. It was an actual place, Todd explained. A place Jesus used as a metaphor for where we'd wind up if we didn't repent of our sin. Almost any industry could serve as a path to the smoldering trash heap. I thought of fracking, and the lake of fire it sometimes summons to our kitchen faucets. I thought of burning tar sands and aerial shots of the Pacific garbage patch.

Then, unbidden, came a memory of tall evergreens shading the banks of the Nehalem River, and how it feels to stand on a beach in the Olympic Peninsula, watching gray-green waves batter the sea stacks. It didn't occur to me in the moment that these were images of home, my personal vision of paradise, but they did give rise to a question.

I asked Todd what his image of God was, and his response seemed a feat of clairvoyance.

He said he imagined an ocean: he's a drop in the ocean, and evil constitutes a few drops, too, but mostly the ocean is love.

Tikkun olam's mystical underpinnings are found in Lurianic Kabbalah, a creation story in which the material world is born from the loneliness of *ein sof* (the infinite love and light that is God's original form); *ein sof* contracted to create space for an other, and the void became a vessel, and *ein sof* radiated into the vessel, which shattered under pressure. But traces of the divine light remain, clinging to the shards, and these form the basis of the material world.

Once upon a time, all was unified, but an empty space gave birth to brokenness, to individuation and binaries. Stern judgment was pulled apart from mercy. But light clings to the places where we are broken. When and if the shattered light finally reintegrates with its source, the world of estrangement will end. Students of comparative religion might read in this story a resonance with Nirvana, wherein reunion with the source obliterates the delusion of separateness that animates the phenomenal world.

For those like me, for whom there is no other world, the collapsing of certain divisions—man and nature, wilderness and settlements, body and mind, us and them—might indeed bring about the end of the particular world we've inherited. I think of an essay on the American jazz composer and polymath Sun Ra, by the poet Harmony Holiday. She writes, "Fear of the end of the world is really fear of the end of the defunct ideologies that sustain Western civilization." Those who are ready to "overthrow the West's dead ideas and the habits they demand" make pilgrimage to a territory that is "*after the end of the world* where our sense of sound becomes invincible and whole and grammar is world building and elemental." In this story, *after the end of the world* there is wholeness, a grammar of "Thou" from which to build the next world.

On my last night in New Mexico, I drove through the dark to the little room I'd been renting with a view of Taos Mountain, feeling unexpectedly bereft. I was inspired and moved by the human efforts I'd seen at TiLT, by the human poetry embedded in their gospel, but the path forward continued to elude me.

I took a shower, poured a drink, and sat at the big picture window watching headlights snake through the foothills and through my bent reflection. I was an orange smear, shot through with light, and the mountain pulsing in the dark somewhere beyond. Fleetingly, I wanted the mountain to get up, come to the window, drop its girth upon me, and make of me a stubbed-out bug. In a way, it would be easier. As the poet Auden observed, "We would rather be ruined than changed."

No doubt, there's a lot to atone for. More than any one life could amend. My own running moral inventory included people I'd hurt, or failed to love; people I'd never met, on whose backs my larders were loaded; a whole lot of dead people, whose blood was in the ground, broken to build the house I shelter in; all the animals and plants without whose flesh I could not have lived. The list was too long for any single person to hold alone—and I felt suddenly, mortally alone. Whether that wilderness was inherited or of my own making, I no longer cared—I was tired of wandering there. But I didn't want a deity to rush the gap; I wanted other people, and in the same breath doubted my ability to commit to them for any sustained length of time.

The psychoanalyst and author Adam Phillips has written that our utopias speak more articulately about the privations of our actual lives than of an external ideal. The question posed by a utopia, in clinical terms: "What would the symptom have to be for this to be the self-cure?"

The Promised Land is a place of the imagination, a novel place that recuperates the known, spiritually wedded to the homes we left behind—Eden, intimacy, oneness with creation. The Promised Land assumes many forms. For some it is their ancestral homeland, for others I guess it's world peace, or the Beloved Community, or the decolonized future after the end of the world. For me, it's something akin to Ched Myers's covenant metaphor: a human love that endures the worst in the other, that sits at the dying person's bedside, that commits to a limit where life can flourish.

Maybe the Promised Land only ever existed in the promise itself. The promise to stop running, to put down roots, to know the stone and valley in all their earthly beauty and imperfection. To nurture that which nurtures you. To help one another find a way home.

4

NOTES ON A LIVING TRAIL

Never trust to general impressions, my boy, but concentrate yourself upon details.
—SHERLOCK HOLMES (Arthur Conan Doyle)

Attentiveness is the natural prayer of the Soul.
—NICOLAS MALEBRANCHE

The night I arrived at Deer Island, I sat in a fifty-foot yurt in the woods drinking Costco brand bourbon and cola out of a travel mug in the company of a dozen men. They were ex-military, volunteering with Search and Rescue or working as civilian police on base. All of them dressed in army casual. The only other female student in the yurt made her living training dogs. Like the men, she dressed in camouflage fatigues and wore a little camouflage cap. She'd brought along one of her K-9 trackers, a fluffy German shepherd that growled like he'd flay your face if you so much as glanced at him.

Fernando Moreira, the man we'd come to the Oregon woods to see, was rumored to be one of the best trackers alive. His students claimed his abilities verged on the supernatural, that thousands of hours in the field had so attuned his eye to the spoor he was capable of trailing a man for miles over solid stone. One student told me that Fernando had never lost a trail. A missing person was sometimes dead by the time he found them, or a trail terminated in a parking lot just before the subject climbed into a car and sped away, but if a hair so much as grazed the earth, he could point to the sign.

A Google search the week before I arrived had produced a 2008 article, first published in "the official peer-reviewed, quarterly journal of the American College of Forensic Examiners."[1] It began like a script for an action trailer:

> He's wanted by the FBI, Special Forces, the Border Patrol, sheriff departments, SWAT teams, and at least a dozen police agencies . . . Law enforcement personnel are aware that he camps in the mountain ranges . . . and that he uses "Grasshopper" as an alias. What makes him so hard to find is his ability to cover his tracks, never leaving a trail . . . Like the strategic chess player, his mind is always several moves ahead of you. The dictionary describes him to a tee under the word *stealth*.[2]

And so on.

This sort of hype is not uncommon in the world of tracking. Student trackers tend to constellate around personalities, and there's a lot of whispering about who's for real and who's a grifter. There are claims of rare competence and an intense desire on the part of students to believe. Of the handful of charismatic tracking experts, most served as full-time figureheads for expensive schools and rarely returned to the field. Guys like my former hero Tom Brown, Jr., or the ten-gallon-hat-wearing Canadian reality TV star Terry Grant.

But Fernando Moreira executed live missions monthly

in between trainings. Unlike those other teachers, he didn't care about notoriety or money or personal comfort, and much of his work was volunteer. He was, reportedly, indefatigable. If a case took multiple days, he'd track to exhaustion, sleep a few hours beside the trail, then rise in the predawn dim to track again.

I'd talked my friend Willem—one of Fernando's protégés—into letting me crash the Tactical Tracking Intensive for free. Willem and I were first introduced to each other in the late 1990s at the wilderness survival school where we were both enrolled (he was in a program for college-age students). Wildlife tracking was a main component of our study, though I was never very good at it. For Willem it had remained an abiding passion. He'd nursed many passions in the twenty years I'd known him: boxing, thermogenesis, Arthurian legend, polyphasic sleep cycles, and, most recently, the history of nomadic horse peoples on the Eurasian steppe. He was prone to enthusiasms but generally a reliable source, and he was certain that Fernando was the *real deal*. Willem, who dressed in a woolen suit and flatcap and smoked a calabash pipe, had taken to calling Fernando the Portuguese Sherlock Holmes.

In the tradition we knew, tracking was less a discrete activity than a total worldview. We didn't just study animal tracks in mud or sand. We tracked animal shit, pulled it apart, studied its composition of fur and berries and plant fibers, and tried to extract from that composition information about the availability of small prey or seasonal blackberry yields. We tracked the paths of plants over the landscape, shifting weather patterns, salmon migrations. We tracked the alarm calls of birds and hypothesized as to the type and whereabouts of the predators that had prompted them. We tracked our emotional responses to natural phenomena. In the mornings, we tracked the previous night's dreams. Or at least we tried to track these things.

Intimate knowledge of the world was the goal, and tracking was the method for achieving it. If you were estranged from your own ecosystem, tracking was a refreshingly straightforward practice for overcoming that estrangement. I never doubted its importance, though I did wind up doubting the abilities of some who were touted as experts. There was so much masculine posing and bluster, there were so many fish stories, it was difficult to know what facility in tracking actually looked like. If Willem was right, if Fernando was the real deal, I wanted to see for myself.

It was late in the evening and the men had circled around him, cupping their travel mugs of booze. The scene had the spirit of a tailgate. Under a string of white Christmas lights, Fernando lit one unfiltered Camel after another. The glow split his face in two. On the lit side, just above his broomlike mustache, I could see the scar jagging up his cheek where a surgeon had cut out a sizable melanoma five years earlier. (It wasn't the excision that hurt, he'd later tell me, but being stitched up again taut as a drum.) He was dressed like his students, in fatigues and a woolly army-surplus sweater, but with one notable exception: he wore a scarf of pale yellow linen wound loosely at his neck. I was taken with this yellow scarf—a romantic flourish—and with the extravagant fluidity of his movement. He told tracking stories continuously through the night, and as he told them, he floated back and forth on his heels in a kind of slow dance.

Given the volume of militarized testosterone in the room, I doubt he performed that rhumba intentionally, and I suppose he thought the scarf harked back to the flyboys of a bygone war rather than to an aged choreographer of Eastern European extraction, which happened to be the effect.

Back home in Reno, Fernando kept in shape by walking in the dry heat with a weighted pack, ten or so miles a day, three days a week. But most weeks he was away on missions.

"I used to average two, three, four hundred missions a year," he told me. "There were days when we'd get two or three calls."

"Wow," I said. "What does your day off look like?"

"I still go out and train." He laughed. And then, as if it had only just occurred to him, he said, "I don't do anything else."

Some expert men exploit their corner of power to make other men feel small or subservient, particularly if there are women on hand to bear witness. Fernando managed to project a humble, democratic air even as he dominated our attention, the addendum of each story amounting to *You can do this, too! I'm just a regular guy.* He was a jovial, constitutionally enthusiastic person—a type we might dub gentle-father raconteur. Anyway, the students adored him and drank in his stories eagerly, prodding for another as soon as he'd finished the last.

I remembered reading a theory that human storytelling and animal tracking were interdependent ventures, evolving in concert over millennia. "Trackers themselves cannot read everything *in* the sand," wrote the evolutionary biologist Louis Liebenberg. "Rather, they must be able to read *into* the sand. To interpret tracks and signs trackers must project themselves into the position of the animal in order to create a hypothetical explanation of what the animal was doing."[3] The act of reading *into* the sand might sound exotic, but wherever human beings have subsisted on the flesh of wild animals, they've tracked. Go back far enough, and that's most people's kin.

By midnight, between the bourbon and the Busch, pretty much everyone in the yurt got popped. Fernando was showing off a pair of custom-made flip-flops: scored into the sole of the left: *Follow Me*. Right: *Bring Beer!*

I saw him sit down just once the entire night, and then it was at the insistence of a student. Of the handful of things in life Fernando disliked—idle time, "bad people"—the thing he most especially disliked was saying no. For this reason, he hadn't taken a day off from tracking in approximately forty-five years. He'd go anywhere in the world to help find a missing person, and he'd work for free, he said, so long as someone covered his travel. He didn't even mind sleeping on a couch or pitching a roll on the floor of a garage.

When probed about the root of this selflessness, he simply said, "Everyone has the right to come home."

Our class gathered early the next morning on a small beach down the road from camp. There were several sets of footprints in the sand, marked by orange flags, each trail about the length of a bowling lane. We bent over these trails as a group and tried to sleuth out what human scenario made them.

It was raining that morning and the wind off the river was brutal, casting icy knives against our necks and into our faces at alternating angles. The rain was making mush of my journal, and my hands were soon chapped and numbed to inoperable claws, which I shoved into the mesh pockets of my windbreaker, skinning several knuckles.

Of this, the first of many tracking exercises, I mainly recall my desire that it end as soon as possible.

Willem came by and asked how I was doing.

"This is fun," I lied. "And cold."

"Fernando doesn't feel cold," he observed.

Down the beach, Fernando was crouched on his hands and knees, reenacting a former triumph. While his assistants huddled around him in the rain, rubbing the chill from their arms, he looked like he was fixing to peel a layer.

"Yeah," I said. "I can tell."

After a while, Fernando approached our group. "You all was able to figure out what happened? Please, what happened?"

One of the more experienced men began. "Whelp, the stride keeps getting larger, as he takes off here. I pictured him taking off running."

"Anything else you see there?"

"Then they come closer together, they're pretty tight together."

As the man spoke, he walked alongside the tracks miming what he described. It wasn't a performance, more like an autonomic impulse. It reminded me of Fernando's unconscious slow dance the night before.

"That's why I think he's running, there's so much pressure

in the front of his feet. And there's something strange about— right here! There's a lot more pressure on his left side, his left print is more pivoted."

Fernando explained that the disturbances toward the center of the trail, where sand was violently kicked from the track, are called "explosions." Because the explosion exited left from the track, it meant the subject pivoted right, toward the water. He said it's a fairly common sign when you're tracking a killer. The subject hauls back in the midst of a run and chucks something into the water: a gun, a pipe, a candlestick—you get the gist.

Fernando demonstrated this throwing motion and stepped out of his tracks.

One of his assistants—a bald, bearded guy from the Ozarks named Steve—gestured for the rest of us to come down low.

"There's actually five lateral ridges here," he told us, pointing inside one of the tracks. "Those are the motions of the arm."

I came in close and squinted but could not see what he meant. It was a familiar feeling.

One of the younger guys gave a strained laugh.

"For real, man," said Steve.

"Oh, I know *you're* for real," the guy assured him. "I know *you* see it."

Maybe the younger guy was marveling at Steve's abilities, or maybe he was checking a minor controversy in the larger world of tracking regarding the reliability of something called "pressure releases," a term popularized by Tom Brown, Jr. According to the myth, Brown's mentor trained him to read minuscule fluctuations inside the tracks, and supposedly these tiny marks told him an animal's age and sex and whether it had eaten that day, or slept, or suffered from a sluggish liver. Some students claimed to see the pressure releases, while others were dubious. I'd never really moved past the identification stage—you know, *deer track, rabbit track*—so those debates were well beyond my ken.

Any interpretation of mood or motive is a higher-level tracking skill. Like most human skill sets, the basics of tracking evolved out of need. For our ancestors, the first step was identification. Hungry people didn't want to track just any old bird or rodent; they wanted to follow the animals they hoped to eat, which meant being able to pick out those tracks in a crowd. Next, they needed to determine the direction of travel, because the likelihood of catching up to the animal they hoped to hunt was slim if they walked in the wrong direction. The ability to age tracks is probably the most intuitive of these skills, but no less crucial. If you're hunting a doe, for instance, and you're presented with two sets of tracks, one of which is clean and clear and the other faded with debris inside it and maybe a dew-adorned spiderweb stretched across the toe, which do you suppose would lead you to the kill? Point being, you won't find an animal today by following a week-old trail.

Our first day of tracking class offered many bleak object lessons. One example, given by Fernando almost in passing, demonstrated what happens to the tracks of a grown man when the child he's abducted tries to fight free of his arms.

There was the story of the missing child Fernando tracked through the night, through a series of arsons, to a torched utility shed where he discovered the boy's charred body, mistaking it at first for a melted plastic dummy. The boy was so obscured by flame-retardant foam that the firefighters who'd applied it hadn't noticed he was there.

There was the story of the fugitive child-porn trafficker Fernando trailed from a ditched car, two miles into the mountains, to a camp where a pile of incriminating photos lay smoldering in a pit. Fernando was so engrossed by the final track that he failed to notice the man was swinging by a noose overhead, having hanged himself. When Fernando stood up, the man's limp feet bumped his shoulders and startled him.

Once, on the search for an abducted woman, Fernando found evidence that suggested she'd been crawling on her knees through the woods, but in the place where her handprints belonged, there were two small, circular depressions straddling the trail. He puzzled over the divots for a while before it dawned on him: they were elbow tracks.

"She was crawling out of there, but the bad guy had hit her with a rock, so she had to use her hands to hold her head together."

I disliked the phrase "hold her head together." It made me think of an overripe melon.

Over lunch, I asked him if the woman had lived.

"Oh yeah," he said, with modest cheer. "She actually survived."

In Fernando's book, survival was a happy ending, no matter its conditions. If the story he was telling involved a person's death, if in the end the tracks led to a "deceased individual," he braced. It was like the story was something being done to him.

For all the "Be a man among men" memes rolling through

his Facebook feed, the guy was actually a bit of a softy—an unlikely candidate, perhaps, for a job so plagued with bashed-in skulls and fugitive pedophiles. Though I suppose there is some solace in the act of reconstruction, a measure of control. Even if a narrative lacks coherence, there's skeletal sense in a sequence of events, in the bald progression of happenings.

A skeletal reconstruction of Fernando's biography might go something like this: He is born in 1960 in the Azores, on the island of Terceira. His family soon relocates to a ranch in the mainland village of Fátima, Portugal, a Catholic holy place where it's said the Virgin Mary appeared to three shepherd children in 1917. Like many of the locals, Fernando's birth certificate reflects that his godmother is, in fact, God's mother, the Virgin Mary. Both his father and grandfather are military trackers, and his mother descends from law enforcement. "Catching bad guys" is a family trade. Around the age of eight, Fernando begins tracking with his father on the family ranch, though he doesn't find much time for it between chores and school. Every morning, the little children in his village gather outside the teacher's house and walk together as a group, nine miles to the primary school in a neighboring town. The trek takes nearly three hours each way. In the evenings, he is tasked with tending "to the potatoes and the tomatoes."

His father pulls him out of school at age eleven and puts him to work on the military base as an apprentice mechanic. The pint-sized Fernando demonstrates no aptitude for the job, but he makes friends with the soldiers, many of whom share his interest in tracking. He's fourteen in 1974 when he enlists in the Portuguese military, fudging his birth year (the official age of conscription is sixteen). Portugal is more than a decade deep in a series of conflicts with various revolutionary forces in Africa. It's the twilight hour of their empire. Fernando is assigned to a light infantry unit that trains him in bushcraft, and for the next two years he tracks men through the backcountry in Angola and Mozambique. His skill swiftly develops, thanks, one assumes, to an unremitting flood of adrenaline.

"If you're not real good, or if you make one little mistake . . ." he says, "you get your entire team killed."

This quote comes from an episode of the TV show *Monsterquest*. Fernando speaks directly to the camera, his brow cinched up with pained intensity. The *Monsterquest* producers cast him as a tracking expert but failed to mention the episode's theme—"Hunting the Sierra Sasquatch"—until cameras were rolling and he was presented with an obvious fake. When Fernando told our class the story, he chuckled and shook his head as if those poor producers must have been the dumbest suckers on earth.

"You gotta *think* about it," he said. "The track they had was an inch deep. If I'm seven hundred pounds, my track is gonna be a lot deeper than that."

He went on to relate a story about a woman who claimed to have preserved a chupacabra in her ice chest. Turned out her "hard evidence" was just a large, skinned, frozen-solid dog.

Except for that nationally televised disclosure, Fernando was reluctant to talk about his time at war. When I asked him about it, he stubbed out his cigarette and shook his head at me. "Listen, ma'am, you gotta understand, those years are a shadow on my life."

The military years, or rather their omission, set a disorienting warp in the story. To have even the vaguest sense of history is to know which side of it Portugal was on. I don't know what memories lie within that shadow, but I know Fernando was fifteen and sixteen years old, far from home, his survival tied to the forestalling of "a little mistake."

Then he's in Boston, his mother and sisters with him. He speaks no English and has little formal education, but he'll serve as paterfamilias for the next three years while his father completes his own military service in Portugal.

He gets a job in a factory spray-painting caskets eight hours a day, and at night he cleans one of the government buildings. Tracking, his principal passion, is confined to his fifteen-minute breaks and to the hour between jobs when he trails pedestrians through Boston's city parks. Sometimes he devotes his break to studying tread patterns at the shoe store, committing them to memory. The saleswomen watch as he appraises the soles of loafers and pumps and espadrilles. When they ask if he needs assistance, he tells them, brightly, "No thanks."

Soon he can track a person from the grass onto asphalt and out into the street. Passersby stop and ask him if he needs help, if he's lost something. He tries to explain with the little English he's picked up at work and from the newspaper, but the people give up and move on.

By the time I meet him, he's been a mechanic, janitor, casket shellacker, dishwasher, busboy, security guard, father, and husband—but tracking, he told me, is the only thing he's ever been good at.

Back in camp, we spent the afternoon and evening on our hands and knees, studying ghostly footprints over stones and over the hardwood floor of the yurt. By a certain cant of the light, you could see where a foot had displaced dust on the hardwood, and you could see a subtle shine where a rubber sole, under two hundred pounds of human pressure, had polished the surface of a stone. This was not bluster or hallucination. I could see it, too. For once, rather than incompetence, I felt an inkling of the possibilities I'd been hearing about for more than half my life. All the while, I was turning Fernando's words over in my mind. *Everyone has the right to come home.*

My own desire to come home was one reason for going to Deer Island in the first place. Beyond the potential practical applications of tracking—hunting, evading bloodthirsty antagonists in the post-apocalypse—I suspected it could serve as a method for overcoming rootlessness, a daily practice for reconnecting with our ecosystems. In the most basic sense, to track is to *attend.*

But I had a personal stake in the prospect, too. Growing up, I'd spent a lot of time outdoors alone—a solitary kid, not always by choice. According to some neighbors and state agencies, this constituted criminal neglect on the part of my parents (who were too busy working to survive to take offense). But it also occasioned some remarkable experiences. I wasn't raised religious, but I wound up inventing a sort of faith from the trees, the overgrown fields near our house, and the fat clouds herding through the blue. In all those hours alone, I was not alone, because I sensed a greater presence. The presence was omniscient and held unwavering interest in me. It pulsed in the backyard oak and bounded from the blackberry. The feeling of this presence resists description—Rilke was close when he wrote, "We're all falling," but there are hands here, too, "holding all this falling." One way to think about it is "force," a force akin to the kiss of two magnets, or the pocket between two bones that gives the body spring where there might have been pure friction.

The force was in the hand and in its falling, but it was also in the holding up and in the space between. I spoke to it, and when I wasn't speaking directly, I performed. My life became a kind of performance for the presence. Lacking as I was in adult oversight, I don't think it's a stretch to assume I was projecting a parental figure on the environment, but in any case, the so-called natural world became a kind of god to me.

In adolescence, books provided narratives for that raw experience. If the natural world was my altar, a venue for unmediated conversation with the god I worshipped, then those books were scripture. *Ishmael*, by Daniel Quinn, and *The Tracker*, by Tom Brown, Jr., in the main. Like Fernando, Brown had contracted for the FBI and law enforcement, but his passion for tracking derived from a love of the earth and all the creatures who moved upon it. In the New Jersey Pine Barrens, where Brown grew up, a conversation was always under way between the deer and bears and birds, a conversation transcribed into the earth like braille. Tracking was a way both to read and to be a part of that conversation.

To be fluent in tracking, like any language, means by-passing the step of translation and inhabiting the sign in real time, as an echo of the quarry. The tracker is in conversation simultaneously with the earth's source material—the sand, snow, and soil that hold the impressions—and with the elements that act on those materials—the rain, wind, and sun that erase the tracks, slowly or violently, keeping time. Weather is the tracker's clock. The earth is not rock but liquid, humus in voluptuous decay, and our movements upon it a slow *pigéage*. We mark everything we touch, and we are marked.

Just thinking that way could make you feel less alone.

In time, I came to doubt the stories Tom Brown, Jr., told about his life. The loss was subtle, but as my faith in his narrative waned, so did my connection to that early presence. The god had been conflated with the charismatic figurehead, and charismatic figureheads can be corrupted or killed.

At the wilderness survival school, self-sufficiency was prized. The men of rare competence exalted the figure of the lone wolf, and their supernatural skills—whether real or invented—kept them isolated from others. Rather than viewing this as the tragedy it was, we admired it and strove to emulate them. As a seventeen-year-old, I'd longed to want what they exalted, but my actual loneliness prevented me. What I actually wanted was other people. I longed to belong to others, and I longed to belong to that old *presence* I could no longer feel.

Kneeling on the hardwood floor of the yurt, watching the men press their faces close to the tracks and to one another in the dwindling light, their inadvertent proximity,

I wondered how individualism ever became a part of the story. It seemed to me that the lessons of tracking were otherwise. The central premise of tracking is that all life marks and affects other life. It is not, in fact, possible to cover one's tracks completely, to never leave a trail. We leave evidence of our existence everywhere we go, and learning these traces of one another, intimately, was to my mind a far more novel endeavor than learning one more way to become invisible.

"As soon as you arrive at the scene," Fernando told us, "you find a clear print of the subject's shoe and then you draw it. Sure, you could take a picture with your cell phone, but it's not gonna stick on your brain!"

It was the second morning of class, and we'd gathered in a field near the yurt, in seated clusters. Our heads were bent reverently toward the tracks while Fernando presided above us.

The man next to me was painstakingly rendering the intricate waffling of a high-dollar-sneaker print in his journal. The print was preserved in a "track trap," generally any substance that holds an impression more clearly than the surrounding substrate. In this case it was a patch of mud, but it might be engine oil on a stretch of asphalt, moss sprung up in a sidewalk crack, or even flower petals. Should you ever go missing and hope to be found, it's a good idea to step in one of these every chance you get.

Fernando's thick, musical accent sounded Russian to my ear but was in truth a polyglot's amalgam. A native speaker of Portuguese and fluent in English, he spoke five additional languages well: Spanish, Italian, Filipino, French, and German. He pronounced the word "length" like *lenck* and "focus" like *fuckus*.

"We must take five measurements of the track," Fernando announced. "We measure the *lenck* of the heel. The *width*. The *arch* to the *toe area*. The widest part of the toe . . ."

"And then?" he beseeched us.

We did not know.

"The lenck of the *whole shoe*."

He walked the field with purpose.

"Everybody needs a little stick!" He exclaimed. "A little stick is gonna help you *fuckus*!"

The "tracking stick" is basically a staff fashioned from wood or a repurposed ski pole with colored rubber bands at each end to measure the stride between tracks. A tracker who lost the trail could plant the stick in the last visible print and use it to narrow the search, like a protractor.

The students took up their little sticks and partnered off. One of the pair was to avert his eyes while the other cut a path through the field. The first student would then look for compressions where a shoe smashed the grass, the dull line where his partner's clothes absorbed the dew as he passed, or the trembling of rebounding blades, agreeably dubbed "the living trail."

"Spoor" is a catchall term for the traces an animal leaves behind: a footprint, a scent, bent foliage, urine or scat, the dregs of a kill, antler scrapes on a tree trunk, a blood trail from a wound—the list goes on. But to interpret spoor, a tracker must possess a lot of other knowledge about an animal: what they eat, where they sleep and drink, where and what they forage or hunt, how they raise their young. Finally, to detect the spoor at all, the tracker must be familiar with the ecological baseline. For example, if you don't know what red osier dogwood normally looks like, you won't notice when a deer has come through and browsed it down. But even within an individual track, there are subtle variations—a chipped hoof, a bent toe, a subtle limp—that allow a tracker to identify animals as individuals.

This is also true in human tracking. Man-trackers must become intimate with their subjects, be they a foe or a friendly. According to Fernando, the average person leaves a clue every eighteen or twenty inches. That clue might be a track, a strand of hair, a bitten fingernail—each of us shedding countless tiny markers as invisible to us as the skin we slough. Good trackers figure out which markers are particular to their subject. If the missing person smokes, for example, he finds out her favorite brand. He also finds out her "second-flavor cigarette," because maybe the store was sold out that day. Maybe he pulls a butt from her ashtray at home and examines the pattern of her draw through the filter to be referenced against butts recovered on the trail.

Sometimes, a subject's family inhibits a case by concealing clues like these, out of shame or fear. "If I have a little notebook and a pen," Fernando told us, "and I ask a parent, 'Is your kid smoking pot?' they're going to tell me, 'Ohh noooo. He's the nicest kid in the block.'"

Families are justifiably reluctant to reveal their loved one's illegal hobbies to law enforcement, but even innocent omissions might mean the difference in understanding the mindset of a missing person, in understanding their physical state, in interpreting their movements. And so the old Alcoholics Anonymous maxim might be adapted to read "You're only as *lost* as your secrets."

Here was an aspect of what facility actually looked like: It looked like intimate knowledge of the other, hours in the dirt with your face pressed up to the sign. It looked like resisting the received or convenient story and turning your full attention on the concrete clues the world was actually giving you.

Louis Liebenberg theorizes that tracking evolved in response to environmental conditions. "Simple tracking" basically means following a set of clear prints over ideal substrates like sand or snow. Simple tracking came first, when humans migrating to arid and frozen landscapes where vegetable foods were scarce found themselves dependent on animal flesh. "Systematic tracking" involves the interpretation of multiple forms of sign—following disturbed leaf litter across a forest floor, for instance, or tracking a path of bent grass over a savanna—and likely arose from trackers entering environments with more difficult substrates, often obscured by vegetation. The last of these categories is "speculative tracking," wherein a tracker has become so intimate with their quarry and environment that they are able to extrapolate a theory of their quarry's location from a handful of signs. Put simply, they don't need to trail an animal track-by-track, a time-consuming process. Once they form a hypothesis, the tracker then makes decisions about how to catch up to their prey, by running it down, for example, or lying in wait, or taking a shortcut.

For the hunter well versed in their environment, speculative tracking saves time and energy and increases the likelihood of a successful hunt. But this is not a good plan for the novice tracker on a search-and-rescue mission where half-baked hallucinations could get a missing person killed. In the field, hypotheses are useful only when they are linked to concrete clues and extensive knowledge of both the environment and the subject. Fernando often stresses this point to his classes, and most of his training exercises demand that we trail a subject track-by-track.

It is a point of frustration for professional trackers that they are usually called upon only after an initial search fails. Volunteer search parties fan out over the landscape, walking in close succession, sometimes with dogs, looking only for the missing person, ignoring their spoor, and obliterating it in the process before the tracker even arrives. These methods of search extend from two distinct worldviews, of which neither party is very conscious. One views the missing person as an alien in a foreign landscape whose rescue depends on subduing that landscape by inundation. The other closely mirrors Liebenberg's view of human evolution. Human beings "cannot be treated in isolation from the environment," he writes. The environment is not a "static background, but an interacting agent, and humans should be seen as a part of the biological community."

The tracking stories Willem and I grew up on, the ones we read in the books by Tom Brown, Jr., affirmed the idea that humans are part of the biological community. But they also preached in the highest rhetoric on the subjects of sylvan communion and animal telepathy, employing phrases like "spirit tracking" and "inner vision" and other mysticisms. Such ideas do not play in a room full of soldiers.

Most of the folks in Fernando's class were there to learn how to track other humans. If there was a fantasy at work, it was of the military variety: Special Forces, commando fiction, Tom Clancy sort of stuff. Much of the money Fernando makes is in contracting for military and law enforcement organizations, and he is sometimes called to appear as an expert witness in court. He is a pragmatist, by default interested in documentable results. To accentuate this position, he often exclaims, "I don't have no magic feather!" He said this in reference to a class he once took from Tom Brown, in which students were directed to manipulate the flight of feathers via telekinesis.

His encounter with Brown came in a period when Fernando was checking out men purported to be great trackers, just to see if they knew something he didn't. In this way he wound up befriending Ab Taylor, a U.S. Border Patrol tracker who created the Hug-a-Tree and Survive program to teach children to stay put if they're lost in the woods.

Then there was Tom Brown, Jr.

"Do you know how much money it costs to go to those classes?" Fernando asked me. He was enjoying a post-lunch cigarette on the yurt steps.

"As a matter of fact, I do," I said.

"Exactly. I'm concentrating more on tracking, he concentrates a lot on the spirit type of stuff . . . And I don't—I don't know, that's not for me. I just want to track and be able to save somebody's life."

The larger world of tracking breaks down along similar lines. "The art and science of tracking" is a common phrase, but individual trackers tend to favor one conceptual framework over another. According to Fernando's website, "Tracking is not a lost art, but rather an underutilized modern science."

In *The Art of Tracking: The Origin of Science*, Liebenberg more or less reconciles the split. While living with the !Xo San and Gwi master trackers of the Kalahari, Liebenberg came to understand that trackers were both empirically minded and creative. "Generally speaking," he wrote, "one may argue that science is not only a product of objective observation of the world through sense perception. It is also a product of the human imagination. A creative hypothesis is not found or discovered in the outside world, it comes from within the human mind."

Anthropomorphism—the "attribution of human motivation, characteristics, or behavior to nonhuman organisms"[4]—gets a bad rap in certain circles these days, as does empathy. And though I find some of the criticisms persuasive, both empathy and anthropomorphism have had their place in the human organization for millennia, so it's my assumption that they serve a purpose, however limited.

I personally view empathy not as a quality someone possesses, but as a practice that results in particular outcomes. A hunter who feels compassion for his prey might make ethical decisions about the manner and frequency of his hunts. But when, during the hunt, the hunter "feels with" the animal, he knows on a somatic level that their subjectivities overlap, that they will be quite literally of one flesh. "The tracker must ask himself what he would do if he were that animal," Liebenberg observes. "In the process of projecting himself into the position of the animal, he actually feels like the animal."

This way of knowing oneself as inextricable from the environment is very old among human beings. In the Cave of Niaux, in the department of Ariège in southern France, a fifteen-thousand-year-old painting of a hybrid being—half man, half deer—might depict a transfigured shaman or the spiritual marriage between the hunter and the hunted. Or it might depict the terrestrial act of a human dressed up as an animal. But all are forms of identification that affirm an essential interdependence.

When night came again to the yurt, Fernando hadn't diminished an iota. He held forth and smoked passionately while the others, hungover from the night before, bone cold from the intermittent rain, climbed into their sleeping bags and slipped into unconsciousness.

I wandered toward my tent and paused awhile at the edge of the wood to watch the nearly full moon strip off her cloud. A dull line snaked through the meadow where some creature had passed from sight, and my eye caught on the twitching blades. Maybe Fernando's skills were supernaturally advanced, or maybe he was just the most dogged guy in the field. Short of vanishing down that trail myself, I didn't know how I would know if he was the "real deal," but I felt certain that some virtuosity was speaking through his body. It was as if the memory of his missions lived in his limbs. The language he used to recount them was almost unimportant.

"Attentiveness is the natural prayer of the soul," wrote the seventeenth-century philosopher-priest Nicolas Malebranche. If we believe him, it follows that whatever commands our attention will determine the form of our god. If we mainly train our attention on the screens of our devices—that's one kind of prayer. If we train it on the dirt, or the birds, or the faces of those we love—that's another. Most of us run a gauntlet of rotating concerns, with little agency over the convulsions of our minds. Or else we forgo agency entirely and remit our attention, via any number of substances, to a high. In any case, our preoccupations become objects of worship.

In the most basic sense, to track is to attend. To be alert to the signs of another—whether human or animal or element—and responsive to their calls. This is a form of worship, but it's also a form of love, a method for overcoming the numbness or the disconnection that allows us to screen out the killing of the world. Naturalists describe this relationship like a kind of cosine law linking attention to intimacy, and intimacy to care. A precept of the Senegalese environmentalist Baba Dioum is often quoted: "We won't save places we don't love. We can't love places we don't know. And we don't know places we haven't learned."

If that's too crunchy for you, try the Tom Clancy version. The most succinct recipe for intimacy I've read came out of a book by a former spy recruiter for the FBI. According to the author, Jack Schafer, the formation of intimate relationship depends on four elements: proximity, frequency, intensity, and duration.[5] Sentiment isn't really part of the equation; neither are good intentions. Relationships depend on a renewing investment of presence and time. When tracking becomes a daily ritual, intimacy develops between the tracker and the earth, whether or not they conceive it as such.

Fernando says, "The ground will tell you a thousand words about the person you're looking for." But those thousand words can't be read from a distance. "You got to go down to your hands and knees to see it."

In the face of ecological collapse, tracking might strike you as a small and insignificant intervention, unless you believe—as I have come to believe—that it is our very disconnection, our habit of abstracting and objectifying the natural world, that has brought us to this brink. To track is to overcome that estrangement, to once again "feel with" the many beings on which our lives depend, and so the casual killing of the planet becomes impossible.

On the last day of class, Fernando told us he had such confidence in our skills that we'd soon be able to interpret the mindset of a subject by examining a remnant of his track, on a moonless night, "by the light of just one little cigarette."

He'd sent one of his assistants running down the old logging road in the far woods, up an embankment, and into the brush, and we were supposed to track him down. The forest floor was still moist from the rains the days before but nowhere near as pliant as mud. Students were pointing out bent pine needles among the leaf litter, but it seemed a stretch to me. Yesterday's gains were suspect in this light. It was a fact that I sometimes saw floaters; maybe the shine on the stones had only been a flaw in my eye.

A couple of students were flustered, hanging farther and farther behind, commiserating sotto voce.

"I don't see it."

"Are you seeing anything?"

"Hell no. I have no idea what they're talking about."

In what was for some the final straw, Fernando demonstrated something called speed trailing. He grabbed up a handful of orange flags and took off running after his assistant, spearing each track with a flag as he passed. When he was finished, we followed the flags. It was difficult enough for me to pick out the tracks while crawling on my hands and knees. Fernando had flagged each one accurately at a dead run. It was shock and awe—and man, it was pretty fucking awesome. But also bewildering, and illustrative of the probably irreconcilable gap between us. Like trying to learn "Chopsticks" from Tchaikovsky.

At lunch, I found Fernando on the yurt steps, blissed out, chewing cold pizza from the night before. I asked if he'd ever received any awards for his efforts.

"Oh, I have tons of awards," he said, then recited them flatly.

World's Best Tracker '88, the Excellence in Search and Rescue Medal, Rescuer of the Year, American Red Cross Real Hero.

"Oh!" He revived. "I was awarded the Dumbshit Award. It actually says, 'Fernando Moreira: Dumbshit.' My team gave it to me because they knew I was afraid of snakes. One day we were out tracking, and I saw a snake, and I beat the shit out of it." His eyes welled with amusement and pride.

Willem chimed in, "Don't forget, you had your picture on a frickin' Wheaties box!"

"I did, I did," Fernando confirmed.

Some months later, he emailed me a JPEG of the box. Sure enough, there he was in Day-Glo-orange splendor, a

Real Hero poster boy, mustachioed and stoical on a box of Wheaties.

"My mission is, before I go, I want to pass on these skills to save someone who needs help out there. I'm fifty-four years old, I'm already an old guy. How long am I gonna be here? Five years? Ten years? I pray every day, and I always pray to God, 'Give me one more day, to teach one more class.'"

"What does God say?" I asked.

"Until this day, I'm still here. I survived the cancer."

I'd slept like garbage the night before, and I was very tired by the afternoon when we received instructions for our final mission. It was a real-time search-and-rescue scenario involving team leaders and "sign cutters" and group strategy. I got myself elected to a grunt position and slacked behind the others.

Willem sidled up and told me I'd missed out on some great stories the night before. Evidently, the precise moment I exited the yurt, Fernando opened up on some top secret Special Forces shit. The upside was that I'd also dodged the evening's more carnal artifacts, those that a dozen men produce when they've subsisted for days on budget beer, cheeseburgers, and warmed-over hot dogs from the country gas station. All night long, the yurt's timbers shook with woodsawing and wind-breaking so foul that not even their copious smoke could cover it.

I wasn't especially surprised to learn that I'd missed those stories. I'd gone to Deer Island as a student but also as a writer. The tracker knew he was being tracked, and he was understandably wary of me and what I might have to say about him. Every time I asked a question about an old case or tried to push into his war story, he diverted to Search and Rescue Tips 101. Details from one story would later pop up in another, and it was tough to pin down his timelines. I suspect this had less to do with faulty memory than with a desire to obscure identifying details of those involved.

I wasn't the only one having this problem. Willem had undertaken to ghostwrite Fernando's memoirs the previous summer but found his stories impossible to disentangle. Fernando can't discuss open cases on the record, and though he's a contractor, discretion is one of the ways he protects his relationships with sheriff's departments and search-and-rescue organizations. It may be an inconsistent and wandering discretion, but it's not like he's out there pitching his own TV show.

"You can't tell half the time what you're supposed to know and what you're not," Willem said. "He loves stories—he just isn't supposed to tell any."

Fernando also worried about a story winding up somewhere a victim or a victim's family might recognize it. He was worried they'd be re-traumatized. Willem heard through the grapevine that Fernando wouldn't talk about the war because he still had enemies from Angola and was worried they'd come after him if they knew he was alive, not to mention the assorted criminals he'd helped to catch and convict stateside.

Whether these threats were real or imagined, I can't say. Maybe there were thwarted pedophiles, drug kingpins, and former freedom fighters lying in wait for a chance to exact revenge. Maybe that's post-traumatic stress talking. Either way, I suspect his dodges were less devious than naïve. The shadow narrative of Fernando's life was emerging, and its theme was atonement. He wanted to spare the aggrieved their pain, spare himself his past. That's impossible of course, but I didn't fault him for trying.

Meanwhile, the real-time search-and-rescue mission was owning our asses. Our team lost the trail in an overgrown pasture almost immediately. We spent the better part of an hour trying to track our way out of the weeds while a rival team receded at a clip through the field and into the woods to victory.

I didn't mind losing. I was glad to be lost in the tall grass, on my hands and knees, zoning out on the inscrutable ground. I could almost catch the edge of something if I blurred my eyes, an old thread I'd dropped a long time before.

Above it all, high in a tree, the scarved impresario was pleased, smoking and surveying the various theaters of search.

"You know what I wish?" he said. "I wish that I was fifteen years old and could start all over again. I'm telling everybody, when I die, I hope I'm reborn a tracker."

We are advised to distrust the stories we tell about the missing. Trust only the tracks, experts say. The tracks are connected, always, to the body that left them. They are a string leading to the ghost we seek. Fellow searchers may speculate—our subject would have climbed a ridge for a view, would have most likely followed the river. Or else the family is adamant their loved one would *never* go to that park, would never take the route under the bridge, never at night. If we believe the stories, we are led astray. Often those who claim to know us best cannot see us with any clarity.

That was the shape of the living trail I'd recovered in the tall grass, and this is where it led me.

I was seven years old and I decided to do what a lot of kids decide to do: I would run away from home. I packed a little bag, composed a note, and stuck the note to the fridge to be discovered by my family. I wish I could remember the contents of the bag or the note, what I most wanted to keep, what I hoped to convey—concrete clues that might shed light on my real motivations for leaving, rather than those I apply in retrospect.

It wasn't unusual in my family to leave a child alone for much of the day, which was the case the day I staged my disappearance. I set out with the bag in the afternoon down the gravel road that connected our rural house to the suburban development where I waited for the school bus each morning. The road was flanked by weedy fields where I often played alone. Each blade of grass held a wad of dew, like spit, where a tiny green insect lived. I liked to look at those bugs and braid the grasses.

After some hours, when the sun was low, I headed back to the house and found it empty, my note still hanging on the fridge. I took it down and went to my room, and like any child might, I told a story about my unanswered bid for attention: if no one came to look for me, it meant I did not matter. I'd been telling myself that story a long time.

I find my mind circling that day, that iteration of family, as it feels emblematic of a larger estrangement: each of us desperate to be seen, each benignly unaware of the presence or absence of the other, each wholly absorbed in the requirements of getting by. The meaning was simpler than I'd imagined. No one came to look for me because no one noticed I was missing.

Fernando had no interest in what tracking had to say about the fundamental interconnectedness of life on earth, or how it might help us to heal our estrangements with one another and the world. He preferred a bootstrap parable about the rewards of hard work and dedication, a story about a soldier who sacrificed himself, as the para-rescue motto goes, "that others may live." And yet it was by virtue of that dedication that he'd become more sensitively attuned to the ground, and all that moved upon it, than any other person I'd previously met. Just as the muscle memory of a mission lived in his limbs, communicating a more coherent story than the one he told in language, he modeled an example of what an embodied relationship with the earth might actually look like—no matter what he believed. It's fine and well to have a lot of fancy notions about the earth as a grand collaborative document of interspecies communication, but if you don't spend your hours in the dirt, on your hands and knees, with your face pressed up to the sign, you'll always be outside that conversation.

The metaphors we use to describe our world, and the stories we tell about our place in it—they're important. But they are no more important than the crucial embodied requirements of intimate relationship: proximity, frequency, intensity, duration. You don't have to be perfect, or even especially good, to have a relationship, but you do have to keep showing up.

There's a question at the center of tracking, and maybe you, like me, have been waiting to be asked it.

Where are you?

Meaning, your absence has been noticed.

Where are you?

We miss you. It matters that you're found.

In one version of the story, there is a person who knows you better than you know yourself. No matter where you go, no matter how far you wander into the dark, that person will find you. It's the version I'd always preferred. As it stands, I'm not sure who's the missing person in this story, but I want to believe Fernando when he says that everyone has the right to come home.

5

THE PROBLEM OF OTHER PEOPLE

It is always possible to bind together a considerable number
of people in love, so long as there are other people left over to
receive the manifestations of their aggressiveness.

—SIGMUND FREUD

have said that my Promised Land is located in other
people, that I suspect our salvation lies in cooperation and
interdependence. But that doesn't mean I think cooperation or interdependence comes cheaply, or that I haven't been
as wounded and as burned by other people as the next guy.
Human beings are social animals, and it's a central paradox
of human life that other people should confront us with our
most difficult problems while possessing our only hope for a
solution. "That's life," to quote Sinatra. A cynic might call
it pharmakon—we are, at once, each other's poison, scape-
goat, and remedy. However you want to cut it, we require
other people to survive, to love, to be loved by, to reflect that
we exist in time. Or at least, we used to.

In a technocentric society, isolation—or the illusion of
isolation—is not only possible, it is increasingly unavoidable. But for most of human history, isolation meant death;
so human cultures, by necessity, developed ceremonies,
laws, rituals, and stories to redress the common conflicts
that arise between people and to teach their members how

to live in accord. Metabolizing conflict while maintaining the bonds of the group was not so much a moral endeavor as a practical one.

What becomes, then, of a people who invent a way to live without relying on others directly? I think we're finding out.

As is true of other survival skills we've lost, social skills atrophy with disuse, and once our survival no longer depends on our togetherness, what impetus do we have to tolerate the conflict, confusion, and vulnerability that are the price of relationship? I'm not certain that it's possible to sustain communalism long-term based on ideals alone. So long as there exists a more comfortable world to defect to—even if that world is laced with depression, anxiety, and isolation—we will be tempted to take the out.

This goes for noncommunal endeavors as well. Time and again I hear stories about idealistic people, wholly devoted to worthy causes, who wind up tearing one another apart over relatively minor disagreements before retreating to their former lives of quiet desperation. "Community is the cure for tragedy." But what if community (or the attempt to build community) becomes the *source* of tragedy? What follows is a small case study of one such instance that unfolded close to home.

It was while walking through Pioneer Courthouse Square one day in 2003 that my old friend Peter Bauer was struck by an idea—a vision really—of "a man living in a post-collapse world, traveling back to the ruins of downtown Portland to observe the ghosts of his ancestors, who sadly had not realized they died long ago and so continued to go to work every day."

This vision of the "working stiff" no doubt derived from Tom Brown, Jr.'s "mindless grey masses," the zombie-death-cult-image we continued to project onto an innocently milling populace. In subsequent years, passing the square on any afternoon between May and September, you stood a decent chance of running across that vision made manifest in "the Urban Scout," a street performer described by one reporter as "a playful response to a real set of problems, from environmental degradation to postmodern anomie."[1] The Urban Scout's cardboard signs read, variously, *The end is here*, *Apocalypse now!*, *Will stalk your enemies for $$$*, and *Will hunt and gather for food*.

Also, less epically: *Will light your cigarette for 25c*. Should you have dropped your coin, he'd have sawed out a bow-drill coal on a nest of tinder, blown it steadily into flame, and lifted it to the end of your cig. Scattered applause.

Did I mention he was nearly naked as he did this? He wore only a thin dappling of mud over the whole of his pale body, and his feet were bare. A rectangle of gray wool clothed his loins. *Mad Max* meets Ötzi the Iceman.

This "pan-global Paleolithic" futurism was such a fixture of my early twenties I hadn't thought to ask what it was devised to achieve. Luckily for me, soon after the character was born, it apparently became incumbent upon every alt-weekly reporter within a hundred-mile radius to spend the day with the Urban Scout, building shelters in public parks, trying their hands at friction fire, commenting on his "mess of dark tresses," or detailing the preparation of roadkill using plenty of tongue-in-cheek gourmand terminology. In one case, the reporter actually butchered and consumed a roadkill squirrel. First, "you must 'release the anus,'" she informed her readers.

A couple of highlights:

> Foraging is more than a pastime for Peter—it's training for the future. He practices hunting and gathering skills to prepare him for life after civilization collapses, he says. That's right, this modern young man is an apocalypticist. But he's not letting it spoil his day.
> —*Willamette Week*[2]

> Peter Bauer has been standing in his front yard, wringing out what looks like a long, fleshy towel . . . "I'd shake your hand," Bauer says, "but mine are covered in brains."
> —*The Southeast Examiner*[3]

Looking back, I'm struck by Peter's preternatural talent for marketing—the difficult balance of ironic and slapstick humor, the earnest thrust—evinced by the all-but-audible rim shot punctuating each article. Those of us on the Gen X cusp were suspicious of overt utopianism, as the failures of our boomer parents had instructed us well, but a mere spoonful of sarcasm sure made the medicine go down.

You understand why it had to be that way. If you extracted the gags, the log line you were left with was uncomfortably familiar: a young idealist, content to slum with the least of us, claims our culture is doomed but is willing to sacrifice himself to "save the world."

Daniel Quinn posed the question "Who can live with a light heart while participating in a global slaughter?"

And the Urban Scout answered, in a nutshell, "Me."

Well, not exactly that, but he was suggesting that preserving a sense of humor is key. "Sometimes we get paralyzed and we can't do anything," he told a reporter. "That's why I have to make this fun."[4]

Over the next year, the Urban Scout's tackle expanded to include a pair of knockoff Ray-Ban sunglasses, a pack of American Spirit Blues, and a tall boy of Pabst Blue Ribbon: hipster props, taken up for the purpose of preaching beyond the choir and attracting new friends to the "preemptive post-apocalyptic" movement (and if he happened to attract a mate, that would be fine, too). Those who dominated the naturalist scene[5] were not so amenable to hipsters, or to the use of multimedia, and suspected ulterior motives on Peter's part, such as fame-lust and profiteering—which would have been comical if their suspicions hadn't so readily spiraled into threats of violence.

The community uniform at the time was basically army-surplus wool and shapeless ankle-length skirts of organic cotton. Peter, by contrast, was an aesthete. He'd learned to sew his own garments from fine woolen fabrics of burnt sienna and forest green. He designed an elegant mackinaw jacket with belt, and tailored his field trousers slim. He wore camo-print high-top Chuck Taylors, and even the raccoon's tail, sewn into the back of his trucker hat, caught the light with conditioned luster as it wagged. King of the rewild frontier.

Why not? had been a guiding question through adolescence, and it was steering us into our twenties. *Why not* master the art of knife throwing? Or eat these only-slightly-expired hot dogs pulled from a dumpster? *Why not* chug the bottle of potato vodka into a blackout and wake up in a stranger's bed, the skin of your arms and legs inexplicably hashed with road rash? Potatoes are paleo.

It was in the spirit of this question that several preemptive post-apocalyptic dance parties were thrown in a sepulchral, four-story warehouse attached to the eastern abutment of the Burnside Bridge.

> Civilization is devouring the planet at an accelerating rate. Let's face it; collapse is inevitable. Most people might poo-poo [*sic*] you with doom and gloom visions of the future but we say, why fear it? Why not celebrate it? Hell, why not take it a step further and prepare for it by celebrating before it actually happens?

The above quote is from a press release that went on to encourage the public to dress as if the end had already arrived and "dance away your pre-post-traumatic-stress to the awesome beats of DJ Copy." The Nuclear Winter Formal was set-dressed in the dun and grayscale of *The Road Warrior*. The Silent Spring Fling was screamingly neon, inviting attendees to "End the silence: wear your loudest clothes." There was a post-apocalyptic costume contest, judged by local clothing designers, featuring prizes like gas masks and DVDs of *Mad Max*. Partygoers could have their photo taken in front of a painted backdrop of Portland's skyline in flames to "document this exciting time in human history."

The Urban Scout, then twenty-three, arrived at the party with his skin painted a camouflage of nuclear orange and radioactive yellow. The remaining partygoers could generally be divided into two categories of punk, though under normal circumstances the twain of those punks would not meet. One group dressed in dystopic civvies: torn black clothing, dirty bandanas tied at the nape—more or less their daily costume—plus a prop, like a siphoning hose. Others, calling themselves steam punks, wore velvet corsets, top hats, and impractical gold-plated welding goggles modeled on nineteenth-century science. Their kink hinged on a kind of ornate obsolescence, nostalgia for the "new-fangled contraption." Or something.

I am persuaded that I attended several of these events because I've seen the sweaty, pupil-blown photos placing me there. Dimly, I recall the singer of a punk band leaping from the stage, soaked in beer, collapsing on the sticky warehouse floor, and doing one of those run-in-a-circle-while-lying-on-your-side maneuvers. His neck flushed red, the tendons in it drawn alarmingly taut, as he screamed into the microphone for a surreally long interval—like some avant reenactment of the birth of Athena.

It's hard to say what these events accomplished. It's unlikely that any partygoers woke the next morning, took their hangover to brunch, and seriously discussed the implications of their agrarian civilization. But they certainly helped to integrate our otherwise incommensurable selves: the selves that were sincerely disturbed by the destruction of the natural world, and the early-twenties selves that lived to get tipsy and flirt with attractive strangers.

In July 2006, Peter was gearing up to run a preemptive post-apocalyptic summer camp, a weeklong class covering skills like gas siphoning, urban camping, foraging, dumpster diving, and lock picking (practiced on Peter's own front door). In a feature for the *Portland Mercury* titled "Apocalypse Soon," the reporter Marjorie Skinner described her immersive day with the Urban Scout and friends, writing: "They are not paranoid conspiracy theorists who hide in basements stockpiling guns, radios, and canned food. They'd rather stockpile beers in the cool embankments of bogs from which they good-naturedly bean you in the head with fetid gobs of mud."[6]

The feature ran with a photo of the instructors, including Willem and Peter, seated on the square's amphitheater stairs, partially camouflaged, and wielding staffs like a posse of Tolkien LARPers. The article concluded with Peter delivering a diatribe against hippies, whom he describes as "pot smoking, peace-and-love-and-sustainability-begging pacifists with no understanding of the power structure of civilization, or even a shred of understanding of the laws that govern the natural world." And stating that, conversely, preemptive post-apocalypticism "is not about peace™ and love™ and sustainability™. It's about survival. It's about adaptation. It's about deep knowledge of place."

> TO THE EDITOR:
> If "Urban Scout" spent more time in the woods honing his skills and less time drinking at the Aalto and pandering to the greenhorn chumps at *the Mercury*, he may have the skills to survive the fallout awaiting our "civilization." But he's too busy kowtowing to the local "alternative" media and engaging in societal masturbation to have done more than play act at being

a hero. I hereby challenge him to a "Live Off" (after Burning Man and his little camp have passed). We shall see who can live in the woods longer, with just a knife. Do you accept or are you too busy kissing the man's ass?
—"Hippie Scout"[7]

The letter was a curious development. The Urban Scout had been publicly challenged to a duel by a person who knew him well enough to cite his drinking habits and where he liked to exercise them, but who was stranger enough to drop his own intention to attend Burning Man without any apparent embarrassment (meaning, he was no one we'd associate with) and who, unaccountably, mistook a breaking-even alt-weekly paper for the mouthpiece of the bourgeoisie.

Peter, Willem, and I set to working out the true identity of the Hippie Scout—an investigation detailed at length on Peter's blog:

> Clue #7: Who says things like "greenhorn" and "kowtow-ing"? I had not heard either of the words before. Lisa is a writer and knew the words, however agreed with me that this is not the language of our generation. Clue #8 Man or Woman? Man. For some reason I just don't see a woman being as big of an asshole. It's a very competitive tone, a very masculine one.

The Urban Scout began as a visual gag, a clown devised to welcome the curious into the world of "ancestral skills." But as the character evolved, he underwent a period of on-tological excavation, discovering his identity by rejecting all that he was not. *The Adventures of Urban Scout*, a blog and proving ground for the Freudian game of *fort/da*, had hundreds of daily readers by its peak in 2008. He discarded the label "preemptive post-apocalypticism," which focused too much on an imagined future rather than what might be done to address our perilous present, and took up "rewilding."

Though the blog is now defunct, a curated artifact of its tenure remains in *Rewild or Die*, a manifesto self-published in 2010—forty short chapters elucidating the spirit of rewilding as the Urban Scout understood it, using a structural conceit associated with professional boxing matches (or, if you're me, with the experience of slumping paralytically stoned on the couch of an acquaintance watching a group of dudes diddle out round after round of Mortal Kombat): Pacifism vs. Rewilding. School vs. Rewilding. Robots, Religion, and Science vs. Rewilding. Dieting, Money, Voting, Pessimism, Denial, Hipsters vs. Rewilding. Rewilding vs. Rewilding. Yes, by the end of the book, Rewilding would be pitted explicitly against everything.

"Rewilding doesn't refer to a way of dressing, or a cool new diet, or a sustainable product you can use to fuel your car, or voting with dollars, or any of that," Scout writes in a chapter titled "Everything vs. Rewilding."

His friendly, slapstick comedy began to veer toward provocation, and readers attributed inflammatory statements made by the character to the actor who played him. His response to his critics—sometimes as Scout, sometimes as Peter—only served to stir the muck and reinforce the conflation. Scout met their criticism with a kind of shrugging self-deprecation, à la the final battle-rap scene of the movie *8-mile*, in which Eminem preempts all trash talk by insulting himself before his opponent can begin to.

DEAR "HIPPIE SCOUT":

First off, shame on you. If you gave a rat's ass about the environment, the Earth, or future generations, you wouldn't have wasted your time challenging someone who is actually making a difference. All you've done is shown that you care more about the size of your dick than the survival of the planet.

Second, if you were trying to make me sound like a drunken hipster . . . well, yes, I have been known to piss on couches at parties, convince people to punch me in the head, and had my fair share of blacked-out bike rides. Who gives a shit? My high functioning alcoholism will crush your ganja-induced apathy any day. That's why the hippie movement never accomplished shit. They were too busy smoking the CIA's weed.

Lastly, maybe you haven't noticed (perhaps you're too busy getting "dosed" at Burning Man) but the world around us is falling apart. You probably have all the time a free-lovin'-commune-livin'-trustafarian-hippie-mooch might have for silly little games, but I don't. Every day, every second, this culture of death comes closer and closer to the crash. That's no game.

—Urban Scout[8]

As Oscar Wilde famously observed, "Man is least himself when he talks in his own person. Give him a mask and he will tell you the truth."

That we can say more with a mask than with our naked, undefended faces explains a lot about the human drama (and the internet), though I'd argue the "truths" we tell are often provisional, contingent upon the moment they are communicated. The mask affords the freedom to be uncertain, to explore what Joan Didion called "the shifting phantasmagoria that is our actual experience" without a whole lot of anxious qualification. We need not believe what we say when we wear it. We may not even know what we believe until we try saying a few things we don't.

In the year 2006, depending on which of my connections you asked, I might have been described as sweet, bitchy, shy, extroverted, funny, too serious, or, most accurately, mercurial. One acquaintance, I was told, attempted to spell his assessment out loud: "Lisa Wells? She's an H-O-R-E."

All *sic*s aside, it was true that I'd loved and wounded profligately, boys and girls and genders undisclosed. And that I'd been loved and wounded in turn. And through all of it accepted my earned portion of guilt. But guilt is something I can stand, a heady and consummately human feeling. Unlike denial, it invites us into closer contact with ourselves and occasions development. In my experience, the most tedious characters are those most committed to the cause of avoiding implication. This was the catalytic magic of the Urban Scout, by my lights: his inconsistency, and the foregrounding of his flaws.

To some, he was an amusement. To others, an opportunistic fake. Some people thought him a hypocrite for having a day job and not living in a debris hut full-time. (He was a barista for a while, then a production assistant, before taking a gig at the paleo restaurant Cultured Caveman.) To others still, he was an inspiration, an antihero for those who wished to resist the plunder of the planet but who were disinclined to enter the puritan fold. To me, the Urban Scout act felt subversive; a simultaneous embrace of idealism and hedonism, the privileging of investment over perfection: how he smoked cigarettes, shotgunned PBR, danced in his raccoon cap to techno at house parties, and attempted no defense for his use of technology or anything else construed as hypocritical. In the current zeitgeist, this would be nothing much special, but twenty years ago environmentalism was much more insular and wedded to its particular form of ascetic fundamentalism.

It was my impression that the all-or-nothing agenda of the purists tended to default to a lot of nothing. But the Urban Scout stood for all *and* nothing, defied the binary, accommodated a spectrum between. You could call it "societal masturbation," or you could call it the performance of an essentially irreconcilable self.

In 2015, an article titled "Geeks, MOPS, and Sociopaths in Subculture Evolution" was making the rounds.[9] David Chapman, its author, articulated a taxonomy of subcultural participants and the typical trajectory of subcultures beginning with their so-called creators and ending in "the death of cool."

I first encountered this sort of authenticity continuum in punk rock. There were those who made the music and those who made the scene, as well as organizers and donors of money, space, and time. There were geeks—those who lived for the music, obsessive collector types (this describes most of the people I hung around). There were the members of the public (MOPs)—the lay term is "poseurs"—who were interested in the wardrobe and in passively consuming the music, but who had limited investment in the scene as a community, and who would, inevitably, move on to a "next thing." In contrast to the MOPs were the "fanatics," for whom there would be no "next thing" save for the snuffing of consciousness. Finally, if a scene accrues enough MOPs, it attracts "sociopaths," those who swoop in to wring cash and other forms of equity from the scene through the exploitation of its membership. A more accurate shorthand for this type might be "capitalist vultures," but in any case, sociopaths herald the death of cool.

I don't know where academics fit into it all, but I know it was a firmly held belief among certain of my fanatic and geek friends that should your scene become the subject of anyone's dissertation, it was already dead.

In 2008, Ursula McTaggart, then a PhD candidate in English at Indiana University, was in the process of completing a dissertation on the use of "primitive and industrial metaphors" in revolutionary movements. The dissertation, later published by the State University Press of New York under the title *Guerrillas in the Industrial Jungle: Radicalism's Primitive and Industrial Rhetoric*, "examines the rhetoric of four social movements, focusing on how they envision utopias by merging metaphors of industrial and 'primitive' worlds: the Black Panther Party, the League of Revolutionary Black Workers, socialist organizations of the 1970s and 1980s, and twenty-first century anarcho-primitivists."[10]

Peter was dating a girl who lived in a cave in the Pennsylvania woods and who blogged about her experiences using the moniker Penny Scout. She soon moved to Portland to be with Peter, and both Scouts kept their blogs regularly updated with artfully staged photographs of their rewilding activities. These provided content for McTaggart's final chapter:

> Penny Scout creates stylish clothes, often by processing animal skins, and she frequently models them on her website.

A report about a survivalist camp, for example, includes photos of her posed in a model-like stance while wearing short shorts, fur wrist bands, a hip belt for a knife, and mock Ugg boots that she sewed out of felt. Urban Scout generates similar photos, which are often stylized in the manner of corporate promo shots.[11]

McTaggart advances the idea that the Scouts, as creators, have inoculated themselves against exploitation by using capitalist tools to spread their anticapitalist message: "By using blogs, YouTube, and red carpet events, they acknowledge the success of corporate, technological strategies of 'selling' ideologies, and they insist that their anti-technological perspective can best be spread through the media that they hope to destroy."

A lofty theory. I'm pretty sure, however, that the objective of their slick media campaign was satire, good old-fashioned entertainment, not a preemptive strike on the capitalists. In any case, it succeeded in convincing many rewilding fanatics—who either didn't get, or didn't want to get, the joke—that they'd commodified themselves and vulgarized the movement.

Fanatics and geeks are understandably suspicious of MOPs. They want to protect the object of their love from predators. Their paranoia leads them to accuse one another of masquerading as fanatics when underneath they are nothing more than MOPs or, worse, sociopaths. In my experience, this sort of policing is just as likely as anything to destroy a group of people. Freud called the phenomenon "the narcissism of minor differences," observing that rather than truly opposed peoples it is "precisely communities with adjoining territories, and related to each other in other ways as well, who are engaged in constant feuds and in ridiculing each other."

Still, one could not deny that sociopaths exist, are bad for communities, and are not always easily identified in a crowd.

One day, Peter received an email from a respected anarchist writer and sometime collaborator of the green-anarchy godfather John Zerzan:

Subject: hip-douches are still douches

Scout,

You and the other 'primitivist' bloggers are fucking douche bags. I'll give you credit for having a sense of humor, but then you err on that side. Trying to make rewilding just some new hipster shit is pathetic . . . Benefits for fucking fashion shows and dance parties? I imagine you might mean well, appealing to other hipsters or what-the-fuck ever, but you're only making a mockery of yourself. Perhaps that's your intent? Urban Scout is, after all, just a character right? Fucking PATHETIC. The rantings, daily affairs, and love life of a fringe blogger do not constitute a primitivist site. The sooner you realize that the better off we'll be when the hype fades and y'all stop trying to co-opt valid shit.

Clearly, this anarchist thinker had designated himself a creator, and had decided that the Urban Scout was at best a MOP and probably also a capitalist vulture. The insult stung, and Peter responded, at first, from his wound:

Though you don't support me, obviously, I support what you do and have enjoyed reading most of the articles you have written . . . Just because we wear different clothes and have a different style doesn't mean we have different values . . . I don't understand why you did this.

But by the end of the email, Peter receded and the Urban Scout took over:

We need solidarity, not divisiveness. That is why I continue to critique the culture of anarchists. Because they send bullshit e-mails to people who should be their friends. Way to make it into my "Anarchists Vs. Rewilding" blog.

Peter assigned his detractor a pseudonym, "Meany Mc-Meanpants," then posted the letter to his blog with a handful of words redacted, inviting readers to complete the Mad Lib and post it in the comments thread for a chance to win "a signed and framed photograph of your favorite celebrity anarchist . . . ME!"

Over the next days, twenty or so responses were posted—many of which could have passed for Oulipo poetry.

Dear Urban Scout,
You and the other 'primitivist' cats are fumigating wombats. I'll give you castle for having a sense of talisman, but then you err on that tree. Trying to make rewilding just some new hipster graveyard is bluesy.

❦ ❦ ❦

In his book *Negotiating the Nonnegotiable: How to Resolve Your Most Emotionally Charged Conflicts*, the Harvard professor Daniel Shapiro writes, "Threats to identity often elicit a divisive mindset that transforms disagreement from a workable problem into a seemingly insurmountable one."[12]

Shapiro, who founded Harvard's International Negotiation Program, calls this dynamic "the Tribes Effect." I think it has a lot to say about subcultural factionalism, but before I proceed, a note on the word "tribe": Much in the same way people conflate "civilization" with "civil society" (any critique of our civilization—a social structure characterized by a dependence on agriculture and exponential population growth—inevitably prompts the breathless plea "But what about *Beethoven*?"); "tribe," in this case, seems to be an extension of the term "tribalism," which has come to denote small-minded aggression and in-group fidelity to the exclusion of rational thought, never mind the fact that tribal peoples, in contrast to so-called statesmen of empire, do not have a global track record of colonizing and converting "the other" on the basis of moral superiority. And so I wish Shapiro had chosen a different term for the Tribes Effect.

Anyway, some years ago, at the World Economic Forum's annual summit in Davos, Switzerland, Shapiro facilitated an exercise for international leaders in which they were split into "tribes" and asked to answer a series of morally divisive questions such as "Does your tribe believe in capital punishment?" Then the groups were brought together and told they would need to choose one of the six tribes—a single value system—to represent the whole group. The exercise would be timed, and they'd be given three rounds of negotiations to determine which tribe they would join, with the addendum that if they had not reached consensus by the end of the third round, the world would explode.

Shapiro characterizes the Tribes Effect as an adversarial, self-righteous, closed mindset, and writes that it "breeds the self-serving conviction that our perspective is not only right but morally superior." He continues: "In this closed system, we come to characterize ourselves and the other side as immutable . . . We critique their perspective and condemn their character. But we dare not criticize our own perspective, for we fear being disloyal to our own identity."[13]

Intrinsic to the crime of disloyalty is the risk of banishment, the loss of belonging, and thus the loss of identity itself. In other words, an argument might strike outsiders as petty, but the anxiety driving it is linked to our sense of safety in the world. Taken to an extreme, the choice between belonging to the group or belonging to oneself—that is, the freedom to exist as an autonomous being with a divergent viewpoint—proves untenable for almost everyone but the unquestioningly obedient or the pathologically contrary. Such pressures can result in the forging of a third way. Misanthropy, for example, or suicide.

I'm reminded of an anecdote in R. D. Laing's *The Divided Self*, in which this anxiety is expressed in exaggerated terms. An argument breaks out in a group therapy session, and one of Laing's patients explodes, "You are arguing in order to have the pleasure of triumphing over me. At best you win an argument. At worst you lose an argument. I am arguing in order to preserve my existence."[14]

When the delegates at Davos reached round three of their negotiations, they spent their remaining minutes arguing

over which was "a more important core value," humanitari-
anism or compassion.

"Moments later," Shapiro writes, "the world exploded."

In 2009, Peter moved out of his parents' house, where he'd
been crashing since the breakup with Penny Scout the previous season, and into a room in a scabby punk house on Portland's Eastside. He'd been living in the house for only a few
weeks when his roommate knocked on his door to let him
know he'd received a package. Right away, he had a bad feeling. He hadn't gotten around to learning his own address, let
alone sharing it with anyone. The huge box was sent anon-
ymously from Emeryville, California, and addressed to one
"Urban Scout, Domesticario Inc."

Given the antonymic relationship of the adjective "domestic" to "rewilding," Peter understood "Domesticario" as
an insult. He didn't want to open the package. "What lies
inside?" he wondered on his blog. "A bomb? Anthrax? Drugs
meant to incriminate me?"

Eventually, a more courageous friend opened it while
he watched from a hundred feet away. Inside the box was
a rock and some packing peanuts. A really big rock. Like, a
twenty-three-pounder.

"What was it supposed to mean?" I asked him.

"It was meant to be a threat."

Whoever sent the rock used a FedEx account number belonging to a corporate clothing chain, making it difficult to track
at first. Peter called FedEx, and they told him the package

was mailed by a woman but, understandably, would not grant his request to see the surveillance footage. He called the Portland police's non-emergency line and filed a report, to create a paper trail should things escalate. He suspected that one of his housemates was involved, in part because few other people knew he lived there, and in part because the guy he suspected—a young guy, in his very early twenties—had just moved to Portland from Oakland, where he'd been part of the vegan-anarchist scene. One day, the kid came home with some Primal jerky sticks, a vegan meat substitute, and Peter ribbed him for it—perhaps a bit too enthusiastically.

It turned out that many people had been using the stolen FedEx account number of the corporate clothing chain. Doing so provided multiple benefits to the sender, including anonymity when mailing incendiary materials, with the additional benefit of financially injuring a company that exploits sweatshop labor. Peter's police report had endangered their modus operandi; that alone was a major assault. But the most damning fact of all was that he'd called the police.

An anarchist website reposted Peter's blog article about the incident ("Horizontal Hostility vs. Rewilding") and the comments began pouring in.

"i don't call the cops when i get robbed or jumped or shot at," read one comment, "and you call them for a fucking rock?, pa-fucking-thetic."

"this kid is a fucking bird and a waste of skin," read another. "hes got nothing to do with anarchism. his website and the work he does is more like a white, rich kid, twenty-something fantasy camp for wieners."

Other comments offered advice. "You're more than slightly neurotic, you're edging over into paranoia. Take a break, go somewhere peaceful and quiet and chill out."

"Anon" commented (they were nearly all Anons), "A few years ago an ex of mine sent me a package full of rotting hamburger meat with a note saying that when I least expected it someone was going to stab me in the stomach. Did I call the cops? No, I did the right anarchist thing to do and dealt with it in a way which we won't discuss on the internet . . . My advice to Urban Scout: If you're concerned about your safety, go buy yourself a crossbow or something. Never give the pigs any excuses to poke around the @ scene, lest you end up with more numerous and serious enemies then you started with."

These vague threats, bizarre anecdotes, and self-aggrandizing outbursts of advice multiplied over the coming days. The thread soon spiraled into infighting, as they do.

One Anon called Peter "a fucking pussy," and another Anon responded, "Right now I'm calling out your sexism and assumed sexuality of this person."

The first Anon replied, "okay, i admit that calling a dude a pussy is a pussy move . . ."

Finally, WeWillWinAnarchy chimed in to deliver a moral to the story: "I would say that strength, in the sense of personal integrity, is a positive thing for everyone regardless of gender or sexual orientation. There is never a good excuse for being a whiny little bitch."

But there was one point on which all could agree: contacting the police was not "the right anarchist thing to do." And Peter's flagrant flouting of their law had fitted him for a snitch-jacket.

"So, what did you say about the kid's jerky?" I asked.

"I made fun. They're called Primal. It's like they're

acknowledging the fact that humans need to eat meat . . . He got all weird and defensive."

"He probably thought he was doing the right thing," I said. It was easy to chalk the whole episode up to karma. I reminded Peter of the New Year's Eve we spent with Matt's family in a cabin on Mount Hood. We were sixteen, probably drunk, and had just become vegans. I don't remember what set him off—maybe one of his parents ate some cheese—but I remember Matt running around outside in the snowy woods and screaming at the top of his lungs, "You're all fucking rapists!" And swelling with emotion as he did, with the slow-clap rush of righteousness that comes when you know someone has spoken truth to power.

As many before me have observed, it's not the unknown that disturbs us so much as *not knowing*. In order to manage the anxiety of not knowing, we tend to fill in the gaps with conviction. This effect is intensified when that not knowing pertains to fundamental questions like "How should a person live?"

That there is no one right way to live was one of *Ishmael*'s principal concepts, but somehow the meaning escaped us, even as the phrase slipped from our lips. I don't suppose Peter, Nick, Matt, or I would have claimed to have knowledge of the "right way to live." Instead, our convictions manifested as rigidly defended stances about other people's wrong ideas: hippies without "even a shred of understanding of the laws that govern the natural world," as Peter had it. These stereotypes served, like all stereotypes, to diminish the individual and deny their particularity, dehumanizing them.

In this, we were not so different from Peter's anonymous persecutors. If *we'd* been living in that house in our teens, we wouldn't have mailed him the rock; we would have sent it directly through his window. Time and experience had humbled us to life's complications and clued us in to the vast amount we did not know, and likely never would.

"We thought we were doing a good thing," Peter sighed. "The reality is, Lisa, there is no such thing as 'good things.' Everything is fucked."

❧ ❧ ❧

One more Urban Scout origin story: Peter had just returned to Portland from wilderness survival school. It was 1999; he was seventeen. He'd heard that one of our fellow survival students had gone barefoot for much of a three-year stretch, aside from wearing flip-flops in winter. Peter wanted to try this out in the city, to "feel the world" with his feet.

He quickly discovered that his days were constrained by the no shirt/no shoes policy enforced by most establishments, including the city bus, his primary mode of transportation. He worked around this rule by cutting the soles from an old pair of Adidas. Then he cut the feet from a pair of socks and sewed their ribbed tops into the ankles of the soleless shoes, and stretched a strap of elastic across each arch to hold them in place.

"Since the shoes rendered my barefootedness invisible," he wrote, "and kept the sensory data feet pick up available, I called the shoes my Urban Scout Shoes. No one ever blinked an eye at them."

He wore the decoys for close to a year.

Peter's objective wasn't so much to build calluses as it was to push the limits imposed by an urban environment. But he grew callous in the process anyway. So it goes: you set out to feel the world and wind up with the impression that everything is fucked.

Eventually, things died down. Though the callout feels interminable to its target, its shelf life tends to be rather short. New enemies were brought to trial, the schadenfreude-induced dopamine kept on pumping. Anyway, Peter had grown tired of the argumentative life.

A man "wears a mask, and his face grows to fit it," Orwell instructs.

When Peter finally burned out, this was more or less how he diagnosed the problem on his blog: "I had to get my own identity back . . . Urban Scout doesn't give a darn what people think . . . My heart just couldn't take it anymore."

In the late spring of 2011, he prepared to embark on a book tour for *Rewild or Die*, which he described as "sort of a swan song for the muse." The Urban Scout was being retired.

Just before he left, he received an email from a bookstore in Seattle dropping him from their calendar: "We've heard some allegations about you calling the police on people and are concerned because we are an anti-authoritarian and anti-police space."

He responded by linking to several remorseful tracts he'd produced on the subject in the two-year interim. He regretted calling the police, he wrote, and he regretted blaming vegans and anarchists for his harassment because, in reality, he didn't know who was behind it. The bookstore never wrote back.

"People don't want to do any problem solving," he said. "They want to critique without action. They could have had me there and directed the conversation like, 'Let's talk about this. What is a snitch? What would you do differently in this situation? What are viable alternatives to calling the police? Let's have a conversation.' You can't solve a problem by pretending it isn't there or by disposing of the people creating it."

In Oakland, he taught a class on friction fire at an urban permaculture event, and when he returned to his car, his windshield was smashed. Someone had punctured his tires with a nail and written SNITCH across the chassis in black Sharpie. This time, he didn't call the police. In fact, while he was waiting for the tow truck to arrive, a police cruiser slowed its roll and he anxiously waved it on.

"I was like, 'Get the fuck away from me.' I didn't want whoever did it to photograph me anywhere near a cop."

I suppose some would view this waving-off as progress, evidence that intimidation had forged a "better" person. I'm not so sure.

A few months later, he was driving around Portland when he was suddenly overcome. He had to pull to the side of the road and sob it out.

"You put all this energy into this thing, and these assholes show up to tear it down and make your life harder—" He stopped, seeming to hear himself with others' ears. "Look. I'm not a victim. I wrote inflammatory blogs and pissed people off. I'm not saying I asked for it, but you play with fire, you get burned. The fact that I was talking shit in that tone to a subculture that behaves violently means I shouldn't be surprised when I'm met with violence from that culture."

Anarchists didn't invent the callout, though you could

say they were enthusiastic adopters. It's important to note that, before the internet, a callout looked a lot more like individuals who knew one another confronting ideas and behaviors, and less like thousands of point-and-click activists piling on relative strangers without having to look them in their human face. In any case, any serious heads in the scene for the long haul had been witness to, if not the subject of, so many skewerings they couldn't help but grow a thick skin. You learned from the lashing, or you weathered it, or you packed up your toys and went home. Meany McMeanpants was a serious head, and he'd raised an important point in his and the Urban Scout's exchange those years before, about the potential utility of these disputes:

> It's obvious you think anarchists are over-critical and over-burdened by idealism. There's truth to that, but it's that kind of hyper-critical shit that forces you to have to think twice about EVERYTHING you say or do and, for those who stick through it, sharpen your own ideas and ability to defend them.

"You know what?" Peter told me. "Rereading these letters, I agree. My responses were subpar."

In time, Peter came to regret having created the Urban Scout. He regretted having talked so much shit about vegans and anarchists, groups that are already marginalized and dismissed or laughed at by the dominant culture. "I regret having conflated a few idiots with a deep political ideology that I actually believe in," he said. Mostly, he regretted having sown division and antagonism where he might have built a coalition.

Fair enough. But this regret fails to acknowledge the good that the Urban Scout also brought about. It wasn't all warehouse parties and internet flame wars. I've heard from many people who were introduced to the concept of rewilding through the Urban Scout, several of whom went on to teach those skills to others, including one young man who formed his own rewilding school in Maine.

In any case, Peter's change of heart struck me as an expression of an archetypal tension, expressed between generations or within a single aging man: a tension between the young and the middle-aged, between passion and prudence, between militant ideals and imperfect compromise. One man might temporarily triumph over the other, but the world depends on the energies of both.

Peter continued to correspond with McMeanpants. Eventually, they made amends and found some common ground. They still disagree on many points, which is fine with them. They don't have to agree on everything in order to cooperate. This is why Peter thinks the Tribes Effect exercise is basically bullshit.

"Putting hope in the idea that we need to get everyone to agree on a single solution is a surefire path to despair," he told me. "Something only a state would conceive: a monoculture. Maybe that world *needed* to explode."

I admitted this hadn't occurred to me.

But agreeing on a single solution didn't seem to me the primary point of Shapiro's exercise. The point was compromise in the face of a grave threat, in the interest of lives beyond your own and your own constituency. The people I knew who cared about living on a just and habitable planet spent much more time and energy negotiating in-group politics, minor disagreements, and lateral aggression than they did confronting those entities that posed the greatest threats. Perhaps it's precisely because those entities are so large, and the threats they pose so grave, that in our overwhelmed state we turn on one another, fixate on the smaller, proximal offenses; on what can be controlled. This would be forgivable if it weren't so often coupled with false equivalence and self-righteous claims of "bettering" one's comrades through a process of public shame and exclusion. Whatever its root, the narcissism of minor differences was a siphon that burned people out, rendering them fearful, bitter, and, often enough, ineffective.

In all likelihood, there will come a time, sooner or later, when the *out* will no longer avail itself to us, and we will once again be left alone together in the aftermath of all we've made. What will we do then about the problem of other people?

"In nature, there is no way to represent a 'whole group' with a single value system," Peter continued. "Life moves toward diversity, toward resilience. Everything is negotiation, compromise, collaboration."

On this we agreed.

"Imagine if instead the requirement of the exercise was to *diversify*," he said, "to come up with a thousand solutions to a single problem."

I could imagine it.

In fact, I've come to believe it's exactly what's required of us.

6

—

TO LIVE TOGETHER

The feeling of my selfishness is absence: the absence from my
life of the trash I leave behind, which becomes the structures
into which others must live, the broken hearts, the warmer
air, the slower fish, the rising ocean: whatever I do not feel
that to others becomes the shape of their world.

—KRISTIN DOMBEK, *The Selfishness of Others*

This is a story with two threads. One thread is about a group in North Philadelphia, and the other, a group in northern New Mexico. Both concern problems of disintegration, addiction, and "the shadow"—the unacknowledged psychic and social material that can impede people's ability to live together in a community. Both pose a question about reconciliation, a word derived from the Latin *reconciliatio*, "to bring together again": What does it take to reconcile a life, or a community of life, that's been fragmented?

I caught the first thread on a balmy afternoon in September. I took a train that day from Penn Station to Philadelphia, then a local to Kensington; I disembarked at Allegheny, descended a stair pocked with old gum, walked under the overpass past Checks Cashed and Diamond Dolls Go-Go

Club, to a triangle block of brick-and-clapboard row houses. 3234 Potter Street.

> I tried to keep facts like "Philadelphia is one of the most violent cities in America" and "there have been over 100 homicides this year" out of my mind as I kept a kung-fu grip on my Jansport backpack holding over $1,000 worth of recording equipment.[1]

I'd run across this account on a Chicago-based blog called *A Daily Miracle*. The blogger had traveled by public transit to visit The Simple Way intentional community, a multiracial group of radical disciples who'd fixed up several blocks of foreclosed and condemned houses in the neighborhood—the place where I was also headed. The Simple Way's stated purpose was to occupy the abandoned places of empire. Its unofficial purpose, I soon gleaned, was to perform resurrections.

The blogger from Illinois had taken in the "sights, smells, and impressions of the inner city," all while keeping a running inventory, not only of her backpack's brand and contents, but also of the "empty bags of chips, candy wrappers, pop cans, and plastic bottles" littering the streets—the discarded husks of former pleasures, juxtaposed with all she held in her "kung-fu grip." And though I'd read her account with smug contempt, stepping off the train that morning, I was forced to acknowledge an impulse in myself to clock the spent bags and bottles, the concrete "pocked" with chewing gum, and so on. Whenever the "out of sight, out of mind" principle is suspended, its suspension raises a reflexive question: What disposed parts of self return to mind when confronted with these sights?

The shadow, according to Carl Jung, contains whatever remains unconscious to the ego—our disowned and refused parts of self. These parts of self that we deny are then projected onto the environment, where we encounter them as disturbance. Stepping off the train, I'd encountered certain passing correspondences to refused aspects of my own formative experience: twice-monthly visits to Checks Cashed with my mother; returning empty cans and bottles for lunch money, hands sticky with hoppy dregs; hands plastered with orange dust when dinner was a bag of nacho-flavored tortilla chips. In certain company my family had been labeled "trash" explicitly, and I was frequently accused of being "dirty" as a child. I'd worked hard, in the ensuing decades, to distance myself from the detritus of my past, but any encounter with familiar expressions of disorder threatened to raise the memory of shame.

I recalled a line from an essay I'd been reading, "Plastics as Spiritual Crisis," by Sasha Adkins: "We tend to project what we loathe onto 'trash,' and then hold to the fantasy that by throwing away what is 'used' and/or 'dirty' we will ourselves be purified . . . This relationship to disposables habituates us to project a similar shadow onto other people."[2]

This projective loathing puts the "refuse" in "refused," and it tricks out in all kinds of ways. The disavowed toxins of industry are exported to rivers or buried in the ground, the repressed trash of the affluent is projected onto the poor, the shit of the pyramid scheme rolls downhill. But the same strategy was also at work in the communities where I'd once found refuge, in the shaming and exclusion of so-called toxic people, in the "shut-the-fuck-up-forever" ethic cycling through my social media feed.

No doubt the lens through which the blogger viewed her surroundings was distorted, potentially deforming to whomever passed through its projections—this was not at issue. But the righteousness I felt in rejecting her was. The farther I pushed her out, the cleaner I felt.

The notion was not exactly novel—that what we fear or loathe or otherwise deem unacceptable does not disappear the moment we banish it, but rather haunts our footsteps and acts on our lives in hidden ways—but recalling it helped me to recognize my self-righteousness for what it was: fear of my own shadow.

There's an old idea that the wound makes the medicine. It predates Jung by a long shot, though he did coin the term "the wounded healer," he whose own pain "gives the measure of his power to heal." This power is the story's second thread.

In 2018, I returned to Taos, New Mexico, to attend the annual Regeneration Festival, described as "a global movement to celebrate and honor children, teens and young adults to help them understand they are loved." Members of the Taos Initiative for Life Together (TiLT) were participating in the festivities and they'd extended an invitation to me. The festival was born seven years earlier, as a response to an epidemic of suicide and drug overdose among Taos youth. Members of the larger Taos community now came together annually over four days to fast, to pray, to break fast, and, on the final day, to celebrate together in the city park.

That same week, a town-wide reconciliation ceremony was scheduled to be held in Taos Plaza. The ceremony would bring together three different groups of stakeholders—Hispanic, Anglo, and Puebloan residents—in an attempt to metabolize historical trauma and imagine a way to live together in the uncertain landscape of the future.

I'd read about other reconciliation ceremonies during the height of the Standing Rock resistance. In one case, U.S. military veterans had traveled to Standing Rock to beg forgiveness from the Lakota People for historical atrocities committed by their units[3] (in a grim turn, it was later revealed that one of the veteran groups "egregiously misspent" money raised through their GoFundMe campaign[4]). At another event, a group of water protectors offered forgiveness to the Morton County Police, not in order to excuse their abuses, the protectors explained, but rather to lay down the burden of hatred.

I'm interested in the limit of forgiveness. Where it is, and why, and how some people are able to forgive those who've done them the greatest harm, often when they haven't earned it.

Just reading reports from Standing Rock, I found my mind drifting into violent fantasy. A part of me wanted the police and the corporate VPs and private security people to feel the pain they'd inflicted, to be hit with hoses in freezing temperatures, to have their snarling dogs turn against them—and it wasn't my home that had been invaded. This was a problem. Not because violence isn't warranted in defense of the planet but because the violent fantasies of a distant observer like me might serve a shadow purpose.

If there is such a thing as evil, I presume Big Petroleum is high on the list. But it's a divided self who daydreams about eviscerating the hocks of an economy in which she participates. And if those violent daydreams provide catharsis, if they serve to further distance her from her own culpability, to mutilate that which implicates her, and thereby help her to dodge the imperative to effect material change—then aren't those fantasies an extension of the evil at hand? And so long as we're at it, why not acknowledge that by *she* and *her* I mean *me*.

In the fall of 1995, the Philadelphia-based Kensington Welfare Rights Union (KWRU), an "interracial organization of welfare recipients and other poor people,"[5] occupied the abandoned Church of St. Edward the Confessor in North Philadelphia. Forty homeless families, mostly single mothers and their children, had taken up residence in the church and were refusing to leave. When the Catholic archdiocese caught wind of it, the archbishop gave the KWRU forty-eight hours to vacate the premises under the threat of arrest.

A group of students from Eastern University read an article in the local paper about the occupation and impending eviction, then drove to the church in Kensington to see how they could help. The families told them a student movement willing to stand in solidarity and risk arrest could make a difference. Eastern is an American Baptist institution with an interdenominational student body, and when the students returned to campus that evening, they appealed to their peers' religious convictions, papering the campus with flyers that read: "Jesus is getting kicked out of a church in North Philly!" More than a hundred people showed up to their meeting, and dozens of students headed to St. Edward the next day to join the occupation. The families, meanwhile, hung a banner in front of the church asking, "How can we worship a homeless man on Sunday and ignore one on Monday?" They held a press conference announcing their intention to stay, telling reporters that they'd spoken to the true owner of the building, and God said they could live there until they found somewhere else to go.

The occupation of St. Edward continued for several months, with intermittent moves on the part of the archdiocese and police to evict the families, and each attempt thwarted, in turn, by the KWRU's summoning of the press and local allies, including students from Eastern. Most of the families received housing in the end, either through government programs or donations from private citizens. A handful of families went on in the early weeks of December to occupy houses abandoned by the U.S. Department of Housing and Urban Development (HUD), correctly predicting that the city would not want to be documented evicting homeless families at Christmas.

Some of the Eastern University students maintained relationships in the neighborhood, and in 1998, they pooled their resources to purchase an old shoe-repair shop at 3234 Potter Street. This became the headquarters of The Simple Way.

I'm not sure how best to describe The Simple Way—it's a bit amorphous. Maybe something like "not-for-profit intentional Christian community." In their materials they write, "We celebrate together. We garden and work to make our neighborhood beautiful . . . When we run into bigger systems that throw obstacles in our neighbors' way, we advocate for systemic change together."

In practical terms, this meant running a food pantry,

providing emergency services, and creating affordable housing through the Simple Homes program—a sister nonprofit that acquires and restores cheap or donated houses in the neighborhood in need of significant repair. Each home was collaboratively rehabilitated by people like the Eastern students ("relocators"), locals ("remainers"), and those who'd been pushed out years before when the collapse of the factory-economy gutted the neighborhood ("returners"). Returners, remainers, and relocators could buy a deeply discounted house on a zero-interest loan through the program, provided they invested a few hundred hours in the restoration. In twenty years, they'd grown into twelve properties.

In the summer of 2007, a seven-alarm fire broke out in an abandoned factory on H Street, and the flames jumped to one end of the triangle between H Street and Potter, reducing the community center, and many community members' belongings, to ashes. The neighborhood got together and planted a park on the ruin, and built a greenhouse where lavender, beets, and kale grew primordially large, thanks to a magical process of cycling fish feces called aquaponics.

So much of the pain and pollution produced by industrial civilization is inflicted at a remove, so much depends on our abstracting that pain as "resource," "product," and "waste." Such direct conversion of feces to food struck me as a blunt form of shadow integration, a direct reckoning with our *materia prima*. Finisia Medrano understood that the subject was charged and took pleasure in detailing the life-giving power of her own feces. Her turds served as self-fertilizing seed-bombs in the backcountry, provided the earth was soft enough to admit them. If the earth was frozen, as it was the week I visited her camp, she shat on a page of newspaper, rolled it up, and fed the "shit burrito" to the woodstove. At the time, I found the idea repulsive. But at the slightest remove, the culturally sanctioned ritual to which I was accustomed— excreting into a porcelain bowl of clean drinking water— sounded preposterous by comparison.

Transformation of this kind is always occurring in the world—decay becomes compost for new life, pain motivates the sufferer to alleviate the pain of others. The Simple Way called it "practicing resurrection," the intentional conversion of vacant houses into homes, ash heaps into edible gardens, and deadly weapons into tools that cultivate life.

There's a verse in Isaiah that reads: "They will beat their swords into ploughshares and their spears into pruning hooks. Nation will not take up sword against nation, nor will they train for war anymore." Several years ago, a neighbor discovered a handgun in their basement. Taking a cue from this verse, the community gathered, fired up a forge, and hammered out a little garden pick from its melted barrel.

To formalize the ritual, they put out a call to the neighborhood and to their extended community: anyone who wanted to get rid of a gun could bring it to the forge. Over the years, people from all walks of life have given their guns to the fire. Military veterans and former cops who wished to disarm brought their guns to the forge. Guns used in suicide had been brought by surviving loved ones, and mothers who'd lost their kids to gun violence came and beat the molten metal with a hammer. The "hammering of the guns," as they called it, was conceived as a political protest, a public grief ritual, and a practical disarmament wrapped up in one. A method for transforming "violence into things that cultivate life rather than take it."

Resurrection is a freighted concept, and frankly, I don't have a handle on all the connotations. The biblical resurrection story, or at least the version I'd heard growing up, the one about a heavenly surrogate in the distant past coming back from the dead—it left me cold. Unless a story is made relevant to the problems of our actual lives, it will lose its power. But the metaphor of resurrection I encountered at The Simple Way—to make "rise again from the dead" by transforming what kills into what cultivates life—was a story enacted as a practice by the people, and thus made alive again on earth.

All along the triangle, brick walls bore colorful murals that looked like pages torn from an enormous picture book; depictions of the lion lying down with the lamb, the boulder rolled away from the cave mouth, a rising phoenix in the key of art deco, a two-story reproduction of Banksy's *Kids on Gun Hill*. If one way to disavow something is to label it "trash" or "shit," then the murals, the shiny tools, the pastel-painted stack of old tires, the defecating fish with incandescent scales—all that bright phenomena seemed to represent the transmutation stage of projection. Transfiguration, in the language of the Church.

"I've had reconciliation in my life and it sets you free," Christalyn Concha, the organizer of the Taos reconciliation ceremony, told me. We were sitting at a café on Bent Street. Many of the good restaurants and coffee shops in Taos were located on Bent, a street named for the slain territorial governor whose death was used as pretense for the massacre at

Taos Pueblo. The next day, they would gather a block and a half away to publicly lament that massacre and others, but for now we sat at a table on sunny Bent Street, eating quinoa salads.

It may be shallow to note, but having met nearly a dozen people in the business of making peace, I can say with some confidence that reconciliation is a hell of a beauty regimen. Forget the creams and injections, friends. Twenty years of sobriety and the belief that you are unconditionally loved by a divine source seems to act as a fountain of youth. When you're sickly and skeptical, you notice these things: vigor, posture, an ineffable radiance in the eyes. That was Christalyn Concha all the way.

Christalyn's father is from Taos Pueblo, but she was raised for the most part by her white mother and stepfather in Albuquerque. On the night of winter solstice in 1996, Christalyn's older brother Anthony was drinking and driving when he hit black ice and crashed. He was twenty-two years old. Days after his death, Christalyn found an entry in his journal saying he prayed "to break the curse of alcoholism" in their family. Her father and uncle got sober shortly after, and though it took a few years, she did, too. In death, Anthony had broken their curse.

After her brother died, Christalyn moved up to the Pueblo to live with her father full-time and began throwing sober dances for the community. At an event at the local arts center, she recounted the story of her brother's death and her subsequent transformation. Her talk was permeated with images of resurrection: "Though there are tragedies, deaths, loss, and suffering," she told the audience, "beneath the darkness there always lies a beauty, a promise of new life, of hope. Where death makes fertile the ground of our hearts, seeds can be sown. Seeds that produce life and multiply, seeds of love."[6]

Saturday, the day of the reconciliation ceremony, Ryno Herrera rose before dawn, dressed, finished the previous night's dishes and laundry, and then drove from the house he shares with his wife to the John Dunn Bridge on the Rio Grande.

Five miles downriver, where the canyon was deepest and the cliffs were sheer, many people had jumped from the Gorge Bridge, falling 650 feet to their deaths. It was still dark when Ryno pulled to the side of the road, parked, and began making his way on foot along a dirt path down the hillside to a hot spring below. When he reached the bank of the river, he undressed and began to dance in anticipation of the rising sun. This was how he began every morning.

Later that day he told me, "There's no greater moment for me than waiting for the sun to come up. I have PTSD from incarceration, so I'm up anyway. I might as well introduce something positive into my stream of life."

We met up at a café (also on Bent Street) and took a table on the patio. It was crowded with tourists, several of whom watched Ryno unselfconsciously. It was my impression that his tattooed arms and long hair signaled something unruly to the tourists, whose hangdog stares and frosted hair communicated to me, in turn, something of the working-class Midwesterner—a gawking-prone people from whom I partially descend.

Ryno was born in Taos in 1973 and raised just up the road in Arroyo Hondo, where his family lived for six generations, close to the land. He helped his father and grandfather gather wood and hunt and tend the gardens. The community was small and tight-knit back then; everyone knew and looked out for everyone else. He grew up running around with the same group of fifteen kids.

When the kids were sent to Taos proper for middle school, they mixed for the first time with Anglos and kids from the Pueblo. He said the groups were territorial and tended to stick to their own, which didn't change all that much once they reached adulthood.

Over the years, things in Arroyo Hondo changed. The Anglos moved in and posted PRIVATE PROPERTY signs, put up fences, and patrolled those fences with semiautomatic weapons.

"Places where my grandfather and father used to hunt as kids," Ryno said. "Now we're chased off the land."

I asked Ryno if working with Todd Wynward and the other Anglos at the TiLT House had caused tension in his family.

"Oh, I'm shaking the adobes at home. They haven't cracked yet, 'cause we got strong mud." He smiled sadly. "It's a hard place to walk. The people in my family are still scared of me building bridges."

Some mornings, there were other people down at the hot spring before dawn, healers from all over—a "world college," Ryno called it. And these healers would all tell him the same thing: *Don't be afraid to cross cultures, to be the one to help change this way of living.*

"Nobody makes it out alive, Lisa. We're all in this mess together, so we have to learn how to live together."

The waitress came by and refilled our coffees and delivered a gooey cinnamon roll the size of a dinner plate. The smell alone sent a flood of happy endorphins coursing through my body, but I declined Ryno's offer to share, as any one of its ingredients was liable to cause me crippling intestinal distress. Ryno had undergone gastric bypass surgery seven years before and could only get through a few bites, so most of the roll remained on the plate when we left, less a symbol of willpower than an offering on the altar of our former lives: what used to soothe our pain now caused us double.

"I was four hundred pounds for twenty years," Ryno told me, "and through therapy I found that food was my first addiction. I was addicted to food, then cocaine and crack, which I used at first to try to lose weight."

He'd been clean without interruption for the last four years thanks to a sobriety program that uses Suboxone, a drug commonly prescribed for detoxing from opioids. The supervising physician of that program had introduced him to Todd Wynward, who in turn introduced him to the Watershed Way. More recently, Ryno had been certified in peer support to help other people struggling with addiction.

Mismanagement of funds at the local detox center had led to its being shuttered in recent months. Ryno was worried. There was nowhere for people to go, and the opioid crisis was hitting the area hard. Down in Española, where he sometimes planted gardens with local kids, he'd picked up six hundred used hypodermic needles.

"Once that needle goes in the arm, it takes everything," he said.

When Ryno was freed from prison for the last time, his father observed, "Wherever you are, you take the best thing out of every situation." The statement felt like forgiveness, but there was truth to it, too. His talent for wringing sweetness from shitty situations was how he came to be called

Ryno in the first place, an acronym that stands for "Rewire yourself with new opportunities." The nickname was given to him in prison on account of his habit of helping others and the many certificates he'd earned over the course of three stints inside on drug-related offenses. He'd trained in such varied areas as information technology, culinary arts, barbering, and fiber optics.

I pointed out that "Rewire yourself" sort of echoed the title of Todd Wynward's book *Rewilding the Way*, though I guessed he'd already noticed the connection.

He confirmed that he had. Todd's book had meant a lot to him, and he'd reread it several times. Over the last year, Ryno and Todd had collaborated on the planting of permaculture gardens in Arroyo Hondo, Taos, and Questa, a town near the Colorado border.

Ryno and his mom used to operate a video store and trailer park in Questa. When Redbox and Netflix came in, they were wiped out. But the land was close to the Red River, and water on the property ran through the old acequias—an irrigation system brought over by Spanish colonizers. Ryno and Todd used that water to grow potatoes, corn, beans, and beets, and they were about to harvest the apples.

The gardens were conceived as a hedge against climate change. Ryno envisioned a future of regional self-sufficiency, in which the gardeners of each area shared their resources in the lean times. "If there's not enough food in Taos, we bring it from Questa, from Hondo. We can take from Taos to Questa. It's an amazing thing if we could all learn to live this way, where we share the issues that we're facing together."

His long-term goal was to build tiny houses in the old trailer park and establish a transitional community for addicts, a place where the recovering could live on sweat equity, on the tending of gardens and chickens, and the building of community structures.

"'Therapy' is a strong word for Hispanic men," Ryno told me, "but if you can have some togetherness as positive people doing positive things, and then bring the kids around—once the kids are involved, we don't have any choice but to thrive. Because they are innocent, they are our future."

On the day I visited The Simple Way, a couple of community members had given me an informal tour of the neighborhood. We concluded in one of their houses. On the kitchen table sat several large jars filled with used hypodermic needles.

The needles, they told me, were regularly collected from local streets. Once the community members had gathered several hundred, they dropped the jars off at the offices of the mayor and the health administrator. Each of the jars was labeled with a message from a neighborhood child. A thirteen-year-old child wrote: *Even though we live in what people call a "bad" neighborhood, there still shouldn't be any needles and guns around because we have families and babies too.* Another child, nine years old, wrote: *I hope the drugs and stuff go away, and the guns. It would be better without them, because there is a lot of drama in Kensington . . . Can you help take the drugs and needles off the earth?*

At the sight of these jars, I was flooded with an uncanny sense of a dream bleeding into waking life. I hadn't slept much in the days leading up to my visit, and I was threadbare and wired. The night before, I'd woken in the dark from a nightmare with a racing heart. In the dream, my grown nephew was still a little boy, and we were camped out in sleeping bags in the basement of my sister's house. *The house is cursed*, he told me with terrified eyes. *We should never have come here.*

My nephew was found a few days after his twenty-third birthday. He was geared up with the TV on and had a lethal dose of an opioid in his blood. In the eleven months between his death and the dream, I'd heard, as if in my inner ear, his kid voice calling, *Aunt Lisa? Can you help?*

Whether or not I could have helped him, the fact was, I did not. *Heal the sick, raise the dead, drive out demons.* The verse had lodged in my mind, like a stylus hitching on a record. I resented the suggestion that the dead could rise, and I felt the ghost of "your" hanging in the gap between "drive out" and "demons." But I also wanted to believe all three were possible.

That afternoon, I went with one of the men of The Simple Way to the corner diner. It was nearly empty. We took a seat and chatted for a while. Our conversation was pleasant enough, but by then I was feeling pretty strange. I couldn't shake the nightmare, or the sight of the jars filled with hypodermic needles, or this new obsessive thought: had I broken my family's curse, driven out its demons, my nephew would have been spared his fate.

When our sandwiches and Cokes arrived, I started stuffing my face, hoping it would normalize me, but the slow clasp of unreality had already taken hold.

"What's your understanding of the figure of Satan?" I asked the man. "You know, demons, evil, these kinds of things?" As soon as the question was out of my mouth, I wished I hadn't asked.

A wave of incoherent speech was swelling on the street

outside. I had my back to the door and couldn't see what was going on, though it sounded like maybe someone was fighting. I kept pushing French fries into my mouth, one after the other, as if by automation.

The man's eyes searched my face. "I'd say I believe those forces are real," he told me. "There's a place in Ephesians where it says, 'We wrestle not against flesh and blood but against principalities and powers—"

He broke off. His attention pulled to whatever was going on outside.

I turned to look where he was looking and saw a white man with a bent spine, hobbling from the door toward us.

"I got a question," the bent man shouted, "'cause I don't hear real good!"

His voice was odd, at once fervent and mechanical. His volume was high, but his eyes were dull. It was as if each word were pitched into his body by an unseen source.

He reached our table.

"Aren't atheists better than these people bickering about religion?" the bent man asked. Then he said something about "Mary Magdalene the harlotote." His eyes were roaming wildly, all around the room. At the mention of "the harlotote," a little alarm bell went off in my spine, and I thought, *This person is possessed*.

In my warped state, the man arrived like a warning. I'd underestimated the principalities and powers. We laid cash down on our check and made for the exit.

The bent man shambled quickly ahead of me, then stood aside at the threshold and waved me through the door with a gallant sweep of his arm.

"If I hadn't had the Bible," he was saying, "I would have survived my childhood but I would have been a serial killer."

He let go a burst of pained laughter. "You would still like me if I was a serial killer?"

I arrived in New York that night physically intact, but other structures were in a process of unraveling. Every face that floated down the aisle of the train was suspect. I'd asked a question about evil, and now, I believed, I'd summoned it. By the time I stepped onto the platform for an F train to Brooklyn, they were angels and demons all.

The subway car was nearly empty, so I sat in one of the two-seaters and tried to make myself a stone. A hulking man boarded at the next stop. He wore a moldering wool duster, wet with rain, and smelled strongly of sour milk and mothballs. There were dozens of vacant seats, but he took the seat beside me. I worried it would draw attention to move, so I pulled my body away from him against the wall. He had his head in his hands, and was shaking it back and forth, like *no, no, no.* I suspected that the unseen person to whom the man was speaking wanted to do me harm. The negative fantasy was quite specific. I imagined he'd pull an ice pick from his coat and stab me quickly in the brain, like gigging a frog, instantaneous lights-out. I imagined he would do this not because he was the evil one, but because *I* was, or because he believed I was. Because he believed I was one of the demons. And how could I be sure I wasn't?

Two seats, two people. One good, one evil. It had all stitched together into a frightening chiaroscuro. I was being "shown" something, something invisible to most people. It stalked me through Brooklyn, up to my borrowed apartment, the forces of evil gathering on the street below the brownstone.

I locked all the doors and windows, grabbed a frying pan and a knife, and set them on either side of the bed.

You should sleep, a voice said—my own voice, the faintest interjection of reason. *This feels real, but if you sleep it won't.*

Thirty or so people had gathered in the gazebo at Taos Plaza on Saturday afternoon for the reconciliation ceremony. Ryno was there, and Todd Wynward and Peg Bartlett. There were members of the local government and a dozen other people who were either Taos residents or maybe tourists just passing through the plaza. We stood in a circle. Occasionally, a pack of small children broke through it, squealing, as if to remind us what all our solemnity was for.

"I have a vision of reconciliation," Christalyn told the crowd, "and that starts with acknowledging the past. When there are stressors, or when there's a breakdown in relationship, it helps us to have a deeper view."

Todd Wynward stood up on behalf of the clergy. He introduced himself as a "recovering Christian" and a "recovering settler," and he talked about the "legacy that has been going on for about sixteen hundred years, ever since the Roman emperor Constantine took the beautiful path of Jesus and turned it into empire."

Next, Ryno came to the mic and read a rousing prayer to San Isidro, patron saint of acequias, finishing with a kind of call to arms: "I'm done with wanting to be destructive and distrustful. How about you?"

The crowd clapped.

"Will we trust each other?" he asked them. "I tell you today I am going to trust, even though it seems crazy. I tell you today I am going to commit to this way of life, this movement we call the Watershed Way. I am going to build bridges across the lines that divide our town, our culture, our races, our religions."

Two of the four Taos Town Council members came. One of the men, a teacher at the local high school named Pascual Maestas, spoke about the "seventh generation" principle. Then he echoed Ryno's call for cooperation. "We are one community, we have a shared destiny, and to move into the future we need to work together."

Christalyn had written up a proclamation for the mayor, who had agreed to read it. She gave me a copy. Here's how it begins:

Whereas, from its foundation, the town of Taos has experienced a violent History, beginning with Spanish Colonization of the Taos Pueblo in 1615. Much atrocities, bloodshed, slavery and acculturation have occurred on Taos soil among Taos Pueblo people. And while people are relatively amicable, the past often surfaces through violence/abuse, drug and alcohol addictions, and present day tensions which can be barriers to cohesive relationships.

Whereas, the violent past, did not originate from the hand of any person in this present day, the stories have been passed down through the generations, the trauma faced by ancestors has left an imprint, affecting the very DNA of people today, commonly understood as Historical Trauma.

Whereas, in order to take steps towards healing for the sake of future generations, and to repair relations, I would like to acknowledge some specific historic events . . .

The proclamation went on to list some specific historic events that had taken place where we stood. On April 9, 1847, after the Americans hurled cannonballs at the little church up at the pueblo, they hanged six men down in the plaza. In the weeks that followed, they murdered twenty-two more men. The proclamation goes on to detail the systematic orphaning and abuse of children through the boarding-school system, and the subsequent damage to family relationships and cultural transmission.

"I acknowledge the injustices, and ask for forgiveness on behalf of my ancestors," the mayor was going to say. "May this gesture be a seed that grows into a greater movement of healing and repair for restored relationships in Taos and beyond."

But the mayor didn't say any of that.

Instead, he read a proclamation of his own devising. It expressed his discomfort with the ceremony and his place in it. He told us he'd been mayor for only a short time, and he wasn't sure how to apologize for things that happened hundreds of years ago. He said the community should work together for a better future. "How can I help?" he repeated. Then he left.

The second town council member in attendance, a man called Fritz (whom I later learned is one of Christalyn's uncles) stood up to say he didn't have patience for speeches, or for people who are "long on the lip and short on the muscle," and if you want to make a difference, if you want "to make a down payment for that seventh generation," you should grab a shovel and climb in a ditch to help retrench the acequias.

In his book *Why Good People Do Bad Things: Understanding Our Darker Selves*, the psychoanalyst James Hollis describes taking his children to visit Dachau, Bergen-Belsen, and Mauthausen. Unable to imagine how anyone could commit such atrocities, he writes: "I finally concluded that such perplexities will remain unsolved, until at least enough of us can confess, '*Such horrors were committed by my countrymen, or my coreligionists, or by my fellow human beings, and even I, who was not there, must nonetheless take responsibility.*' Only then can any real healing begin."

Of course, real healing also depends on putting a stop to ongoing injury. I didn't know much about reconciliation ceremonies before attending the event at Taos Plaza. After I returned home, I read critiques describing these events as "Kumbaya" bullshit for settlers hoping to be let off the hook with no real investment in correcting ongoing injustices. Though, just as often, such events were described as transformative or profound. I assume it depends on who shows up and how, and on whether or not formal acknowledgment is a prelude to material change or just another opportunity to maintain the status quo.

In Taos Plaza, it seemed to me that the mayor and councilman battled straw—as if it were impossible for a person to both dig a trench and acknowledge injustice at the same time, as if what happened before is unrelated to what is ongoing. Ours is not a choice between word and deed but between consciousness and unconsciousness. If you want a situation to transform, you must first acknowledge that it exists.

As Jung puts it, "One does not become enlightened by imagining figures of light, but by making the darkness conscious. The latter procedure, however, is disagreeable and therefore not popular."

Ryno Herrera and I were walking down Bent Street the next day. I asked him what he made of the reconciliation ceremony.

He said he found it interesting that all these politicians were invited, but most of them didn't show up. "We the people showed up," he said.

I pointed out that the mayor came, though he did seem to vanish the moment he completed his speech.

"The mayor should have stayed," Ryno said. "Maybe if he was Hispanic he would have."

I said I couldn't tell if he was or wasn't.

"That's because he was speaking Spanish, let's work *con juntos* and all that, but he's an Anglo . . . I guess he's Italian? Anyway, he should have stayed around to listen, not just make a proclamation and leave."

Just then, we passed a white family of five in matching Red River T-shirts.

"You guys like the Red River?" Ryno asked them.

They looked away and moved past us, apparently in shock. Someone finally murmured the affirmative.

"You know those guys?" I asked, once they were out of earshot.

"Nah," he said, smiling. "They're scared of me, but I'm the nicest guy in town."

"You're really nice," I agreed. Then, after a moment's

thought, "The weird thing is they're scared of each other, too."

It was Sunday morning, and the Regeneration Festival's big concert was gearing up down the street in Kit Carson Park. Kit Carson was a famous American frontiersman known by some for helping to "settle the West" in the mid-1800s, and by others for his scorched-earth method of starving and burning out Indigenous peoples from their ancestral lands. In 2014, the Taos Town Council had voted to change the name of the park. People were understandably offended that the park bore the name of a man who'd helped execute the Long Walk of 1864, the forced march of Navajo peoples from the four corners to Fort Sumner's Bosque Redondo, a concentration camp known in Navajo as Hwéeldi, a place of suffering.

Others in town, Anglo conservatives for the most part, claimed Carson was a victim of revisionist history, that in fact he'd resisted the scorched-earth campaign. One of Carson's biographers even weighed in, claiming his subject was "a friend to all the pueblos" and "no Indian hater," citing as evidence Carson's first marriage to an Arapaho woman. As if marriage has historically precluded hatred of a wife's people, or for that matter, the wife herself.

But other Anglos in town agreed with the activists and wanted healing on the issue. A woman from Kit Carson's lineage apologized to Christalyn Concha, who stood on behalf of her Pueblo lineage.

"This woman had been harsh with me," Christalyn said, referring to interactions before the apology. The experience confirmed her suspicion that the past exerts a powerful hold on the present. The old dynamics cycle back, even if we're mostly unconscious of their origins.

It was a good day for the festival, bright blue skies and warm. I arrived at Kit Carson Park at half past ten, thirty minutes late, but only about two dozen people had shown up, mostly booth minders still in the process of erecting their tents. There was a dunk tank in progress, and a face-painting booth, and people roasting corn. The teen homeless shelter had a booth, as did a teen-run suicide prevention group. Once the microphone was up and running, people took turns talking about sobriety and the importance of taking good care of the earth. Teenagers and their parents trickled in.

Christalyn had grown up spinning records in the rave scene, and now she ran a mentorship program for young DJs. Some of her teen mentees took the stage, while kids and parents danced barefoot in the grass.

During the second DJ's set, an enormous dark cloud came down off the mountain and ceiled the blue day, dimming the world in an instant, like a scarf thrown over a lamp. I'd never seen a clear sky cloud over so quickly, and I lived a couple of years in the land of monsoons. Moments later, thunder clapped and the cloud broke open unleashing a torrent of rain, flooding the festival grounds.

People sprinted for cover or for their cars. A handful ran joyfully into the deluge. Curtains of water came sheeting off the tents; wet gusts soaked the booth minders' pamphlets and the piles of donated clothes. The DJs kept spinning, and once the initial shock wore off, children and adults came out from under cover to dance again, their faces and hands up-turned to the sky.

I'd ducked under one of the tents and was watching the dancers. I couldn't remember the last time I'd seen a group of human beings who appeared so vital, submitting their bodies to the rain, no frazzled parents trying to usher their children inside. Even among those who'd sought shelter, not a single face was bowed toward a smartphone screen.

"It's not a coincidence this song is playing," said the young man sheltering next to me, a smiley teenager with a ponytail and a penchant for elliptical philosophical statements.

We'd met earlier in the day. I'd learned he was a descendant of Tecumseh, and that he was currently Christian, but lately he'd had his mind blown by "this atheist guy named Erich Fromm." He said something about how the word "rain" was related by obscure etymology to "love."

"Can you hear it?" he asked.

A chipmunk-voiced electronic dance tune was escalating in the speakers. I could hear it. Here's what I heard: *Put your love on me, put your love on me.*

A month or so after my return from Philadelphia, I still hadn't made any meaning of my demon experience. It troubled me, and I preferred not to think about it. I was disturbed by the ease with which I'd figured ordinary people for monsters, but more by how close it still felt, just under the surface, and the fear—still alive in my nervous system—that those people actually were possessed.

I consulted my bookshelf and pulled out *The New*

Dictionary of Kleinian Thought, a compendium of writ-ings on the Austrian-British psychoanalyst Melanie Klein.[7] I turned to a section on psychological splitting and read: "The chief characteristic of the paranoid-schizoid position is the splitting of both self and object into good and bad, with at first little or no integration between them." Klein is referring to a developmental process in infants, but like most early processes, it can show up in adulthood. Klein describes the process by which an infant splits off negative emotions and projects them into the mother, the "psychic equivalent," as the Kleinian psychoanalyst Michael Feldman has written, "of expelling dangerous substances from the body."[8]

The infant expels these "harmful excrements" and projects them "in hatred" into the mother, and later, in adulthood, into other charged figures, such as co-workers, politicians, ex-lovers, or random strangers encountered in diners. Negative feelings are transferred to an external fig-ure that threatens, menaces, persecutes. "These excrements and bad parts of the self," Klein wrote, "are not meant only to injure but also to control and take possession of the object."[9]

The evening of my meltdown, I'd locked all the doors and windows in the borrowed apartment, grabbed a frying pan and knife to set on either side of the bed, and heard my own voice say, *You should sleep.* When I finally did fall asleep, I went deep, as if bludgeoned, and woke to find the panic mostly gone. I made a morning flight to Tucson, hungover from stress-induced cortisol, the residue of my delusion draining off as the plane climbed, and by the time I arrived home I felt I'd outrun it. The binary of good and evil as it was presented to and by my terrified self was convincing, though I don't believe in evil.

I don't believe in evil, and yet, at various times in my life I've felt that I was in the room with it. How does one talk about serial killers, or people who derive pleasure from hurting children without employing the word "evil"?

This was on my mind in part because I'd just seen a documentary about sex offenders called *Pervert Park*. The men and women in the movie, who'd done evil to children, had also been abused as children. I felt more sympathy toward them once I understood their contexts. This was, of course, the motive of the documentarians and the predictable outcome of allowing a monster to take off his mask and speak. There was an almost palindromic logic to it: their personal histories did not excuse their behavior, nor were those histories guaranteed to produce their behavior (the proximal case in point: I was molested as a child, and did not grow up to become an offender), but their behavior had nevertheless grown out of their personal histories.

In other words, our compulsions have roots that extend beyond the self. The "perverts" could not be treated without recognition of this basic fact. Most of us know this, but sometimes it's simpler to pretend we don't. Treating complex trauma and seeking restitution for extreme violations is a far more uncertain process than, say, flipping the switch on the electric chair.

James Hollis writes about working with chronic abusers, noting that "much of their survival depended on numbing themselves, transferring the pain to another, and learning coping adjustments that bury, desensitize, or disassociate the suffering."

In this case, it's the abuser's vulnerability and sensitivity to others that are relegated to shadow. Empathy requires resonating and feeling with another, but if the prototypical other is not safe to resonate with, to be vulnerable to, one learns to numb. "As there is no abuser who has not been abused," Hollis writes, "the capacity to feel empathy for their victim, rare as that may be, is the only hope for their healing."

My doubt about evil, or at least my received notion of evil, is that it casts destructive energies with terrestrial origins in a supernatural pall, estranging it. Calling something evil severs it from context and elides whatever humanity remains, however corrupted, within the evildoer. It is not a victim's responsibility to rehabilitate her abuser, but it is the responsibility of the larger culture to try. If instead, as a culture, we dehumanize and excommunicate our monsters, the possibility of their finding access to healing goes from slim to none. Handily, it also serves to split off and expel the evil within those performing the excommunication.

The banishing of excrements is both literal and figurative. You press a handle and banish your actual excrement through a vortex leading to who knows where. Or you call someone a piece of shit and you take control of them, dismiss them, flush them out of sight and mind. But where do they go then? This practice of rejection, disavowal, and exclusion has been applied to so many our culture deems harmful that I fear our shadows have reached maximum density. In certain dire situations, exclusion, even execution, might be necessary to minimize harm, but let's not pretend that those are scalable solutions or that they address the root of a systemic problem. If we believe the First Law of Thermodynamics—that energy can neither be created nor destroyed—then it's safe to assume the untransformed energy we've rejected will return to us down the line.

I wanted to understand the obstacles that prevent a community from coming together, but how much could I realistically expect to learn from a day, or a week, or even a few months of conversation? These were not my communities, and I wasn't going to think or talk my way past a surface understanding. (In order to learn how to live with others, it turns out you actually have to live with them.) In both instances, I believed that I was encountering the world, when in fact my most salient interactions were with my own unconscious projections.

So I still don't know what it takes to reconcile a life, or a community, that's been fragmented, but I think I've found some partial answers. One basic lesson being that unless we reckon with what we've denied, unless we risk obliteration by bringing the shadow to light, those forces will persist in affecting our lives and relationships and nothing will transform. When we reconcile the divisions in ourselves and our communities, when we face our histories, the intractable begins to move and we spare our children the burden down the line. New stories and rituals are born to serve the people, not in a hypothetical future crisis, but right now, in the ongoing crisis of the present.

"Only out of disaster can the longing for the saviour arise," Jung writes. "In other words, the recognition and unavoidable integration of the shadow create such a harrowing situation that nobody but a saviour can undo the tangled web of fate." But the division between our conscious lives and our shadow, he went on to say, is answered through *relatedness*.

I've lost interest in saviors, but I do long for transformation, for relatedness. And I do have faith in these believers, in Christalyn, in Ryno and TiLT, in the people of The Simple Way: in all those who would live into the purpose the word "religion" describes: *re*, meaning "again," and *legare*, meaning "to bind, bond, or bridge," as in "ligature." This was the ideal function of religion, the analyst Robert Johnson observed, "to bind together again. It can never be affixed to one of a pair of opposites."[10]

7

IN THE GARDEN

Notre jardin is never a garden of merely private concerns into
which one escapes from the real: it is that plot of soil on
earth, within the self, or amid the social collective, where the
cultural, ethical, and civic virtues that save reality from its
own worst impulses are cultivated. Those virtues
are always *ours*.

—ROBERT POGUE HARRISON, *Gardens: An Essay on the
Human Condition*

D riving through California's Central Valley in the
summer of 2017 felt like watching previews of coming attractions. Though Governor Jerry Brown had
announced the end of the state's six-year drought, the road
proffered contradictory images. Once-fertile agricultural
lands were as parched and cracked as desert playa. Dead or-
chards lined the highway for miles, and for miles the hyp-
notic flash of gray and defoliated fruit trees, still upright
in their rows, cycled through my window. On other par-
cels, the snags had been uprooted and stacked in mounds.
When glimpsed at high speeds, in the whitish cast of midday
light, these mounds resembled piles of twisted bodies. The
pale limbs seemed to reach. I couldn't resist the double image: the superimposed specter of human remains. Whoever

had worked in those groves was gone; only their signs persisted. Placards stabbed in the dirt along the highway read, NO WATER = NO JOBS and STOP THE POLITICIANS CREATED WATER CRISIS! But the time for such protest had ended. In this wasteland, the only signs that made any sense were purely interpretive: most ubiquitously, CONGRESS CREATED DUSTBOWL.

On the color-coded drought maps comparing one year to another, a red wound appears in California's side and spreads fast. Within a year, the blood has soaked the fabric. The matter of what or who was to blame for dealing that blow was up for debate. On the left, activists called for an end to fracking, claiming the industry wasted two million gallons of water a day. Some blamed the bottled water industry or conventional agriculture. The vegans blamed the carnivores, and drew up charts comparing water use among California almond growers (10 percent) and the meat and dairy industry (47 percent).

On the right, they blamed environmentalists for impeding the construction of new dams. One California assemblywoman, addressing a banquet hall of pro-life activists in Sacramento, allegedly suggested the drought was God's retribution for legal abortion. "Texas was in a long period of drought until Governor Perry signed the fetal pain bill," she was quoted as saying. "It rained that night. Now God has his hold on California."[1] This prompted local pro-choice advocates to mock up a spoof campaign shirt for the assemblywoman, bearing the slogan *I made a desert with my abortion and all I got was this lousy T-shirt.*

In the final tally, somewhere in the neighborhood of 570,000 acres were idled, and eighteen thousand farmworker jobs were lost. Most parties agreed, if tacitly, on one thing: water is life.

But none had reached the source of the issue. The only complete narrative I'd heard was articulated by Native American activists who'd located the problem in far older events. Namely, colonization. In the case of the Owens Valley Paiute (or Nüümü), one big problem was Los Angeles County and how they'd acquired their water in the first place, an original sin in the city's design, from which much current suffering descended. The essence of that defect could easily be extrapolated to the rest of the state—indeed, to all the cities of the world, and in fact could be credited for the very existence of cities: the problem of urban centers looting resources from surrounding lands.

For millennia, the Nüümü of Owens Valley managed an intricate system of irrigation ditches that routed snowmelt out of the Sierras into the valley. This system spanned some sixty square miles. After the so-called Owens Valley Indian War of 1863, surviving tribal members returned home to find their lands and irrigation system occupied by white settlers. The Nüümü were told they'd need to apply for water rights, but it was understood that anyone who attempted to do so would be made to suffer for it, if not summarily killed. It was that year, in fact, when a mob of white settlers and soldiers drove thirty-five people into Owens Lake, gunning them down or drowning them.

In 1913, the celebrated mercenaries Fred Eaton and William Mulholland completed the aqueduct that would channel the Owens River to the city of Los Angeles—220 miles across the Mojave Desert. Agriculture in the valley began to suffer immediately, and within thirteen years the once-expansive Owens Lake was almost completely desiccated. Until ongoing litigation forced the city to return some of the water, it was not uncommon for the sky to be swallowed by a tsunami of carcinogenic dust drawn up from the dry lake bed. Today, wide swaths of the lake bed teem with halobacteria, forming a dark red brine that appears on the cracked surface of the salt flats like platelets under a microscope, or in the aerial view like gobs of clotted blood.

Eaton and Mulholland made a bleeding desert with their avarice, and all they got was a handful of monuments. But once upon a time, the valley was a very different scene. In the words of the elder and activist Harry Williams, "The whole valley was our garden." That was before the Los Angeles Department of Water and Power pumped "the life and color out of the area" and "turned everything gray . . . sent all that life and that color down to L.A."[2]

The Nüümü name for Owens Valley, by the way, is Paya-huunadü (Land of Flowing Water). Dick Owens, the white man for whom the lake and valley were named, never so much as set foot in that place.

I'd met Harry Williams in Tucson, Arizona, at a screening of the documentary *Paya: The Water Story of the Paiute*. One of the main subjects of the film, Williams had spent decades trying to establish the history of that ancient irrigation system and thereby return some of the valley's water to the tribe by proving "first use." His personal story, which bore the mark of predestination, began with the discovery of a mysterious object. He was out hunting rabbits as a child in the foothills when he came across a hunk of carved wood—an ancient irrigation diverter as it turned out, though it would be years before he understood its original purpose.

In *Paya*, the camera follows him into a dense tangle of brush, which he pulls apart to reveal a trench in the earth. The trench corresponds to maps drawn by one A. W. Von Schmidt, an ill-fated civil engineer of Prussian extraction, contracted by the U.S. government to survey the area in

1856 and '57—a man who'd reported to his masters that the Owens Valley soil was poor and "worthless to the White Man."[3]

At the time of the screening, the Owens Valley Nüümü were engaged in a protracted legal battle with the Los Angeles Department of Water and Power, and the tribe would submit Von Schmidt's journals as evidence that the Nüümü were "using" their water long before the settlers arrived.

To screw the whole story together in one's mind was to enter a Kafkaesque rat maze of imperialist logic: from massacre and occupation; to desertification; to the courtroom where the people of the valley had to prove their right to exist, the very valley's right to exist; to those profiting from their destruction, based on the premise of "ownership" by "use," and not through their own testimonies or oral history, but through the scribbles of a colonial tool who spent less than two years in the valley.

"*This* is our ethnography," Williams had said at the film screening, meaning the land. The land itself was the authoritative text.

Throughout the summer and fall of 2017, I watched the great fires unfurl in the west—Pocket, Atlas, Tubbs, Nuns. California has always served as a kind of petri dish for the new, and once again it was showing us our future. Roughly 240,000 acres burned in California in the month of October alone. Thousands of structures were destroyed, and forty-two people were dead.

Meanwhile, a series of smaller, more personal disasters unfolded around me. Fernando Moreira's cancer came back. He didn't volunteer a prognosis on the Facebook post announcing the bad news, only the characteristic all-caps vow that he would "NEVER GIVE UP." When last I spoke to him, he was in the midst of a search for a missing hiker in the North Cascades, having just completed a search through the California wildfires the day before. As far as I know, he has yet to take a day off from work.

Next came news of Finisia Medrano's busted-up joints, the loss of her horses, and her return to Babylon. Sufficient funds had been raised to purchase a truck—a 1987 Mazda 4x4, dubbed the "stink bug"—and get it running again. She was using it to replant lands torched by the wildfires rolling through the state.

"I'm hauling all these exotic domesticates out into the wild, rewilding these burns out here," she told me over the phone. "People are like, 'They're not native!' I'm like, 'They're going to feed the wild, and you don't give a shit anyway, so fuck off.'"

She was still in a lot of pain and by then living on disability, but like Fernando she refused to give up her life's purpose.

"I'm going to keep doing what it hurts me to do," she said.

Autumn crept toward winter as one emergency followed another. I turned on the radio one morning to dead air. A man's voice finally spoke into the silence. "California . . ." he pronounced, "is *burning*."

In December 2017, the largest wildfire in California history burned more than four hundred square miles of coastal and National Forest lands in Ventura and Santa Barbara counties. I received a group email from Ched Myers at Bartimaeus

Cooperative Ministries, describing the chaos unleashed on the Ojai Valley and his community:

> Stuck it out in Oak View until the mandatory evacuation about 1:30 pm yesterday. We did not think our home was in danger, but the mountain a half-mile away was completely on fire. No one was fighting this fire because resources are spread so thin . . . Watered everything down around the house, directed traffic at our corner (the main evacuation artery) for several hours, packed up necessities, and checked in with elderly neighbors. But finally the smoke got too bad and we left, with divided hearts.
>
> Today: We got home to Oak View about 10 am. Fires still burning along the 101. Ash like snow, smoke as thick as fog here in Oak View; but all is fine. Power is on, we even have (spotty) phone service. Wearing particulate masks . . . Elaine is down in Camarillo to escape the smoke. I am spending the night here because the winds are supposed to pick up tonight, and that could be sketchy again.
>
> Please pray for fire fighters and those many who have already lost homes and in a few cases, lives. This is all part of the "new normal" under climate crisis.
>
> This is why we fight, this is why we sing.
>
> —Ched & Elaine

By the time you read this, the Thomas Fire will have already receded from public consciousness—though not likely from the minds of those affected. How could it be otherwise? The next round of "largest," "coldest," "hottest," "costliest," and "deadliest" was already cued. The end of the world would come again to California less than a year later, speeding over the land at the rate of eighty football fields per minute, incinerating a town called Paradise. *Ash like snow, smoke as thick as fog.* The new normal.

On April 24, 1776, passing what we now call Ventura, the Spanish military governor of California, Fernando Rivera y Moncada, noted in his journal: "The gentiles destroy and consume the pastures with their burnings."[4] Traveling near San Gabriel some time later, he lamented the lack of graze for his pack animals, blaming the "great fires of the gentiles who burn the fields as soon as they gather up the seeds, and that [burning] is universal." The people he refers to—in this particular case, probably the Chumash People—had been observed executing that "universal burning" up and down the California coast by scores of explorers, missionaries, and military men over the years. In an oft-cited 1991 paper bearing the heavy-metal subtitle "Pyrodiversity Promotes Biodiversity," the fire scientists Robert Martin and David Sapsis estimate that between 5.6 and 13.0 million acres burned annually in California prior to colonization.[5] That's roughly 13 percent of the state. The majority of those fires were set by either lightning strikes or Indigenous fire regimes. It would not be wrong to say that California has *always* been burning.

California tribes burned—and continue to burn, when not impeded—for many reasons. They burned to increase the health and numbers of shoots used in the production of cultural properties like baskets, cordage, and clothing.

Smoke from their fires fumigated shrubs and trees, diminishing disease, parasites, and insects. They burned to decrease the fuel load in the understory, and to increase the density of edible plants, roots, berries, and seeds. They burned to make clearings to facilitate hunting and to increase feed for wildlife within those clearings, promoting generational return. These are called feedback loops.

California has always been burning, but fires of the magnitude we've seen in recent decades exist in large part thanks to hundreds of years of colonial fire suppression in concert with climate change. Whereas low-intensity fires recycle nutrients and give life to plants adapted to fire, catastrophic fires sterilize the soil, contribute massive amounts of carbon to the atmosphere, and threaten a forest's very survival as the inferno rages through the canopy. When smoke from these fires reaches the Arctic, dark soot is deposited on the ice, conducting rather than reflecting the sun's rays and speeding the melting process—causing the earth to absorb even more heat, exacerbating drought, and increasing the likelihood of future fire. This, too, is a feedback loop.

The "new" idea making national news—that fire will be with us no matter how we fight it—is in fact very old, though rarely had it issued from the mouths of public radio announcers. In 2017, more than a million scorched acres later, the notion was finally dawning on the general populace that, as one news story had it, "Scientists say more low-intensity wildfires are needed to clear out overgrown forests to help prevent bigger fires."[6] I imagine news of this "scientific discovery" was somewhat frustrating to Indigenous peoples who've practiced low-intensity burning for centuries.

The seeds of longtime fire suppression are now coming into bloom, at 1,500 aluminum-melting degrees. What goes around comes around. If you suppress fire, fuel will accumulate.

Maybe children of younger generations receive better information on these matters, but when I reflect on my own instruction, I recall no mention of my country before the first end rhyme—"Columbus sailed the ocean blue." Everything after 1492 is a diorama, peopled with stiff Puritan bonnets and tough ears of corn, everyone starving and cold. Whether or not these fictions were explicitly contrived as a means of control or passively accumulated down through the generations, the idea that our civilization has saved us from the cruelty of the wild world is one embedded in, and transmitted by, every sector of our culture. Life outside the city walls is struggle, discomfort, mortal fear—a necessary illusion. If the world outside the walls is abundant, and more or less socially level, how do you keep your masses from defecting? If food is always underfoot, freeing one to move, how do you convince people to stay put and labor for it? The short answer is that you can't, and that's why there is, simultaneous with the colonization of the Americas, a hidden history of dissidents, defectors, and dropouts among settlers.

Legend has it that the Spanish name for California was Tierra del Fuego (Land of Fire), not only on account of the burning but also for the vast coastal expanses of poppies, so vivid a galleon could navigate by their glow twenty-five miles off the coast. "California is a land of superlatives," writes the ethnoecologist M. Kat Anderson at the outset of *Tending the Wild: Native American Knowledge and the Management of California's Natural Resources*.[7] For the next three hundred pages, she details the stunning biodiversity of the state around the time of European contact, the methods by which tribes enabled that biodiversity, and the destruction that followed within a couple of generations of colonization.

Again and again these superlatives burst from the reports of explorers, missionaries, anthropologists, and interviews with tribal elders as they describe mind-boggling horizons of wildflowers, visited by "clouds" of butterflies. Tens of millions of birds, miles of geese that so blanketed the earth they tricked the eye into thinking it was "clothed with snow." In 1833, the trapper George Yount observed of a great flock, "When disturbed, they arose to fly, the sound of their wings was like that of distant thunder."[8]

The European landscape, at the time of contact, had been relatively denuded, and one detects in the colonists' journals something like disquiet underneath their thrill as sight breaks against the limits of imagination: bays so filled with shrimp one could reach in and pull out handfuls, rivers so thick with salmon they shone silver, "rocks matted" with "shellfish of innumerable forms." The pools left behind when the tide went out were "the most populous aquarium to be imagined." Herds of antelope, elk, and deer so large they "darkened the plains for miles."[9] The descriptions go on and on, in continual rebuttal of the myth that life outside the city walls was governed by scarcity and struggle.

California's extraordinary abundance and diversity was true of people, too. At the time of Spanish colonization, somewhere between five hundred and six hundred tribes lived in California,[10] with more than three hundred thousand people, speaking up to one hundred mutually unintelligible languages.[11] Traveling in the San Joaquin Valley around 1833,

Jonathan Trumbull "Juan Jose" Warner, marveled at the size and number of villages lining the rivers. Some of these villages had populations of up to twelve hundred people. "The population of this extensive valley was so great," Warner wrote, "that it caused surprise, and required a close investigation into the nature of a country that without cultivation, could afford the means of subsistence to so great a community."[12]

So fused was Warner's notion of cultivation with the sight of crops grown in rows that he had no referent to explain the scene.

The conservationist movement of the mid-to-late nineteenth century absorbed this blindness as they annexed huge swaths of the state, essentially evicting in perpetuity the human beings who'd tended the land there and attributing the fruit of their gardens to God's exclusive handiwork. These Edenic cathedrals called "wilderness" were places for man to periodically worship and "cleanse his spirit," as John Muir wrote, but were not places to live in, belong to, or shape. The cathedral-of-wilderness mythos is one reason I am neither disturbed nor surprised when people confess to numbness or discomfort in nature. It's difficult to connect to something that has nothing to do with you. When the cathedral-of-wilderness notion was invented, a veritable gallery of trees, human relevance was clipped from the picture. The lone human being might find a place there, but only episodically, and at a reverential remove. There is no place for the human social organization in a "wilderness," and the promise of social creatures is not generally fulfilled when severed from their groups, flocks, herds, troops, and so on.

Many of California's former meadows and oak savannas—described in the journals of early colonists as verdant, parklike spaces, teeming with wildflowers and butterflies—are now degraded and compacted from circumscribed herding and ranching, or overrun with brush and conifers thanks to fire suppression. The disappearance of those landscapes within the bounds of protected wilderness was in part due to National Park and U.S. Forest Service policies that promoted densely packed trees over the diverse patchwork of ecosystems tended by California tribes, and in part the consequence of dispossession and genocide. Gardens need gardeners to thrive.

It was high noon in the middle of June when we reached the meadow. Joanna Clines, a botanist with the U.S. Forest Service, had come along with Ron Goode, a North Fork Mono elder who'd helped bring the meadow back to life by burning it. Ron and various partners had worked to restore a handful of meadows in the Sierra over the last thirty years. I wanted to visit one of these meadows, because I was moved by the accounts collected in Kat Anderson's book and in Ron's own writings, but until I put my body there, the landscapes themselves would remain abstractions.

When I first wrote to Ron, he was welcoming, but mention of my vocation set the gears of the bureaucratic machine in motion, and I was punted up to a Forest Service administrator, whose electronic signature alerted me to the threat of prosecution should I reproduce any part of our correspondence, the gist of which was this: I could visit the meadow on the condition that I withhold its name and location from this book. This policy was for the meadow's protection. As the depletion of goldenseal, white sage, and many other plants teaches us, even herbalists and back-to-the-landers who profess to care for the earth have a habit of harvesting plants from public lands without acting in the best interest of their health and propagation. Whether this is a case of entitlement or ignorance or both, the fact of depletion remains. So I hope it will suffice to say that we were standing, that afternoon, somewhere in the wide influence of the Sierra Nevada.

The climate in the Sierra Nevada can be mercurial, especially in the shoulder seasons, when even a minor elevation gain might shift the scene from spring to winter. There had been some concern in the weeks leading up to our visit that we would not be able to make the trip due to snow, but the high that day wound up reaching 94 degrees.

Fall color had overtaken much of the forest, though we were less than a week from the summer solstice. Because I was a stranger in those foothills, I did not register the death in them. The logging road leading to the meadow was clotted with illegally dumped debris and snags downed by Pacific Gas & Electric after a recent wave of tree death: the bleak meaning of the orange trees. Since 2014, more than a hundred million trees had died from drought and beetle infestation. The beetles are native, but they boom during droughts, and their natural predators—cold winters and the praying mantis—have diminished. Winters have been steadily warming in the Sierra, and the praying mantis population has declined in step with the insects' favored habitat: meadowlands. Conservative estimates say 50 percent of meadows are degraded in the Sierra and around 25 percent, according to Ron Goode, have been deemed "non-existent," meaning they no longer function as meadows due to grazing compaction and evergreen encroachment.

We pulled our cars to the side of the gravel road, parked, and began to survey the damage on foot. Industrial-sized bags of landscaping debris were piled along the road amid mounds of cut snags, all of it thrown carelessly near or on top of native plants. Ron suffered from an injured hip and got around slowly with the aid of a cane. The debris was making it difficult.

I asked him where it all came from.

"It's people clearing other peoples' land. They get paid seventy-five dollars to go take it to the dump, and they pocket the money and come out here."

Ron and Joanna debated whether they should put up NO DUMPING signs, or install cameras to monitor the area.

"I think we should put up a sign," Joanna said. "*Go ahead and dump your shit, but you're on camera.*"

I'd only known Joanna for about twenty minutes, but already very little about her conformed to any category of person with which I was familiar. Superficially, she was manicured and magazine pretty, and spoke with the clipped high-rising terminal of a California surfer girl, swear words included. This did not compute with any image of "botanist" or "park ranger" I had on hand. But when I listened past her—should I call it an accent?—I came to realize she was like a living encyclopedia of plants.

She'd announced as much on arrival. "So let me just tell you, like, I am a completely nerdy botanist."

But I was still disoriented each time a lengthy, Latin-studded explanation of complex biological processes un-spooled from her pink and cheerful mouth.

This mystery was later deepened when she told us she used to be a "juvenile delinquent."

"Is that when you formed a relationship with the plants?" I asked.

She raised an eyebrow. "Just one plant."

"I think I know the one you mean."

She'd been in the process of flunking out of Fresno City College when her biology professor cut her a break and let her grade papers for extra credit. She enrolled in his field biology course the next semester and "just fell in love with it."

Ron Goode learned about the local ecology and traditional land-tending practices from his mother. His mother had learned from her grandparents, with whom she'd lived after running away from a residential school in the eighth grade. You could tell from Ron's articles on Traditional Ecological Knowledge (TEK) that he, too, was an expert, though he did not use Latin and frequently chided Joanna to "speak English!"

The logging road led to a clearing a few acres wide, dotted with a handful of large trees and shrubs. At the far side of the clearing, a shallow creek ran parallel to the road. Watching Ron cane his way through the wrack into the clearing, it dawned on me that we were not about to hike toward some majestic alpine meadow, as I'd imagined. This was the meadow. We'd already arrived.

It didn't look like much to me at first, but as I trailed Ron, he began introducing me to the plants and the scene fleshed out in the way a painter builds an image by layers. He introduced me to black oaks with twisted sprawling branches that would one day be heavy with acorns that served as a staple food for his and many other California tribes. He told me how you burn off the pests in the duff, how you burn out some saplings so the big trees get bigger and produce more acorns, and how you leave some saplings for the deer to graze. He showed me deer grass, an important basketry material—a deep green bunch with long pale plumes, home to songbirds and wintering ladybugs. He showed me mint and clover. He showed me milkweed, a plant with long stalks topped with delicate pink flowers, and the primary source of food for monarch caterpillars. (A related plant is the orange-flowered butterfly weed.) I remembered that in the wilderness survival school we would split the stalks of milkweed, strip them for fibers, and twist the fibers into cord.

Yarrow lived in the meadow, a plant with feathery leaves and top-heavy clusters of white flowers. Yarrow's Latin designation is *Achillea millefolium*, named by the taxonomist Linnaeus after the Greek hero Achilles, who was said to heal the battle wounds of his men with mashed poultices of yarrow ("nature's Neosporin"). And indeed, in addition to using it as an analgesic, North American tribes used yarrow to promote clotting and stanch hemorrhage.

Manzanita ("nature's calamine lotion") lived in the meadow, and blackberry, sedges, soap root, and native grasses grew high among the invaders—which were handsome in their own right: primordial-green bunches of curly dock, softly waving velvet grass.

"I'd pull it out," Joanna said of the curly dock. "But sometimes the species that arrived with the Europeans ended up being incorporated because they were useful."

She was visibly disappointed by her own restraint. Among her breezier attributes, Joanna nursed a blood lust for invasive species. Within moments of our arrival, she was vigorously yanking Scotch broom up by the roots with an intimidating, saber-like implement.

Scotch broom is a perennial shrub, native to much of Europe and northern Africa, with long green stems, yellow flowers, and black seedpods. Like many of the species we call invasive, it's incredibly prolific and hardy, capable of thriving in acidic sandy soils, in the wakes of clear-cuts, on roadsides, and in other degraded environments. It is, quite frankly, a bitch to get rid of.

"Eh. I just come out in the spring and yank 'em up by hand," Ron said.

"But these are bigger ones," Joanna said, feverishly uprooting a broom.

"I love her little tools, though," he teased.

I said, "Your mother must have been pretty brave to run away from the boarding school."

"Yeah," Ron agreed. "She was pretty stubborn, too."

Joanna snorted at this. "I have a real hard time picturing that."

"Hey!" Ron pointed to his feet, clearly tickled by this banter. "I see a broom over here!"

"Oh good," she said. "Why don't you use your pinky and pull it out."

Later, Ron would gush that Joanna "just knows so much."

When I asked Ron how the land had changed since he first burned it, he told me, "Fifteen years ago you could not see the creek. It was totally inundated." He said it had looked more like "a tree plantation," a phrase critics commonly use to describe landscapes managed by the Forest Service. The meadow was not so much a meadow back then, but a stand of conifer choked with brush and illegally dumped garbage.

The restoration was slow to get started. The first time he came out, the Forest Service allotted Ron and his volunteer group only four hours on-site. A loose consortium of local teachers, tribal members, and Forest Service employees showed up to help, 120 people in all.

"I think we hauled off five truckloads of trash," he said.

"There were laundry machines," Joanna said, on her knees by then, weeding by hand. "And piles of oleander . . . I mean, *oleander*?" She shook her head in disgust.

Oleander is native to Southwest Asia and the Mediterranean; it produces beautiful flowers, but it's pretty poisonous.

Sixteen years ago, Ron and the volunteer group took an inventory of the area and identified six cultural properties: traditional sources of food, or materials used for crafts. According to their most recent inventory, there were now close to a hundred native edible, medicinal, and cultural plants, plus ladybugs and butterflies, wild pigs, turkeys and turkey vultures, and hawks, with new species in evidence each time they visited. Perhaps most miraculously, a few years after they burned, a spring returned. It just bubbled up in the meadow's center. Now it was close to three feet deep. The spring had probably existed in the past but was sucked dry over the decades by brush and conifer encroachment.

Low-intensity fire maintains meadows by clearing saplings and brush that would otherwise shade out riparian plants, suck up the water, and block rain and snowmelt from sinking. Meadows, in turn, provide natural firebreaks and act as giant sponges, percolating the water coming down out of the mountains and holding it in the land before releasing it to the sea, helping to prevent erosion and drought.

All that fresh water had returned to the meadow thanks to fire. All those new plants and animals had returned, and Ron's group didn't bring in a single species from the outside.

"If you build it, they will come," Ron said. "When we open this meadow up, the bird brings in new seed, bear brings in seed, deer brings in seed . . . Everything will come back to the meadow if you get it restored."

Bigger mammals were also returning. We came upon mud with a fresh bobcat track. Ron found a fisher track.

"And you have generational return from the deer," he said. "It's quite often that we come back and find a mother and her fawns laid out here someplace. And we've even seen bear up there laid out."

"When you say 'laid out,' you mean hanging out?"

"I mean, lying down. Belly up. Just flat-out enjoying."

❦❦❦

That afternoon, the three of us had stood beneath an apple tree, looking up into its branches, admiring its first fruits, when Joanna said with perfect comic timing, "See, if it were up to me, I'd cut that down."

The more I read about restoration ecology, the more Ron and Joanna's banter seemed to reflect two distinct world-views in the field. Joanna was in love with the plants, but she was a purist and did not conceal her desire to tear up all the non-natives from the meadow by their roots. Ron, by contrast, was inclined toward moderation and incorporation, curious about whatever species showed up there, so long as they weren't too disruptive. He sent along an essay he wrote, which includes a story about a time he irritated certain Forest Service employees by electing to leave invasive bull thistle in one of the meadows:

> All the species on the meadow and in the forest are considered relatives in the tribal lifeway. The cultural practice is to always take food when visiting a relative and when you do visit a relative they will always feed you . . . So why come to the meadow where all our relatives live and remove their entire food source . . . Even though rain and snow came early this year, late growing sunflowers and bull thistle still matured. This gave all those who feed off of them something to feast on before winter sets in.[13]

To a layperson, this dynamic might be surprising, that white Forest Service employees should so loathe the colonizers while a Native elder preaches tolerance and incorporation, but Ron's approach was pretty representative of traditional land management ethics, as far as I understood them. "Purity" has always been an imperialist obsession.

I'd been reading a book called *Beyond the War on Invasive Species* by the permaculture designer Tao Orion. Working on restoration projects in Oregon's Willamette Valley, Tao had become disillusioned with the use of insecticides, herbicides, and other denuding agents regularly enlisted by restoration ecologists in the "battle" against invasive plants.

Tao was asking questions like: Is Japanese knotweed really so bad that we're willing to dump gallons of poison into the earth, into the watershed, into the bodies of our children and all other species who live in that place, in order to contain it? Invasive species arrive in context, typically in already degraded landscapes, and as Tao points out, dumping a bunch of poison on knotweed in the hopes of restoring a landscape makes no sense if there is a chemical plant or clear-cut upstream creating untenable conditions for native plants.

She goes on to present an emerging body of research that demonstrates invasive species can actually have beneficial effects on damaged landscapes: for example, breaking up compacted soils, filtering poisons, holding nitrogen in the soil, providing habitat and graze, and generally improving conditions for the return of native plants. This has also been demonstrated by invasive species of aquatic life. Take the Great Lakes, where toxic industry has decimated native mussel species but created the conditions for a single invasive mussel, the zebra, to thrive. Each zebra mussel filters carcinogens, heavy metals, and other toxins from the water at the rate of up to one quart per day. Or consider Montana's Berkeley Pit, one of the most toxic places known to man, where at this very moment invasive algae are consuming heavy metals and rendering them biologically inert.[14]

Migration should not be confused with colonization. Colonizers seek to control, exploit, and suppress life; migrators seek to cooperate and coexist. So-called invasive species can become naturalized; natives and invasives can evolve together and establish a new equilibrium. One study, for example, looked at native plants overtaken by cheatgrass (Finisia Medrano's nemesis) and found that the offspring of the native plants developed traits that suppressed the growth of the cheatgrass. Point being: Ecosystems are not static. Their stability is characterized by constant modification and adaptation.

"Systems are self-organizing and self-preserving and maintain these traits through feedback processes," Tao writes. "In the human body this is known as homeostasis, whereby the body system stays alive by maintaining a dynamic equilibrium through the regulation of both negative and positive feedback processes." Adaptation and development are how we know a system is alive, but there are limits to what any given system can sustain. "These feedback processes are finely calibrated to ensure the continued existence of the living human body; if they are excessively amplified or inhibited it can result in death."[15]

A human allegory: In his 1980 memoir, *A Way of Being*, the psychologist Carl Rogers wrote about his personal evolution from the repressions of childhood to a flexible maturity. Rogers was born to a family of fundamentalist Baptists, a family in which human expression was strictly controlled. Each child was raised according to the same rigid set of rules, and like a monocrop they stayed in line. No dancing, singing, drinking, or cavorting of any kind was allowed in the family home. This imparted, to young Rogers, a belief that "man was essentially evil."[16]

He described the process of coming alive as one of acknowledging and welcoming all feelings, experiences, ideas, and impulses, no matter how inappropriate or unseemly. He writes that, while he did not plan to act on all of those ideas and impulses, accepting them made him more *real* and, in turn, capable of creating a climate of authenticity for his patients. It was Rogers's belief that "persons and groups in such a climate move away from rigidity and toward flexibility." Whereas rigidity inhibited life, flexibility promoted it. He explained:

> Whether we are speaking of a flower or an oak tree, of an earthworm or a beautiful bird, of an ape or a person, we will do well, I believe, to recognize that life is an active process, not a passive one. Whether the stimulus arises from within or from without, whether the environment is

favorable or unfavorable, the behaviors of an organism can be counted on to be in the direction of maintaining, enhancing, and reproducing itself . . . Indeed, only the presence or absence of this total directional process enables us to tell whether a given organism is alive or dead.[17]

The therapeutic relationship, as Rogers conceived of it, was essentially a conversation wherein this process could be supported. He neither overdetermined a patient's growth by imposing a prescriptive agenda nor receded like his analytic forebears to the blank screen. Interventions were made as needed, specific to the emerging process at hand. We take it for granted these days, but once upon a time, Rogers's approach was revolutionary.

"The actualizing tendency can, of course, be thwarted or warped," he writes, "but it cannot be destroyed without destroying the organism."

He recalls that in the basement of his childhood home, potatoes stored for winter sprouted in their bins and sent out shoots, though they lay in the dark and had no soil. Ghostly pale, weak, and spindly, the shoots grew long and twisted in their pursuit of what little light filtered through a small window:

> The sprouts were, in their bizarre, futile growth, a sort of desperate expression of the directional tendency I have been describing. They would never become plants, never mature, never fulfill their real potential. But under the most adverse circumstances, they were striving to become. Life would not give up, even if it could not flourish.[18]

The good news is that biological systems, like people, are far more resilient than most of us imagine. Thirty years after the 1986 disaster at the Chernobyl nuclear power plant, radioactive lynx, foxes, wolves, elk, and bison have returned to the exclusion zone. Were you to pluck a hair from the coat of one of those wolves and swallow it, you'd be poisoned. Their offspring, too, set the heart of the Geiger counter racing—but watching those wolves play together, you'd be hard-pressed to tell them apart from their nonradioactive counterparts. The exclusion zone is an extreme example of the miracle of adaptation and resilience—radioactive animals reclaiming a ruined earth within a generation. Even under the most adverse circumstances, life keeps reaching.

When I followed up with Joanna Clines after our meadow visit, she wrote, "I'm completely fascinated by the ability of the land—that meadow is a great example—to heal itself by popping up native species that have either lain in the soil seed bank for decades, or recolonized due to birds and mammals moving them back in."

As for the role of non-native species, she continued, "I get that it's complex. I am passionate about removing *damaging* non-native plants, knowing that many non-natives in the Sierra Nevada are either mostly harmless and/or are incorporated into Native American cultures . . ."

What about cutting down the apple tree?

"The apple tree comment," she wrote, "was no doubt meant to goad Ron ☺."

I mentioned at the beginning of this book that in the winter before my visit to Finisia Medrano, I had suffered from troubling physical symptoms—unexplained fatigue, itchy skin, hair loss, stabbing stomach pains—and that doctors had had difficulty locating a cause. Without knowing I was ill, Finisia had intuited that I was "as poisoned as the landscape" around me. And her diagnosis turned out to be more literally accurate than she could have known.

After a year of knocking on the door of the medical establishment to no avail (my whispered diagnosis, I suspect, belonging to the category of "hysteric"), I turned to a naturopath. My blood, stool, saliva, and urine were analyzed, and I discovered that I had severe deficiencies in vitamins B and D, bacterial overgrowth in my small intestines, leaky gut (associated with food allergies and inflammation), chronic Epstein-Barr virus infection (due to the same virus that causes mononucleosis), flatlined adrenals, and elevated levels of mercury and lead in my body. The combination of my symptoms is sometimes gathered under the catchall diagnosis of chronic fatigue syndrome.

The language my naturopathic doctor used to describe these conditions invoked dualisms like "good bacteria" and "bad bacteria," the "native microbiome" and "invasive species of yeast." By default, I interpreted my poor health as evidence of a personal defect. If only I could sufficiently cleanse and detoxify, I'd return to a state of purity or "wellness."

Then, one evening in 2017, I attended a lecture and reading titled "Climate Change & Poetry" given by the poet Brian Teare, who also lives with chronic illness. One part of his lecture challenged the archetype of the wilderness poet, and I hadn't realized until that moment how completely I'd accepted the myth's premises.

"In the literature, all the naturalist bodies are healthy," he said, "marching up a hill, diving into a marsh." He was interested in the "pressure on the naturalist" to be healthy, "because so much of our national ideology around the natural world is that you go there for health, because it's inherently healthy, and we can't actually argue that anymore." No part of the planet, no matter how remote, has been left untouched by human-produced toxins. Emerson's wilderness, defined as "essences unchanged by man," does not now exist, if it ever did.

"There's no such thing as a single system operating on its own," Teare said. "It's important to remember in the Anthropocene, all human systems and industry are intertwined with biospheric processes. They're concurrent."

The effects of humans on their watersheds, and vice versa, provide stark examples of this interconnectivity. In Philadelphia, where Teare lived at the time, the Schuylkill River serves as one of the city's primary sources of drinking water. For more than a hundred years, it's received toxic effluence from the oil and mining industries, and has caught fire at least once after spills from the Point Breeze oil refinery (officially shuttered after several explosions and a catastrophic fire in 2019). We are what we drink, and for Philadelphia residents, "the amount of pollution each of us carries is pretty high," said Teare. He had his blood analyzed and found heavy metals and certain industrial toxins in higher concentrations than the national average. The thrust of his lecture—that we are permeable to the world, and the world to us—is by no means news, but it's easy to forget day to day.

That evening, I understood my illness for the first time as *natural*—not aberrant, but rather evidence of my essential inextricability from the world. One needn't have had my particular history to have developed these ailments—indeed, they're increasingly common across demographics—but the ream of test results nevertheless served as an ecological history of my life. Early trauma and poor nutrition gave on to chronic childhood infections, treated with many rounds of antibiotics, which wrecked my guts and my ability to absorb vitamins B and D. That, in turn, impaired my immune function and paved the way for viral infections and opportunistic yeast, overworked adrenals, rotten teeth, and a consequent mouthful of mercury fillings. As for the lead, it was in the water at school and in the paint on the walls of the rentals where I lived my first thirty years. I used to sit in the dining room of one of those old houses, talking on the landline and idly peeling paint from the wall the way you might chip polish from your fingernails.

Now I take supplements and eat a restricted diet, and I feel better thanks to these interventions, but I don't expect to ever again feel *restored*. And why should I? I'm a body after all, dependent on other bodies—an ecosystem within ecosystems. It's not lost on me that my diet, which is described as "plant-rich," a variation on the so-called paleo diet, resembles in no way the nutrient-rich diets of my Paleolithic ancestors. It doesn't even resemble the diets of preindustrial Europeans. M. Kat Anderson notes that the gardens of California were so diverse at the time of contact that the Sierra Miwok, for example, regularly ate forty-eight different species of greens. You and I, by contrast, choose from around twelve different species of greens when we shop for produce. Even if we "buy organic," the domesticated plants we eat are weak in comparison to plants grown in mineral- and bacteria-rich soil that has benefited from millennia of nutrient recycling.

I'm not suggesting that invasive species be left alone to proliferate unchecked, or that those people with chronic illness should give up on ever again feeling well—that's just the flip side of war, the same old false dichotomy of abandonment or annihilation—but I am suggesting that both imbalances should be worked with and understood in context. To name one small example of this principle in action, my friend Peter's organization, Rewild Portland, runs a whole class series on harvesting and utilizing invasive species, including basketmaking with English ivy and Scotch broom, and cooking with Japanese knotweed—which is not only nutritious, he informs me, but tastes like rhubarb. In one fell swoop, students learn new skills, remove invasives from the landscape, and avoid stressing already depleted native plant communities.

In *Beyond the War on Invasive Species*, Tao Orion imagines some remarkable scenarios in which severely degraded lands could be creatively restored by employing invasive species and permaculture principles. She imagines, for instance, planting tree of heaven groves around defunct coal mines as a form of bioremediation; these ornamental trees, imported from China more than two hundred years ago, thrive in degraded soil and accumulate mercury and sulfur dioxide in their tissues and leaves. In another scenario, she imagines a farm overgrown with kudzu vine. In a business-as-usual situation, the farm owners might douse the kudzu with gallons of Agent White—a carcinogenic mixture of the herbicides 2,4-D and picloram used by Americans during the Vietnam War as a defoliator when they were short on Agent Orange. In Tao's scenario, the farmers might instead invite goatherds to let their animals graze the vines, which are high in protein, in exchange for milk. The kudzu vines could be chopped up and sold as fertilizer, or cooked in local restaurants, or used by acupuncturists in the treatment of vertigo and tinnitus. In this scenario, the kudzu serves multiple purposes while the farmers meanwhile encourage the growth of trees that will one day shade it out.

Our health depends on more than our individual choices; we are affected by webs of interactions and conditions over which we do not have complete control. The metaphor of "battling" chronic illness is just one more variation on a theme: the adulterated at war with the pure, the disease process with the healthy body, the settlements with the wilderness, the locals with the immigrants. Obviously, neither of Tao's scenarios alone are going to "save the world," but her way of thinking might. If we approach a problem in context; if we ask ourselves how we might work with its source rather than against it; and, above all, if we dare imagine a world of relationships beyond the adversarial—we'll actually stand a chance at seeing that world be born.

Listening to Teare's talk that evening, I did not feel defeated by the idea that there would be no magical state of health to recover; rather, I felt relieved. It means I'm not alone. My health and the health of the world are intertwined. Our fates hang together.

I'd arrived at the meadow and perceived an unremarkable clearing with a few scattered trees. But every plant I met that afternoon, once connected to a set of relationships, grew more vivid. It is one thing to understand this web of interactions theoretically. It is another to travel that web with your feet, to know your purpose there, and to touch that purpose with your hands. There was a lot to learn, and yet much of it was pretty simple. In an article on Traditional Ecological Knowledge, Ron wrote, "Our gathering philosophy is our ecological policy. Gather what you need, leave some for the next gatherer, leave some for the animals, leave for seed, leave some for the bush itself—no one wants to be left naked."[19]

These weren't especially noble ideals; they were practical considerations and common courtesies. But unless one formed a real, authentic relationship with a place, they were just words on paper. "I can come and sit in a meeting and talk until I'm blue in the face," Ron told me. "But if I'm actually *showing* what can be done . . . That's the driving thing for me. *What can I do that my people have taught me? How can I apply it?*"

I've shared with you as much of Ron Goode's backstory as I know. I can't tell you his age, for example—though, were I to guess, I'd say he's somewhere in his seventies. I know that he's a black belt in judo, and that on the day we visited the meadow he was walking with a cane on account of an injured hip and knee. I can't tell you much more than that because, as Ron put it, that's "information you don't need." But what I have shared may disclose more about the character of the man than any personal history ever could.

In an era when most of us manage public profiles in the vein of wannabe celebrity or self-appointed politician, when individual identities and backstories are traded as social capital, it feels almost radical to assert your right to withhold the personal from the public. It makes me wonder about the larger question of legacy. Namely, once the grid fails and all the shiny baubles vanish, and the relationships conducted at a distance in 2-D cease to matter—how will we know we existed? It's a grim irony of the era that each of us should at once be so visible, so surveilled, so confessional, and—simultaneously—so unnecessary, so likely to vanish from the earth having left behind no meaningful trace save an anonymous conglomeration of damage. On some level, I'm sure we already know as much, and our related anxiety fuels this pageantry.

Toward the end of our time in the meadow, Ron pointed out a patch of wild strawberries and said that he and Joanna used to argue about their nature. "She'd say, 'These are dormant strawberries.' I said, 'They're only dormant because they've never had fire to them.' God didn't make dormant plants. Every plant had a use and a purpose. Every species put here had a purpose." Ron believed this was true of humans, too.

I can't say whether future generations will know the name of Ron Goode, but I do know what his legacy will be: a series of biodiverse meadows; landscapes that were choked with brush and busted appliances transformed into habitats for dozens of species, with more returning each day, including the human beings who show up to learn how to be part of the legacy. This was his joy and his purpose, fulfilling his human ecological niche. What more did I need to know?

You can learn something about relationships by reading a book, but you can't *have* a relationship that way. Just as intimacy between people depends on proximity, intensity, frequency, and duration, so do our relationships with the greater-than-human world. While planting a bunch of native species on degraded land is a decent impulse, if you don't continue to tend them, if you don't understand the broader context in which you've placed them, you've wasted your time. This was a major point of frustration for Ron. Well-meaning organizations would invest manpower and money in restoration efforts only to leave a site when they were done planting and rarely, if ever, return.

"Why plant a garden, if you're not going to tend it?" he'd asked with genuine confusion.

Showing up, again and again, is what it takes to know and to be known by someone, to belong to someone or to somewhere. Just because we've forgotten how to belong to our ecosystems does not mean our particular human efforts are not missed. The radical fact of the meadow's resurrection is that it depended on the intervention of human hands.

To become beneficial remediators of ecological damage is, in my opinion, a story worth living into—and one available to all, no matter how lost or wounded, how motley or ruderal. I can't help but notice the wrecked knees, bad backs, scars, and trauma-etched faces of the people I've met while writing these pages. In many cases, it was the adversity they'd survived—their very woundedness—that pressed them into the service of others. I had a therapist who called this "the price of admission." Or as the Rumi line goes, "The wound is where the light enters you."

But we cannot do it alone. Pain can be the precursor to empathy, adversity can strengthen our structures, but too much, too fast, and we collapse: we cease to reach, or we reach for what harms us, or we bend our reach inward and mutilate the self. We need others to reach back and *hold up all our falling*. Whether we languish or thrive depends on this, on tending and being tended by others.

To tend a garden, to tend one another, is to move beyond chaos and rigidity, beyond abandonment and domination, and into a third way. Life flourishes between imperfect beings, in a dance of give-and-take, in the volley of call-and-response, when those beings trust they will not be abandoned, oppressed, or arbitrarily destroyed. At its best, this exchange is full and flexible and in constant fluctuation, not tallied on an abacus. Being in relationship means never settling the accounts.

Sometimes Peter described industrial civilization as akin to a catastrophic wildfire: there would be no stopping it; it would die when it burned through its fuel load. In our case, the "fuel load" was a nonrenewable resource called petroleum.

Other times, he likened it to a prison.

The character of each metaphor obviously differs. One imparts a feeling of impersonal inevitability; the other, the intentional oppression of some beings at the hands of other beings. But even in the latter case, once a few generations have passed, it may seem to the workaday wardens that this is just the way things are done. Their reference is also limited to the walls of the cage.

Either way, if we hope to survive as a species, a good first step might be to recognize that not only did plenty of human cultures refrain from destroying the ecosystems on which they depended, but their cultural practices supported biodiversity. This most crucial paradigmatic shift can also be the most difficult to make: human beings are built to be beneficial contributors to the earth, just like the bees, the streams, the bears, everyone, all of us—why would we be the exception?

When we engage a landscape as it is, rather than imposing our own agenda, as Tao Orion has written, in "a futile attempt to regain an imagined past," we stand a better chance of reversing the desertification of the land. There will be no return to innocence, but we can work together to remediate the damage we've caused the world and one another. We can support the world and one another as we integrate and flourish in unpredictable ways. This will be especially important as we face the uncertain but inevitable effects of climate change in the years ahead.

A handful of permaculturists and ecologists are already experimenting with "assisted migration," looking for ways to preserve what biodiversity remains on the planet, based on climate change models. One ecologist in British Columbia, for example, has planted an experimental garden based on this modeling, incorporating windmill palms and ginkgo trees, species that were native to the region fifty-five million years ago, when average temperatures were 40 degrees warmer than they are now and alligators flourished in Alaska. On her own homestead in Oregon, Tao Orion has planted species from the three nearest climate zones in each direction, as well as from farther-flung analogous climates, like Japan, New Zealand, and coastal Chile—planting nonnative foods like figs, persimmons, peaches, and nectarines among the native edibles. She's had luck, for example, with *Ceanothus* varieties (species of shrubs and trees in the buckthorn family) native to California, but those native to Oregon have not been doing well.

"We've had a few big ones die in the past few years," she told me. "We're starting to see these trends. I think it's time to start moving some plants north, or up in elevation, and see how they do."

I'm unqualified to say whether or not these experimental gardens are a good idea in practice, but their premise intrigues me: climate migrations will happen for plants as surely as for people, but some of them will need our help to move. Like Noah in the old story, building an ark—or many thousands of arks—to preserve biological diversity in advance of the coming deluge.

Of course, it's always possible that permafrost at the end of the world will continue to warm and explode, and all the methane and carbon released will superheat the atmosphere to apocalyptic effect. But for every one of these frightening scenarios, there is someone out on the land, sowing life where there was death, creating feedback loops in service of future generations, and they can use all the help they can get.

Leaving Ron Goode and the meadow that afternoon, I did not feel discouraged by the piles of snags or patches of invasive grass. I felt amazed and moved by how much life had returned to that place and in so short a time. The span of a single human life is almost no time at all, and yet we can do so much to keep our world living.

8

—

RESTORING PARADISE

How is it possible to rejoice in the world
except by fleeing to it?
—FRANZ KAFKA

"The end of the world" is a relative term. It comes for different landscapes and different species at different times. When one takes into account earth's ice ages, assaults by asteroid, and our near history of wars and plagues—it's natural to wonder if one's apocalyptic fears are a form of hysteria, as myopic as Chicken Little's. I've wondered this about myself throughout the years. It's not my fear that I'm suspicious of, but the intoxicating effects of worst-case scenarios, click-bait headlines, and social media platforms that capitalize on communicable dread, and the potentially fatal presumption that "sharing" our fear and anger is in itself a course of remediation. Emergency is the aesthetic and, regrettably, the anesthetic. With every blow we are benumbed to the new reality.

What constitutes "the end" may be subjective—partly due to the fact that what constitutes "the world" is subjective—but when it comes to the biospheric processes that make life as we know it possible on earth, the data is unemotional. It tells us that our fears are founded, that our moment is unique—a crucible that will determine the habitability of the planet for centuries to come. It's not a case of sensationalist reportage, though there's been some of that. It's not just imagination. One emergency *has* followed another, each an expression of the larger crisis and each evaporated into the ether before its extent can be fully comprehended. "Apocalypse" is an appropriate description of our moment if we reach past our contemporary understanding of the word and into its Greek root: to "unveil" or "reveal." Our moment is apocalyptic in that it tears at the scrim of so-called progress and reveals what we, on some level, have always known to be true: infinite growth is not possible, we are not above the laws of ecological reciprocity, and we are not as independent as we once believed.

On the morning of November 8, 2018, Matthew Trumm had just pulled into his driveway in Oroville, California, when he began to receive the news. He'd dropped his daughter off at school that morning in Paradise, a ridge town twenty miles away.

"I remember seeing the smoke in the distance when I dropped her off," he told me, "but we have so many fires I didn't think anything of it."

By the time he arrived home, the Camp Fire, which began on the edge of Plumas National Forest, had ripped through the rural community of Concow and reached the edge of Paradise. Texts from friends were rolling in: the fire was serious, and the hospital in Paradise was being evacuated.

What followed was what some survivors have described as a vision of hell on earth. Smoke blackened the sky, turning day into night. Harrowing videos of narrow escapes show cars barreling through walls of smoke and flying cinders. Stalled vehicles burst into flame, spilling silver rivers of molten aluminum. In one video, a tornado of fire a hundred feet high explodes over the road. It is slender, an iridescent red, as if what lay behind this world were pure magma pulsing through a torn sky.

As the fire closed in on evacuation gridlock, people attempting to flee on foot or still trapped in their cars were overtaken and burnt to char. Within six hours, the community of Concow and about 90 percent of Paradise were reduced to ashes. In the end, 154,000 acres burned and eighty-five people were dead, all civilians.

It was hours before Matthew Trumm received news of his daughter—she and her mother had managed to escape, but barely. They'd had to swerve to avoid flaming tree limbs falling into the road

As of this writing, the Camp Fire remains the deadliest U.S. wildfire in a century. Several extraordinary conditions contributed to its intensity: Spring rains had yielded an uncommon profusion of grasses, but by November the area was deep in a drought, with almost no rain in six months and the grass desiccated to straw. Fifty-mile-an-hour wind gusts combined with that mass of tinder to make, in every respect, a perfect storm. In a feature for *The New York Times Magazine*, the writer Jon Mooallem called it "an almost vengeful-seeming confluence of circumstances, many of which had been nudged into alignment by climate change."[1]

"Vengeful" is an evocative word. The most terrifying manifestations of climate change—the superstorms, the baseball-sized hailstones, the annual hundred-year floods—are not beyond the explanatory capabilities of science. But a more ancient part of the species is waking from the hubris of its anthropocentric dream to discover that the old nature gods are alive and well and still speaking their old tongue.

Whether or not the magnitude and strange behavior of that apocalyptic inferno in Paradise should have been anticipated, confronting the actual spectacle was another proposition entirely. And while more advanced warning might have produced a better outcome, I doubt human efforts to fight the fire would have appeared any less feeble. To those attempting to escape, the fast-moving intensity and the pitiless totality of the destruction must have felt as if the fire were somehow directed and intentional.

Climate change "nudged" the inferno, and the inferno nudged back, releasing approximately 3.6 million metric tons of greenhouse gases into the atmosphere. Meanwhile, the Woolsey Fire, which started on the border between Los Angeles and Ventura County on the same day as the Camp Fire, and burned for nearly as many days, released 2 million metric tons of greenhouse gases.[2] When forests burn regularly—whether they're ignited by humans or lightning strikes—the fuel load in the understory is decreased and the resulting fires are lower in intensity. Mature trees are scorched, but most survive. With high-intensity burns, like that which smote Paradise, not only do the trees release carbon dioxide and methane as they burn, but many of them die and then are no longer capable of sequestering carbon in the future.

Two weeks before the fire, Trumm had watched a video made by one of his heroes, the land restoration expert and documentarian John D. Liu. As Paradise burned, Trumm remembered something Liu had said in the video, and it gave him chills: "We need to gather around the campfire and restore paradise."

In 2017, Liu founded Ecosystem Restoration Camps, an international coalition that establishes rehabilitation working groups on degraded lands. They currently run nine camps on five continents with a goal of expanding to one hundred camps by 2030. At each site, team leaders and educators train campers in skills like restoring soil, controlling erosion, and capturing and sinking water. In exchange, campers donate time and labor to healing the land.

As Trumm turned Liu's phrase over in his mind, he began to feel that the last decade of his life was culminating in that moment. He'd grown up a city boy in San Francisco's East Bay but had moved off the grid in 2008. Like many Americans, he'd felt disillusioned by the government and banking industry in the wake of economic collapse and wanted to become self-sufficient. He was basically a prepper when he started—he bought a shipping container and started collecting canned food—but in learning to garden, he came on the writings of people like the Japanese farmer and philosopher Masanobu Fukuoka, a grandfather of the permaculture movement, and it revolutionized his thinking.

After experimenting with low-intervention gardening on his own land, Trumm wound up studying with the permaculture expert Penny Livingston-Stark, and later got a job as a farm manager for Dr. Elaine Ingham—a pioneer of soil microbiology who articulated the concept of the soil food web in the 1980s. Ingham taught Trumm about composting, knowledge he used to create a program in Oroville, gathering waste from restaurants and supplying the cooks with vegetables grown from that waste in his garden. After years of living in isolation off the grid, he moved into town, having become convinced that ecological sustainability was fundamentally a social project.

During the Camp Fire, Oroville was evacuated, too. As Trumm made his way out of town, fleeing home for the third time in as many years, he called John Liu from the car and told him, "John, this is the spot. Paradise is lost—we need to restore Paradise."[3]

Like the abyss at the *end of the world*, the fact that a tsunami of fire leveled a town called Paradise was an irresistible allegory for many reporting on the disaster, myself included. And the proposition of restoring that lost Paradise proved irresistible to John D. Liu, who already had a penchant for Old Testament allusion.

In a 2012 documentary on large-scale land restoration efforts, Liu visited cradles of civilization in Ethiopia, China, and Jordan—places where logging, agriculture, cattle grazing, and climate change had made deserts of formerly fertile "lands of plenty." In the Tal Al-Rumman area, near Amman, Jordan, he'd documented the efforts of Princess Basma bint Ali, founder of the Royal Botanic Garden, to restore degraded woodland habitats in danger of desertification. "This was the land of milk and honey," Liu tells the camera. "This was the Promised Land."

In a 2019 article titled "The Holy Grail of Restoration," Liu proposed regreening the Sinai Peninsula, noting how in satellite photos the peninsula "looks like a beating heart, with arteries and veins . . . If one knows how to read this landscape, it is possible to see that rivers flowed through the Sinai over vast evolutionary time."[4]

Here's his description of how that beating heart bled out in the first place:

> All living matter on the Earth is part of a web of life that has taken a lifeless molten rock surrounded by what for us are poisonous gases, and over enormous time, through continuous photosynthesis, transformed it into a beautiful planetary garden with an oxygenated atmosphere, a freshwater system, rich fertile soils, and amazing biodiversity. My observations and the results of numerous studies show that when you lose the vegetative cover, respiration through photosynthesis is reduced; the surface temperature and evaporation rates massively increase, causing spiraling negative feedback loops that can and do destroy functional ecosystems.[5]

For Liu, to seek "the Holy Grail" is to cultivate and pursue the vision that "we can mend our collective broken heart and live again in the garden."

John Liu was born in Nashville in 1953 and raised in Bloomington, Indiana. He traveled in 1979 to China, where he was hired to help open the CBS news bureau in Beijing. Over the next decade, he learned journalism on the job, covering the major geopolitical events of the day. In 1995, he went on assignment to the Loess Plateau, an area of 250,000 square miles in north-central China, where the government was undertaking a massive land restoration project in collaboration with the World Bank.

The Loess Plateau was the birthplace of Han Chinese civilization, an important ancient hub for travelers on the Silk Road, and home to the earliest imperial dynasties. As Liu tells it, the plateau had been extraordinarily fertile for millennia, but the abundance that gave rise to civilization there three thousand years ago had been stressed by centuries of overgrazing and agriculture. By the twentieth century, much of the plateau had transformed into a desert of yellow silt. Each year, billions of tons of silt are carried by rain into the Yellow River, and by wind in great storms of dust that roll across the continent, blanketing faraway cities and rendering the air hazardous to breathe. Desertification is a global problem, but it's an acute concern in China, where deserts have grown by an estimated thirteen hundred square miles each year.

The restoration site in Jordan is located in the Fertile Crescent, a semicircle of land stretching from the southeastern Mediterranean to the Persian Gulf. To the south lies the Zarqa River (the biblical river Jabbok, which Jacob crossed before wrestling the angel), now heavily polluted by industrial waste. Human stories have always dealt in paradoxes, in the collision of the sacred and profane, and in the Fertile Crescent lies both the first sentence of Western civilization's story and possibilities for its conclusion. Archeological sites have unearthed the two-million-year-old bones, hand axes, stone spear points, and knives of the crescent's hunter-gatherer ancestors. Some of the earliest cities were born here ten thousand years ago, along with writing and the wheel. Literatures of antiquity describe thriving ecosystems throughout the crescent, including forests of cedar, oak, and pine. Today it is largely desert, but it is also home to innovative regreening efforts.

Whether or not the transformation of those ecosystems was primarily anthropogenic or the consequence of a natural warming trend that began at the end of the last Ice Age is debated. Some historians say that the idea that human activity created deserts in the Middle East is a "colonialist canard," though they tend to allow that it had *some* effect on environmental shifts.

By my lights, it's not an either-or proposition. It is impossible to fully untangle "naturally" occurring climatic shifts from human activity. As Brian Teare summed it up, "All human systems and industry are intertwined with biospheric processes." Some human systems support biodiversity, others deplete it. Deforestation and other land-use changes were likely transformative to the Fertile Crescent, but no more than they were to the Spaghetti Western abandonments of Almería, or to the 1930s Dust Bowl of the southern Great Plains of the United States.

What we do know for sure is that biodiversity promotes resilience in the face of climate change, whether "natural" or "man-made."

Desertification is not only a by-product of Western civilization; it is also one of its formative myths—the oldest recorded story. In the four-thousand-year-old Sumerian *Epic of Gilgamesh*, a mortality-obsessed king jealously clear-cuts the immortal forest and beheads the demigod Humbaba, who guards it. "Only the gods dwell forever in sunlight," Gilgamesh laments. "As for man, his days are numbered, / whatever he may do, it is but wind."[6]

A few nights before Gilgamesh enters the sacred forest, he is given a prophetic dream:

> The skies roared with thunder and the earth heaved,
> Then came darkness and a stillness like death.
> Lightning smashed the ground and fires blazed out;
> Death flooded from the skies.
> When the heat died and the fires went out,
> The plains had turned to ash.

The beheading of Humbaba catalyzes a violent flood, and further retribution from the gods is promised in the form of drought and fire.

A standard interpretation of *Gilgamesh* is that it's about a man who learns to accept his limitations, to "forget death and seek life." But we might also read a more specific warning in the story. As some accounts have it, the Sumerians overgrazed their domesticated animals and clear-cut their forests, causing silt to build up in their waterways. Over the course of centuries, their crops were devastated by erosion and salination. "The earth turned white," according to one cuneiform tablet. Malnutrition and disease took hold. Lands were abandoned.

In *Forests: The Shadow of Civilization*, Robert Pogue Harrison observes that Gilgamesh is an "enduring archetype," nearly the personification of Western civilization itself:

> [Gilgamesh is] a sort of grand summary of the spiritual afflictions that arise from the inner, alienated core of civilization. The Sumerian hero's stern individualism; his obsession with death; his tragic and futile quest for personal immortality; his childlike rage against the absurd; his monumental will to power—this profound psychology of finitude which pervades the epic cycle.[7]

If fear of death drives Western civilization—if it's the root of the will to hoard and control resources—then the *Epic of Gilgamesh* is a people reminding themselves that the consequences of resisting death are death writ large; that the pursuit of stockpiled wealth and immortality will bring about the death of the land and of one's people.

Another epic—one I've thought of often since I first encountered it—is told by the German director Wim Wenders in the 2014 documentary *The Salt of the Earth*, a sweeping portrait of the Brazilian photographer Sebastião Salgado. Like that of Gilgamesh, Salgado's life is a myth for his century, a digest of its central themes. It is a cautionary tale, a story of loss and redemption, his fate intertwined at every step with the major environmental and geopolitical events of his time.

Salgado was born in 1944 and raised on his family's farm in southeastern Brazil, a large and verdant tract of land with rain-forested hills and waterfalls. At age fifteen, he moved to a boarding school on the coast; met his future wife, Lélia; and eventually undertook a master's degree in macroeconomics. He and Lélia participated in the leftist politics of their day, protesting the military dictatorship that assumed power in 1964 by coup d'état. Essentially exiled for their political views, the couple emigrated to Paris, where Salgado worked as an economist and was sent on assignments throughout Africa by the World Bank. He began taking a camera with him and, in 1973, quit economics to make photos full-time.

Over the next forty years, in collaboration with Lélia, he documented the brutal working conditions of the industrial world and the parallel plunder of the earth: perilous gold-mining operations in South America; Canadian firefighters battling burning oil derricks in Kuwait, their bodies shining with crude while towers of flame explode against charred skies; Bosnian women and children fleeing genocide; and the great droughts, famines, civil wars, and migrations in northern and central Africa.

Salgado returned to Africa in the mid-1990s to document refugee camps on the Rwandan border, and was there at the start of the genocide. But his years of bearing photographic witness to immense suffering had taken its toll: the sight of the dead, the miles of road strewn with corpses, and the masses of mutilated women and children broke his will. He vowed to quit photography, and humanity in general.

"We didn't deserve to live; no one deserved to live," he told Wenders. "When I left there [Rwanda], I no longer believed in anything."

When the Brazilian military dictatorship finally lost power, Salgado and Lélia decided to pick up stakes and go home. They returned to the farm of his youth and found it had become a wasteland. His father had sold off his timber to fund his children's educations, and the cattle had grazed what remained into oblivion. The cattle were then also sold. The birds and animals were gone. The forest, waterfalls, and streams were gone. The earth was "bare crust." The desertification of Salgado's inner and outer life was complete.

Some of Salgado's critics might have predicted the gutting and enervating effects his vocation would have on his life. They'd accused his photos of inducing those same effects in their viewers. In a 1991 essay, the writer and critic

Ingrid Sischy took exception to what she viewed as Salgado's aestheticization of suffering, his "finding the 'grace' and 'beauty' in the twisted forms of his anguished subjects," concluding that "beautifying human tragedy results in pictures that ultimately reinforce our passivity towards the experience they reveal."[8]

In her 2002 article "Looking at War," Susan Sontag wrote that the problem with Salgado's photographs is "their focus on the powerless, reduced to their powerlessness," and that because the powerless are not named in the captions, his portraiture "becomes complicit" in reducing his subjects "to representative instances of their occupations, their ethnicities, their plights." Harrowing photos, according to Sontag, shock but fail to impart understanding. "Narratives," in contrast, "can make us understand."[9]

These are valid critiques, though I wouldn't be so quick to set narrative apart from this particular limitation. Having reduced thousands of years of Western civilization to a series of problems in service to an argument, I know how the casualties of narrative's campaign to "make us understand" stack like cordwood against the inevitable limits of understanding. I'm inclined to agree with the sentiment that representation is a form of violence. But violence is not the only power representation wields, and because I am unwilling to surrender its other possibilities—beauty, narrative, source of instruction or meaning, comforter or discomfitor, subconscious dousing rod, and so on—I can live with its limitations, not always easily. At a minimum we might say: *All representation is, by some measure, false.*

So maybe it's a case of poetic fallacy, but it nevertheless feels true to say that as we desertify the world, a desert grows within. This is a lesson we can take from both *Gilgamesh* and the life of Sebastião Salgado. To be exiled from the earth is to be exiled from fundamental aspects of our selves. The "spiritual afflictions that arise from the inner, alienated core of civilization" have real-world effects on our communities, our families, our inner lives, and the land. Just as the mythic king's killing of the immortal forest catalyzed actual droughts and floods, our fate and the fate of the world hang together.

Until recently, it would not have occurred to many people that humans had the power to alter the seasons or the weather they bring. We used to sort disasters into the categories of "natural" and "man-made." Floods, wildfires, and hurricanes were natural. Nuclear meltdowns and oil spills were the purview of man. Now we acknowledge that our industry can affect the climate, though for many of us the connection remains hazy.

But the condition of our local ecosystems has farther-reaching effects than most of us imagine. Dr. Millán M. Millán, the director of the Center for Environmental Studies of the Mediterranean, has shown that hemispheric-sized feedback loops originate with fine-scale processes in particular ecosystems. Millán conducted a metastudy of meteorological data on the European continent gathered between 1974 and 2011, and reanalyzed it in context of "a perceived reduction in summer storms around the Western Mediterranean Basin."[10] He found that land-use changes in the Mediterranean—the draining of coastal marshes, the expanding of agriculture, the building of dams—triggered the siphoning of moisture from the land and sea into the upper atmosphere, where it could not precipitate as rain. This, in turn, caused drought and salination in the basin and elevated the surface temperature of the sea. The moisture accumulated in the upper atmosphere then moved over central Europe, where it manifested as extreme summer storms and flooding.[11] In short, major meteorological events were set in motion by land-use changes, not only locally but hundreds of miles away.

John Liu puts it simply: denuded lands conjure drought.

"Temperature differentials on the surface cause enormous thermal drafts . . ." he told the Global Earth Repair conference in 2019. "You're essentially creating a vacuum that sucks the moist air up and shifts wind direction."[12]

Just as the degradation of distant ecosystems can have a profound impact on our local environments, Liu believes that restoring those ecosystems could shift climatic trends across whole regions so that our grandchildren might, as he imagines, "live again in the garden."

John Liu was introduced to the proposition of regreening the Sinai by Ties van der Hoeven, a Dutch hydrologic engineer. Ties began his career in dredging, working on liquefied natural gas terminals for the oil and gas industry. "I was a young fool who wanted to make money and party with my friends," he told me. "I was good in finances, but I was getting empty in my soul."

Ties claims the idea was mostly "intuition," the result of his "being stupid and naïve." He first raised the idea with his friend Malik Boukebbous, country manager for a major dredging operation in Egypt. Every time he discussed it with his engineer friends, they became excited. They took it seriously, added their own ideas to the mix, and enlisted more help—including Millán, whose research confirmed his intuition. Together they formed a group called the Weather Makers.

The Sinai is situated between two big drainage basins, Ties explained: the Indian Ocean ("which has a lot of moisture") and the Mediterranean basin ("which has not enough moisture"). If the peninsula is "regreened," the Weather Makers believe, it will shift wind direction and return moisture flow to the Mediterranean, parts of China, the Middle East, and the West Coast of the United States. The group zeroed in on a lagoon called Lake Bardawil, on the peninsula's north coast, separated by a narrow sandbar from the Mediterranean Sea. Once a forty-meter-deep nursery for marine life, the lagoon is now so filled with sediment it's just two meters deep and highly saline.

Because Bardawil is a coastal edge-system, the Weather Makers believe that restoring it would have ripple effects across both of its borders, land and sea. It would "kick start the hydrological cycle," they say, and "simultaneously enrich the fertility and productivity of the water and soil."[13] It's essentially a fulcrum within a fulcrum. Ties refers to these strategic restoration sites as "climate crucibles."

For the last three years, the Weather Makers have been meeting with Egyptian officials who are purportedly enthusiastic. They are, according to Ties, "getting very close" to beginning initial stages.

The restoration work itself is rather blunt. The first steps proposed for restoring Lake Bardawil involve mobilizing dredging machines to restore the inlets and lagoons to their former depths and shapes. After that, Ties says, the group won't need to do much planting "because the dredging will recycle the nutrients and the aquatic ecosystem will restore itself." Eventually, they'd like to use fog nets in the adjacent hills to capture moisture, and build check dams to prevent flash floods and sink water.

The project further aims to restore seagrass and reed beds, remove sedimentation, and relocate it to the shoreline where it will be planted with grasses, shrubs, and trees to sink water and hold back erosion. By doing so, John Liu says, "we can change the surface temperatures. We can begin to hold the moisture in the lower atmosphere, and when we do this, we can turn the winds around, bringing back the moist air from the Indian Ocean, which would change the whole region."[14]

The prospect is exciting but also largely untested. I asked Ties if anyone was nervous about the impact of such intensive interventions.

Initially, he told me, people had responded to the idea with fear. "For a long time," he said, "the eco folks would say, 'You cannot create nature. You can only protect what you have.' But you cannot keep what you have unless you restore these systems."

In other words, at this point in history, region-sized feedback loops must be shifted or the life in those "natural" areas will become impossible to protect.

Being that I am neither a scientist nor an Egyptian citizen, I'm in no position to assess whether or not the project is a good idea. But I do think the broader idea of land restoration in key places—so-called "climate crucibles"—is important and warrants consideration.

Ties likened our situation to a person dying of heart failure. "You can treat all the adjacent systems," he explained, "but unless the heart is healed, the person's life will be imperiled." The time for thinking small is over, he asserted. Your backyard no longer matters.

Paradise, like the end of the world, is subjective. But it's striking to me that, for so many of us, the word conjures natural beauty, be it in the background or the fore. Put another way, paradise is where we already live, or at least some unspoiled version of it. Not a biosphere on another planet, not even the glassy half-mile-high monuments of our own civilization. Surely for some, paradise is a coke-fueled night of fellatio on the Vegas Strip. But I doubt if anyone imagines paradise as the Pacific garbage patch, or a valley of wilted grain, or a tsunami of dust swallowing a megacity, or a tornado of fire touching down on the neighbors, or the rain forest of youth reduced to a parched expanse of clay. For most, these are visions of hell.

Some forms of paradise are not arrived at so much as returned to: a return to love before the fighting and betrayal, to unshaken faith, to the mother before she proved fallible or abandoned us to our fate by dying—forms of paradise are, of course, impossible to recover, what is meant by the maxim "You can't go home again." This is paradise rooted in nostalgia—not the wistful, sentimental "nostalgia" of modern English, but the lethal ache of the Greek: *nostos* (homecoming) and *algea* (pain), a homesickness so severe it was a formal medical diagnosis in the nineteenth century.[15] Sailors fell ill with nostalgia. More than seventy Union soldiers officially died of it in the U.S. Civil War.[16]

To look to ancestral ways of life as exemplars of sustainability is to risk being accused of nostalgia-lite—the sentimental, wistful sort. But to my mind, there is nothing especially sentimental or noble about relating to one's place as a community of subjects, as opposed to objects. If a people wish to prevent overtaxing their ecosystems, nothing could be more practical. Our desire for the earth, for the ur-mother, is a longing of an older order—it is transpersonal, encoded in our bodies and in our ancestral memories—if for no other reason than that our survival depends on it.

Maybe we can't go home again; maybe there's no returning to the paradise we've lost. But that doesn't mean paradise can't be restored, or that a home can't be made. This was John Liu's answer to the question "What's a story worth living into?" Akin to what the Christians call repentance: to reverse destructive feedback loops, "to turn history around."

Here's how they did it on the Loess Plateau.

China's Loess Plateau was considered, by some, a land "beyond help."[17] Loess soil is highly erodible, and centuries of agriculture and grazing had destroyed the plateau's vegetative cover. With no barrier between the soil and the elements, the area was prone to devastating floods and dust storms. Juergen Voegele, global director of the World Bank's Climate Change Group, had visited the plateau in the 1980s in the capacity of an agricultural economist and described it as "a desperate place."

In the 1990s, in collaboration with the World Bank, the Chinese government assembled a team of experts in hydrology, soil health, forestry, and agriculture. Over the course of three years, they developed a plan. They began by banning grazing, logging, and planting on slopes. Restoration project leaders then approached local farmers and pastoralists, now forced to rest their lands, and hired them to terrace eroded hillsides, to plant native species and trees on the terraces, and to build sediment retention dams. By the time Voegele returned to the plateau to work with the restoration team in the late 1990s, he couldn't believe the gains they'd made. "This was absolute desert," he said. "A few years later the whole thing came back. We saw birds, butterflies, insects—the whole ecosystem began to recover. Even after hundreds of years of complete devastation, the seeds were still in the ground and things began to happen very quickly. We did not expect that."[18]

Not all of the restoration efforts on the Loess Plateau were perfectly executed; the initial plantings were not very diverse, which rendered the ecosystem more vulnerable to environmental stressors. And in some areas, newly planted trees failed to thrive or even died. But there were many successes, too. Within ten years, the perennial vegetation cover had doubled. One hundred million tons of sediment were now prevented from eroding into waterways each year. The land began to hold its water again. Within fifteen years, the collaboration had succeeded in rehabilitating more than thirteen thousand square miles of land, an area larger than the country of Belgium.

The before-and-after effect of the restoration site is nothing less than astonishing: it's a dun-colored moon on one side and a lush green patchwork of grasslands and forested mountains on the other. John Liu was so moved by the transformation that he resolved to devote his life to large-scale land restoration. In the years that followed, he was recruited by several agencies—the World Bank, the Global Environment Facility, and the British Department for International

Development—to help influence action on ecosystem restoration in Ethiopia and Rwanda.

Famine and war ravaged Ethiopia throughout the 1980s. Hundreds of thousands of people in the East African nation died. Hundreds of thousands of refugees fled. Two hundred thousand children were orphaned. Civil war and government corruption may have catalyzed the famine, but it was soon compounded by catastrophic drought and crop failure. When the rains finally returned to sub-Saharan Africa, they hatched plagues of locusts, and the nightmare took on a shade of the eschaton. As *The New York Times* reported in 1986, "The locusts rise into the air, eclipsing the sun and riding the wind in a mass onslaught on forests, crops and grasslands."[19]

Ethiopia's Tigray region, once home to the ancient empire of Aksum, was one of those hardest hit. The village of Abraha Atsbeha, about forty miles north of Tigray's capital city of Mekelle, was decimated by drought and famine. Many locals died or were forced to flee, and life was a struggle for those who remained. In a 2013 interview, the village chief Ato Gebremichael Gidey Berhe remembered, "We lived in extreme poverty. Rainfall had totally eroded the degraded soils, and sand was all that was left. We couldn't harvest anything anymore and all the people of Abraha Atsbeha village were dependent on food aid, including myself. The situation was shocking and we were ashamed."[20]

In 1998, there came a choice. The Ethiopian government told the remaining villagers that they could elect either to relocate, or to stay and attempt to rehabilitate their land with assistance from the government, local scientists, and international nongovernmental organizations. They chose to stay.

"The first step was to close the area to livestock and humans," Ato Gebremichael remembered. "The second step was to build terraces. We managed to save our soil from erosion and to capture water in an underground water reservoir for irrigation."[21]

John Liu's documentary *Green Gold* features a visit to the village. In just six years, the once-withered earth that "blew as dust" had been restored to rich, dark soil. A forest had returned, a natural spring and stream had returned, and the water table had risen from fifteen to three meters deep.

"The land has become fertile again," Ato Gebremichael tells Liu. "Our fruit trees were shriveled up, now they're growing again . . . Wild animals that had disappeared have returned, even the leopard." And locals forced to flee in the 1980s and '90s were returning, too. Restoration was the path back home.

In a talk given at the 2019 Global Earth Repair conference, Liu thanked the residents of Abraha Atsbeha and those who took part in similar projects in Rwanda. "We have now a great deal of data," he said. "We've seen that it's possible to rehydrate dehydrated biomes, and that it's possible to revegetate areas that have been massively degraded over historical time."[22]

In Jordan, Princess Basma bint Ali and her collaborators began with even fewer initial interventions. They simply fenced off the restoration site from grazing for the first three years. "It allowed the land to breathe, to take a breath," she told

Liu. "We didn't interfere, we didn't do any planting at the time, just to see how it reacts."

Incredibly, species of plants last recorded in the 1800s and long thought to be extinct, had come up out of the earth of their own accord. They'd been waiting, dormant, for the right conditions to rise.

When land is continually grazed, there's no filter between the sun and soil. "Just by making a fence around this place, you'll get back grasses. That's what's so extraordinary," says Liu. The grasses block and filter the UV rays, giving microbial life a chance to return. "You'll have perennial root systems, and they all spread out and you'll have microbial communities living and growing in this microclimate that's created."

Soil restoration is not only important for plant life but also protects us from climate change. Whereas living soils store carbon—up to three times the amount of carbon as aboveground vegetation—degraded soils release it. Twelve thousand years of agriculture and cattle farming have caused the topsoil to release an estimated 133 billion tons of carbon.[23]

The current rate of soil degradation threatens a global famine. In 2019, the UN Convention to Combat Desertification warned that an estimated twenty-four billion tons of fertile land are lost each year globally.[24] According to its Global Land Outlook, "A significant proportion of managed and natural ecosystems are degrading: over the last two decades, approximately 20 per cent of the Earth's vegetated surface shows persistent declining trends in productivity, mainly as a result of land/water use and management practices."[25]

As soil degradation continues to reduce agricultural

productivity, human populations and food demand acceler-
ate. In 2012, the theoretical biologist and soil scientist Dr.
John Crawford estimated that a "business as usual scenario"
would result in a 30 percent loss in food production over the
next fifty years. "This is against a background of projected
demand," he said, "requiring us to grow 50% more food, as
the population grows."[26]

No national border could possibly hold back the tide of
human suffering that would follow such a famine.

If overgrazing and clear-cutting our sacred forests has
brought floods, droughts, and fire upon us, maybe affor-
estation could reverse those loops, sinking water and calling
back the rains. This has already been happening in the Loess
Plateau. In 2019, John Liu returned there with Ties van der
Hoeven and had this to report:

> We drove many hours through thick, diverse forests that
> cover what 25 years ago was bare earth. We sat outside of
> our cave hotel in Yan'an when a huge rainfall event drove
> us back indoors. We were forced to consider what it meant
> when you watched barrels of rain come down in an area
> that had been thought by most people to be a desert only
> 20 years before. To see that this water was absorbed into
> the biomass and into the intact soils and that these were
> the methods that had reversed traditional desertification
> was clearly apparent.[27]

Unlike some drivers of climate change, soil degradation
is not a matter beyond our control. Certainly, we should

boycott and pressure the mad kings of the oil and gas industry, but I personally find the prospect of sowing life where there was death more inspiring than resisting death's fervent merchants. And though I don't view it as a binary proposition—it's obvious that we have to work on all available fronts—restoring degraded land may present fewer barriers, and in the case of "climate crucibles," doing so may be just as crucial to our survival. I don't pretend to know whether or not greening the Sinai is feasible. But I have read about the transformation of the Loess Plateau in China, and Abraha Atsbeha in Ethiopia, and the initial gains made by the Ecosystem Restoration Camps—ideas that were once criticized as harebrained or doubtful but that have come to fruition because someone dared to imagine them possible.

If paradise is ecological abundance—the basis of life itself—why do we spend our days constructing Gehenna? What was it that drove the project of Western civilization to begin with? These two questions are probably unanswerable. But it seems to me there is a chilling resonance between the traumatized person's approach to negotiating perceived threats and our civilization's approach to the land: chaos or rigidity, two poles, each untenable, between which a threatened person swings.

At times, I have felt so overwhelmed by the existential chaos we face that I've been soothed to imagine: *Maybe this is just the way things were always going to be. Maybe twelve thousand years ago, events were set into motion over which a single human has no realistic control. What agency has a single locust in a swarm?* Isolation and emotional overwhelm can lead to profoundly antisocial sentiments. I forgive myself the fantasy, but I will not indulge the part of me that would like to use it as an excuse to crack foamers and watch TV all day.

We see chaos in the overwhelmed individual manifest itself as addiction and disengagement. We see it in the culture, in rapacious consumption, in the abandonment of damaged lands, in the annexing of so-called wilderness. We see the rigidity of domination and control in the clear-cut, the factory farm, the miles of nuked soils and monocrops. Meanwhile, between these extremes lies a vast interrelated world.

Here's how James Hollis describes the formation of certain neuroses that I don't mind extending to the character of our civilization itself:

> When the environment floods its boundaries, the child learns, irrevocably, its own powerlessness. In service to survival, the adaptive capacity of the child adopts attitudes and behaviors designed to promote survival and enhance the possibility of need gratification. Such a child may organize this provisional identity around the task of gaining power greater than that possessed by the environment.[28]

Enter Gilgamesh.

Maybe a natural disaster—some original trauma—led the progenitors of empire to feel that the environment had flooded their boundaries, that the ur-mother had become unresponsive, withholding. Maybe they bucked against their dependence in a "childlike rage" and turned away. We'll never know. All I know is, the antidote for an "inner, alienated core" is relationship, and the answer to exile is finding a home.

✤✤✤

I was out for a walk not long ago, turning these ideas over in my mind, when I came across a hedge covered in delicate white flowers, their stamens heavy with pollen. As I leaned in closer to smell them, I realized the hedge was filled with bees, hundreds of them, drunkenly wallowing in the flutes of those flowers.

This bee bacchanal called to mind a phrase the permaculture people sometimes say: "Everyone gardens." Squirrels garden when they bury acorns, and bears garden when they shit out seeds, and these bees, in all their pleasure and drunkenness, were gardening, too. The gardening impulse was not an appeal to better angels; it was built into all living beings. Just as paradise is not a spectral kingdom reserved for the "good," but rather creation's birthright on earth. Here were the blossoming roots of "Eden." One root extends from the Aramaic: "fruitful" and "well-watered." The Hebrew grows from "pleasure."

In Paradise, California, human gardeners have been central to the recovery. The first meeting of the Camp Fire Restoration Project convened in the "burn scar" in the spring of 2019. Survivors had been feeling hopeless; many of them had lost their homes and livelihoods in the fire and were uncertain as to whether they ever could, or would want to, return. Butte County officials had held a public meeting that February to kick off their updated Hazard Mitigation Plan, which included interventions like improving mass warning systems and secondary evacuation routes. But their plan to "reduce disaster losses" was predicated on the belief that floods, drought, wildfires, and other natural hazards "cannot be prevented."[29] And while those hazards may be inevitable in the strictest sense, Matthew Trumm and John Liu know that human intervention on the land can prevent catastrophic wildfire and massively reduce the negative effects of lower-intensity fires, droughts, and flooding.

"Ours was the first meeting that was looking at positive solutions," Trumm told me, "which we learned later is a huge part of trauma therapy, to have solution-based action that people can engage in."

Hundreds of locals, exiled from their homes and lives by the fire, would be trained in the skills of damage remediation, erosion control, and fire-safe green building. They'd build swales (shallow contoured areas) to hold water in the ground and combat drought; they'd plant stands of bamboo and restore meadows to act as natural firebreaks. It was a chance to fundamentally reimagine how they lived and how to prevent future disasters.

Trumm views their situation as a kind of crossroads: Now that they've felt the full catastrophic effects of climate change, will they continue on living as they always have, or will they shift course? What new lives will they build in response to the new reality? How, then, shall they live?

The Camp Fire Restoration Project became the first Ecosystem Restoration Camp in the United States. Because the destruction in Paradise was so shocking, many people outside the town, and even outside the state, were moved to donate to their efforts. In one year, with less than thirty thousand dollars, they were able to distribute thousands of straw bales and wattles and hundreds of yards of wood chips to stabilize damaged soil, prevent erosion, and support the return of native plants.

Unlike some of the other Ecosystem Restoration Camps, which have convened on private property, the recovery of the Paradise burn scar would focus on public places. Matthew Trumm told me that the problem with restoring private property (ditto wildland restoration) is that "people can't see it." People need to see the recovery unfold if they're going "to appreciate ecological function." The recovery, he emphasized, "should benefit everyone in the community."

The first ten-day camp was devoted to restoring the grounds of one of the only surviving schools in the area. That school was their first priority because children who'd escaped the fire months before now had to travel through the post-apocalyptic ruin of their former lives to get there each day. Trumm and the volunteers built swales, planted a vegetable garden and a small food forest, built benches and a shed, and rebuilt accessibility ramps and handrails. The school is now a bright spot in the rubble thanks to their efforts, even if the journey there remains bleak.

More than two hundred volunteers showed up to the next ten-day camp, working to restore ten different locations in the area. In the future, they hope to enlist experts to train residents in using biochar and bioremediation to mitigate pollutants—chemicals, plastics, and other toxic materials that seeped into the groundwater during the fire. "Mycoremediation," for example, involves using fungi to absorb and remove heavy metals, benzene, and other toxins from the earth.

Human beings are capable of causing enormous damage, but we're also uniquely equipped to undo the damage we've caused. As Matthew Trumm has said, while singing the gospel of composting: "Nature takes 500 to 1000 years to create one inch of topsoil. I've done two feet in three years."[30] There's no question that the earth will continue to transform and go on, with or without us, and with or without our help, but we could greatly speed its recovery.

This is why the Camp Fire Restoration Project includes mental health counselors at every camp. Equal emphasis is placed on human recovery based on the premise that if humans don't recover, they'll only keep remaking the disaster. "The biggest restoration," Trumm told me, "needs to happen in our minds."

Restoration was the method by which Sebastião Salgado's life was eventually saved.

"When we inherited this piece of land," he told a reporter in 2019, "it was as wounded, as dead, as I was."[31]

In 1998, Lélia proposed that they "rebuild paradise," that they try to replant the barren farm and make it a rain forest again. They didn't really know what they were doing at first, but they were able to solicit help from an expert forestry engineer named Renato de Jesus, who designed their restoration blueprint. The first plants were donated by a local nature reserve, and the first planting was done by student volunteers. Donations began to come in from a variety of sources, including the Brazilian Biodiversity Fund, a cosmetics firm called Natura, and the Lannan Foundation. Their first nursery was donated by a local conservation nonprofit, and within a few years they were sprouting hundreds of thousands of native seeds.

In the early days, Sebastião Salgado had nightmares that everything was dying because the soil was so poor—and in fact the farm lost 60 percent in the first planting and 40 percent in the second. But slowly, things began to take root. Twenty years later, a young diverse forest spanning 1,754 acres had grown up from the dust. As in the Loess Plateau, the visual transformation was astounding. Natural springs and a waterfall had returned to the land, as had 15 species of reptiles, 15 species of amphibians, 172 species of birds, and 33 species of mammals—some of which are endangered.

The farm has been declared a Natural Heritage Reserve, and the Salgados' foundation, Instituto Terra, trains students of ecology in restoration and supports local farmers who wish to repair erosion and replant their lands. Millions of native seedlings have since been raised in their nursery, and they've helped to rehabilitate an estimated seventeen thousand acres of degraded land in the region.

"The land was as sick as I was," Salgado said, "then all the insects and birds and fish returned and, thanks to this increase of the trees I, too, was reborn."[32]

When we were kids, my friends and I went looking for a unified and stable theory of *how to live*—propping up idols and knocking them off their pedestals. As if such a theory, if it existed at all, would be unified or stable when the law of life itself is diversity and fluctuation. The people we idolized succeeded in articulating a set of difficult problems, problems that were invisible to most, and in such a way that most could understand them. But it was the very nature of those problems that both made them possible to articulate (the homogeneity of an expansionist system) and impossible to solve—at least by a single important person. There is no *solution* to the problems we face, but there are *solutions*: multifarious, collaborative, egalitarian, localized. For every so-called end of the world, a thousand smaller worlds must be born.

How, then, shall we live? The question is impossible only because—as the people in these pages have helped me to understand—it was never meant to be answered. Death was always standing at the threshold; the question was always an invitation to face it. Meaning in death comes down to legacy: What manner of persons ought we to be, knowing we will die? Will we sacrifice the world in vain pursuit of immortality? Or will we give life to that which has sustained us, work to restore a paradise we may not live to see?

The threats we face are overwhelming, paralyzing even, but a watershed, an ecosystem—these are limits where life can flourish. We sow life where there was death, and a garden grows within; we perform the resurrection, and we, too, are reborn. To form a covenant with an ecosystem, to restore the life within that limit—this is a manageable path for believers and skeptics alike, with potential benefits that exceed the local ambit. The problem of other people, of how to live together, poses a greater challenge, but the basic approach is the same. You wouldn't have to be perfect to live into that story, or even especially good, as long as you listened to what the world was telling you and responded to its calls. As long as you kept showing up.

The weight of the world is love. My friend Aisha has this sentence tattooed on her thigh; it's the first line of her favorite poem by Allen Ginsberg. I recall a couple of drunken, melancholic dawns in our early twenties when she recited this poem, inspiring rapt silence in the afterparty. So perfectly had the poet described a core and previously ineffable yearning—an absence, she said, to which her heart was soldered—that she'd had it permanently committed to her flesh. This struck me as an apt gesture, since poetry is a form of music, a bridge between the body and speech. The poem's title, after all, is "Song."

Lately, I keep thinking about this poem and the absence it weeps into. About the pain of disconnection, the yearning for connection, the yearning that prompts us to reach for one another in spite of the risks because:

> Under the burden
> of solitude,
> under the burden
> of dissatisfaction,
>
> the weight,
> the weight we carry
> is love.

These ruderal visions are as close as I come to faith: the dandelion pushing through the crack in the asphalt, the long-dormant seeds waking from their desert sleep, the potatoes reaching out from their bins toward such minor light, how my own warped structure shapes the life that comes through me in particular ways. Life keeps reaching, "in all the excellence / of its excess."

In my own life, I know I'd be dead were it not for the interventions of other people: an interested teacher, the nurture of my friends, the nurture of the land and its many presences, writers I'd never meet but whose words would guide me through. Often these interventions were small and basic and not always perfectly executed, but they added up, and they held the world together long enough for me to *become*. I believe we have that to give to one another, and to the place we live. And what we have to give is also the weight that we carry.

Returning to the earth and to one another will require more from us than a conceptual shift; it will require embodied practice. It will mean powering down the intermediaries that train us to regard ourselves and others as two-dimensional outputs of content—and return to the three-dimensional world, to imperfect exchange, to call-and-response, to lived relationships with water and plants and soil. This will sometimes mean being ugly, inconsistent, vulnerable, anxious, clumsy, fucking it up. It will mean fighting and reconciling and reaching across the divide of mutual misapprehension to try again.

Call it love, or life, or the spirit of goodness, or the total directional process. Whatever it is that animates this world does not care that we are broken, soldered to longing, sad, addicted, confused, "crazy"—it wants only to reach through us into the world. Future generations do not depend on our perfection or guilt or fear of failure; they depend on our love. A love that recognizes the other for who they are rather than what we wish them to be. A love that sits at the dying person's bedside. The kind of love that labors with a cane through the heat to midwife a meadow; that crawls through exhaustion to find the shine on a stone, the tangle of hair in the leaf litter; that pursues a living bread, on hands and knees, though it sometimes "hurts to do."

This love is not fixed but evolving. It is not prescriptive but responsive. It's not right or wrong, us or them, but is born from the space between: pupils dilating in sympathy, skin flushing against skin, the mirroring of neurons, the tremor of song in a cochlea. It is fingers in dirt, hair streaming in water, breath entering lungs. It does not castigate and disown; it reincorporates, rehabilitates, accommodates dissonance, guides the excluded back into the fold. It's the Maglite sweeping the dark wood and the voice calling, *Come home.*

AFTERWORD

At the end of *Ishmael*, the human narrator has a premonition and returns to the fairgrounds where his gorilla mentor has been imprisoned, only to find his cage is empty. An elderly carny breaks the bad news: "It was the pneumonia that got him—your friend the ape."

It's probably difficult to believe, but I, too, had a premonition. Walking the dog one morning with my husband, I said, "Something is going to happen. I don't know what."

Later that day, Daniel Quinn's wife, Rennie, posted to Facebook that she'd moved Daniel to hospice. As with his avatar, it was the pneumonia that got him.

"It's here, in a large room with a high ceiling and a wall of windows overlooking trees and a lush green courtyard, that Daniel is entering the 'fire of life,'" Rennie wrote.

He died the next day.

Hundreds of comments poured in from all over the world, most on the order of "*Ishmael* profoundly changed my life" and "You have changed the way I see, sir."

———

That summer, I was living in the desert, where temperatures broke records day after day—118, 121 degrees. I stayed indoors and read and made do with the food on hand. The house came to feel like a biosphere experiment: *How long could she resist taking out the trash?*

One evening, during an "extreme heat warning," I found a fledgling bird on the front step. At first glance he appeared to be dead, but when I bent closer I could see his sleepy little eyes were blinking. I used a towel to transfer him from the hot pavement to a shoebox, sprinkled cold water on his downy head, and left the box outside. He didn't move but to breathe. All that night, I feared the bubble of the house would malfunction and I'd be cooked inside my skin in my sleep without the slightest resistance, like a slowly boiling frog. I was a creature of absolute dependence—on air-conditioning, on water from a dammed and warming river—and I'd done unto myself as I'd done unto the world.

When I checked the next morning, the fledgling was gone, carried off on his own power, or else in someone else's jaws. I didn't know which, but I took it as a sign to get moving.

I write to you now from my home in Seattle, in the midst of a global pandemic, nine months pregnant and eighty days into isolation. Outside my front window, people pass in masks and the cherry trees that line our street are heavy with extravagant masses of white and pink blossoms, as if it were all the world's wedding day. Much will be written about this time—and on the subject of disaster I think I've said more than my fair share—but I will add that the need for social distancing seems a special perversity. To survive this particular plague, we must fight our best human impulse: to pull close together in a crisis. This has been especially painful for those who've lost loved ones; we cannot touch the dead or hold one another in our grief.

On April 2, 2020, Finisia Medrano posted a video to Facebook of a chipmunk eating acorns: "Had a bad heart attack three days ago in my favorite desert, healing now. Meet my doctor." She'd been planting with a couple of friends in southern Nevada, a home she'd always hoped to return to.

The next day, she posted again, this time a photo of a dead deer: "This painful dying just keeps coming in waves."

In the comment thread a friend asked if she was okay.

"No," she replied, matter-of-factly. "I am dying."

One friend urged her to see a medical doctor, another suggested she eat "cayenne powder" as it "cleans up arteries and the heart."

She told them that she'd only puke the cayenne and that "dying is already painful and miserable enough." As for the prospect of a medical doctor: "I won't see them at the Covid dispensary."

Then she stopped replying.

Finisia was the toughest person I'd ever met, and it struck me as implausible that she would just lie down in the desert and die for fear of catching COVID-19. Surely she was fucking with us. But then I typed her name into the Facebook search bar and pulled up a half-dozen posts written that day in memoriam. A little while later, Peter called, tearful. He'd spoken to Jesse and it was true.

Of course, upon further reflection, I realized it would have been far more implausible for Finisia to die in a hospital. She'd lived her own life, emphatically, and in the end, she'd died her own death. It would never have gone any other way.

Permit me a brief digression on the subject of heroes: in my experience, the more strident the claim to virtue, to totalizing solutions—the denser the shadow self, and the greater the likelihood of its sudden eruption on the surface. All heroes disappoint eventually. All are proven hypocrites. And yet, when evidence of inconsistency, vanity, dishonesty, ignorance, selfishness, lust—any of the usual human defects—is located in an admired leader, the backlash can be intense. In some cases, homicidal. This leads me to believe we're asking more of our heroes than we're willing to admit; it means we are asking them to bear parts of our own psychic life, to be impervious to our own disavowed desires and flaws.

Pretty much the instant *Ishmael* was published, readers began pressing Daniel Quinn for instruction. Sometimes they asked with determination, anger, or desperation, but the question was always the same: "What do we *do*?"

In other words, it's not enough to articulate the problem; you must also solve it, then lead people by the hand through your solution, while they pick it apart, flaw by flaw. He'd tried to answer them over the years, but neither he nor they were very satisfied with the result. *Now what?* The question would not leave him be.

Finisia had an answer to the question, but not everyone liked to hear it.

"The name of your hatred is fear," she told me the last time we spoke. Just by living the way she did, she said, "traveling through your world in the opposite direction, giving life to what you'd kill," it caused some people to become enraged. "They'll see what's happening, what their choices are, and they'll be mad at me, like I made those choices for them."

The cycle of worshipping idols, investing them with our disowned energies, becoming disillusioned, then lunging for the pedestal we placed them on—it's a dead end, numbing in its repetition but not inevitable.

In the days following Finisia's death, her friends and self-proclaimed "frenemies" began posting remembrances to Facebook. A handful of these remembrances trafficked, untempered, in the Finisia Medrano myth. But I was struck by the number of people who posted conflicted accounts of their relationships with her. Ways I'd not heard people describe her in life, at least not publicly.

"In no way am I attempting to place Finisia upon a pedestal," one of her friends wrote. "She well understood that was only a prelude to being knocked off and brought down low . . . Her shadows were dark and deep and I know that she was not always kind or gentle in her walk in this life. Do you hate the wave that crashes down to wash away your home, built too close to wild waters?"

"I always saw her as a force of nature like a tornado or wildfire," Peter wrote. "You can learn a lot from them, and they can be revitalizing through their disturbance. Just like the land-tending practices she espoused. It's too complex to wager one personality of hers over the other . . . She was both horrible and amazing in many different ways."

"Fin, honestly, fuck you for the ways you abused people," wrote another mourner. "I say this because not saying it dishonors the full reality of you as I see it. And thank you. For giving me eyes to see. For breaking me so I could live with an open heart. So I could try and fail and try again to live a life of reciprocity."

We are taught not to speak ill of the dead, but here was condemnation, beauty, betrayal, and gratitude—all together, resembling life. The mythic figure can only ever be partly human, and so is held at a remove. But allowing character defects to enter the story, telling the truth about those we love, brings them closer.

Reading these accounts, I couldn't help feeling that finally, in dying, Finisia had received the intimacy she craved.

When we relinquish our saviors, we invite a reckoning with ourselves and, consequently, a good deal of discomfort. Confrontation with the realities we'd outsource to an authority, the realities of our own wills and deeds, talents and failures; our selfless virtue and selfish posturing, the goodness of our professed values and the banal evil we daily do unto the world—it is a confrontation that can leave a person feeling powerless. To view oneself clearly through the distorting prism of the psyche takes extraordinary effort, whereas an idol can be shined or smashed in an instant, by anyone with hands.

Now what? One of the many lessons of our moment—whether through pandemic, ecological collapse, or climate-related catastrophe—is that it's time we stop investing our hope and disappointment in saviors and charismatic leaders, in prime ministers and presidents, and start investing in our neighbors and watersheds.

The Weather Makers are right when they tell us that our concern should extend beyond our own backyards. But I don't think a backyard (or a vacant lot, as the case may be) is a bad place to start, to cultivate a direct relationship with "ecological function," to begin stoking what Daniel Quinn called "the fire of life." The poet Rumi instructed, nearly eight hundred years ago: "Let the beauty we love be what we do. / There are hundreds of ways to kneel and kiss the ground." That's about as prescriptive as I care to get.

Of the fire that burns inside every living thing, Daniel Quinn once wrote: "To each is given its moment in the blaze, its spark to be surrendered to another when it is sent." It's my hope that the stories in this book throw a few small sparks. Long live the blaze.

NOTES

INTRODUCTION

1. Peter Sinclair, "Polar Melting: 'Methane Time Bomb' Isn't Actually a 'Bomb,'" *Yale Climate Connections*, January 29, 2019, www.yaleclimateconnections.org/2019/01/methane-time-bomb-isnt-actually-a-bomb/.
2. "Nature's Dangerous Decline 'Unprecedented,' Species Extinction Rates 'Accelerating,'" Intergovernmental Science-Policy Platform on Biodiversity and Ecosystem Services (IPBES), May 2019.
3. Kevin Loria, "CO2 Levels Are at Their Highest in 800,000 Years," World Economic Forum, May 2018, www.weforum.org/agenda/2018/05/earth-just-hit-a-terrifying-milestone-for-the-first-time-in-more-than-800-000-years.
4. Susan Clayton, Christie Manning, Kirra Krygsman, and Meighan Speiser, *Mental Health and Our Changing Climate: Impacts, Implications, and Guidance* (Washington, D.C.: American Psychological Association, and ecoAmerica, 2017), 27.
5. Eduardo S. Brondízio et al., *Global Assessment Report on Biodiversity and Ecosystem Services* (Bonn, Germany: Intergovernmental Science-Policy Platform on Biodiversity and Ecosystem Services, 2019).

1. ACROSS THE DESERT OUR BREAD IS BLOOMING!

1. Finisia Medrano, *Growing Up in Occupied America*, ed. Seda Joseph Saine (self-published, 2010), 19.
2. Ibid., 147.
3. Edna Rey-Vizgirdas, "Nineleaf Biscuitroot," U.S. Forest Service, www.fs.fed.us/wildflowers/plant-of-the-week/lomatium_triternatum.shtml.

4. Franz Boas, *Kwakiutl Ethnography* (Chicago: University of Chicago Press, 1966).

5. Nancy Chapman Turner and Marcus A. M. Bell, "The Ethnobotany of the Southern Kwakiutl Indians of British Columbia," *Economic Botany* 27 (1973): 257–310.

6. Brian Meilleur, Eugene Hunn, and Rachel Cox, "Lomatium dissectum (Apiaceae): multi-purpose plant of the Pacific Northwest," *Journal of Ethnobiology* 10, no. 1 (1990): 1–20.

7. *The Propaganda for Reform in Proprietary Medicines*, vol. 2 (Chicago: American Medical Association, 1922).

8. Douglas Duer and Nancy J. Turner, *Keeping It Living: Traditions of Plant Use and Cultivation on the Northwest Coast of North America* (Seattle: University of Washington Press, 2005), 112–17.

9. M. Kat Anderson, *Tending the Wild: Native American Knowledge and the Management of California's Natural Resources* (Berkeley: University of California Press, 2005), 300.

10. Alexander Irvine, ed., *The Phytologist: A Botanical Journal*, vol. 4 (London: William Pamplin, 1860), 18.

11. Edward Lee Greene, *Landmarks of Botanical History: A Study of Certain Epochs in the Development of the Science of Botany*, Part 1: *Prior to 1562 A.D.* (Washington, D.C.: Smithsonian Institution, 1909), 51.

12. David G. Lewis, "People of the Mammoth Steaks and Giant Sloth Flanks," *NDNHistory Research*, January 25, 2016, www .ndnhistoryresearch.com/2016/01/25/people-of-the-mammoth -steaks-and-giant-sloth-flanks.

13. Douglas Deur, *Pacific Northwest Foraging* (Portland, Ore.: Timber Press, 2014), 66–68.

14. Meriwether Lewis, June 11, 1806, *Journals of the Lewis and Clark Expedition*, University of Nebraska–Lincoln, Center for Digital Research in the Humanities, www.lewisandclarkjournals .unl.edu.

15. Ibid., May 9, 1806.

16. John McAllister Schofield, *Forty-Six Years in the Army* (New York: Century, 1897), 428.

17. Tanya Eiserer, "Wagonmaster 'Pulling for Christ,'" *Abilene Reporter-News*, December 5, 1997.

18. Christy Lattin, "Nomadic Woman Passes Through Fallon in Horse-Drawn Wagons," *Nevada Appeal*, November 28, 2007.

2. ON THE RISE AND FALL OF A TEENAGE IDEALIST

1. Phil Busse, "Crime Scene: Out on a Ledge," *Portland Mercury*, July 20, 2000, www.portlandmercury.com/news/crime-scene /Content?oid=22485.

2. Leslie James Pickering, *The Earth Liberation Front: 1997–2002* (Portland, Ore.: Arissa Media Group, 2007), 30.

3. Rebecca Taylor, "Arsonist's Sentence Cut in Half," *Eugene Register-Guard*, February 29, 2008.

4. Will Potter, *Green Is the New Red: An Insider's Account of a Social Movement Under Siege* (San Francisco: City Lights, 2011), 69.

5. "Eco-terrorism Specifically Examining the Earth Liberation Front and the Animal Liberation Front," U.S. Senate Committee on Environment and Public Works, May 18, 2005, www .govinfo.gov/content/pkg/CHRG-109shrg32209/html/CHRG -109shrg32209.htm.

6. Ibid.

7. Vanessa Grigoriadis, "The Rise and Fall of the Eco-Radical Underground," *Rolling Stone*, August 10, 2006, 75.

3. PROMISED LANDS

1. Hakim Bey, *T.A.Z.: The Temporary Autonomous Zone, Ontological Anarchy, Poetic Terrorism* (Brooklyn, NY: Autonomedia, 2003).

2. I first wrote about the "opening map" for a collaboration with the photographer Bobby Abrahamson, which culminated in an exhibition and limited-run gallery book called *The West Behind Us* (self-published, 2014).

3. Peter Bauer, *Rewild or Die* (self-published, 2016).

4. Daniel Quinn, "Have You Heard of the Great Forgetting? It Happened 10,000 Years Ago & Completely Affects Your Life," October 5, 2013, www.filmsforaction.org/articles/the-great-forgetting.

5. "Islamic Declaration on Global Climate Change," 2015, IFEES/ EcoIslam, www.ifees.org.uk/wp-content/uploads/2020/01/climate _declarationmmwb.pdf.

6. Rabbi Elliot Dorff et al., "A Rabbinic Letter on the Climate Crisis," The Shalom Center, 2015, www.theshalomcenter.org /RabbinicLetterClimate.

7. David Benkof, "Liberal Orthodoxy, Not Jewish Orthodoxy: 'Repairing the World' Isn't in the Torah," *Daily Caller*, December

10, 2014, www.dailycaller.com/2014/12/10/liberal-orthodoxy-not-jewish-orthodoxy-repairing-the-world-isnt-in-the-torah.

8. Rabbi Nicole Roberts, "Plain as Day: Our Bible's Call for Social Justice," sermon delivered to the North Shore Temple Emanuel, Sydney, Australia, July 20, 2018.

9. "What Is the Watershed Way?," Taos Initiative for Life Together (TiLT), www.taostilt.org/thewatershedway-taos.

10. Ched Myers, ed., *Watershed Discipleship: Reinhabiting Bioregional Faith and Practice* (Eugene, Ore.: Cascade Books, 2016), 5.

11. "Some 'Marks' of the Watershed Way," Taos Initiative for Life Together (TiLT), www.taostilt.org/thewatershedway-taos.

12. Robin Wall Kimmerer, "Speaking of Nature," *Orion Magazine*, March/April 2017.

13. Nathan Joel Ehrenkranz and Deborah A. Sampson, "Origin of the Old Testament Plagues: Explications and Implications," *Yale Journal of Biology and Medicine* 81, no. 1 (April 2008): 31–42.

14. Exodus 16:2–3, as paraphrased by Ched Myers, *Who Will Roll Away the Stone? Discipleship Queries for First World Christians* (Maryknoll, N.Y.: Orbis, 1994).

15. Exodus 15:26, New International Version.

16. Rabbi Jeremy Schwartz, "Tikkun Olam, Unpacked," Reconstructing Judaism, December 1, 2016, www.reconstructingjudaism.org/article/tikkun-olam-unpacked.

17. Naomi Dann, "Expelled from the Promised Land: Exploring Exodus and Zionism," *Huffington Post*, April 9, 2015, www.huffpost.com/entry/expelled-from-the-promised-land-exploring-exodus-and-zionism_b_7029866.

18. An enlightening account of the Pueblo Revolt period can be read in a dissertation by the archeologist Joseph R. Aguilar: "Asserting Sovereignty: An Indigenous Archaeology of the Pueblo Revolt Period at Tunyo, San Ildefonso Pueblo, New Mexico" (PhD diss., University of Pennsylvania, 2019), www.repository.upenn.edu/edissertations/3465.

19. Meriwether Lewis, July 24, 1805, *Journals of the Lewis and Clark Expedition*, University of Nebraska–Lincoln, Center for Digital Research in the Humanities, www.lewisandclarkjournals.unl.edu.

20. Romans 7:19–25, New International Version.

4. NOTES ON A LIVING TRAIL

1. I later learned that the American College of Forensic Examiners no longer exists. After years of bad press, including an undercover exposé by ProPublica, the college's founder shot his girlfriend to death and then himself. See Radley Balko, "The Emperor of Junk Science Has Died," *Washington Post*, August 31, 2017.

2. Mark Withrow, "America's Most Wanted: Staying on Track and Learning from the Best," *Forensic Examiner* 17, no. 1 (2008): 56.

3. Louis Liebenberg, *The Art of Tracking: The Origin of Science* (Cape Town, South Africa: David Philip Publishers, 1990), v.

4. Dictionary.com, s.v. "anthropomorphism," www.dictionary.com/browse/anthropomorphism.

5. Jack Schafer, *The Like Switch: An Ex-FBI Agent's Guide to Influencing, Attracting, and Winning People Over* (New York: Atria Books, 2015), 4.

5. THE PROBLEM OF OTHER PEOPLE

1. Katherine Sharpe, "Survival of the Grittiest," *ReadyMade Magazine*, August/September 2007, 50–51.

2. Laura Parisi, "We're All Gonna Die Anyway," *Willamette Week*, January 24, 2006.

3. Mike Klepfer, "Rewilding and Surviving," *Southeast Examiner*, May 2012.

4. Sharpe, "Survival of the Grittiest."

5. What to call the scene? The terminology is always in flux. "Naturalist" is not quite correct. In the 1990s we said "survivalist." "Rewilding" was common for a long time, a term recently co-opted to sell weightlifting programs and supplements. "Ancestral skills" is the term in vogue at the moment.

6. Marjorie Skinner, "Apocalypse Soon," *Portland Mercury*, August 17, 2006.

7. Hippie Scout, letter to the editor, *Portland Mercury*, August 24, 2006.

8. Urban Scout, letter to the editor, *Portland Mercury*, August 31, 2006.

9. David Chapman, "Geeks, MOPs, and Sociopaths in Subculture Evolution," *Meaningness*, May 29, 2015, www.meaningness.com/geeks-mops-sociopaths.

10. Ursula McTaggart, *Guerrillas in the Industrial Jungle: Radicalism's Primitive and Industrial Rhetoric* (Albany: State University Press of New York, 2012).

11. Ibid., 155.

12. Daniel Shapiro, *Negotiating the Nonnegotiable: How to Resolve Your Most Emotionally Charged Conflicts* (New York: Viking, 2016), 23.

13. Ibid., 24–25.

14. R. D. Laing, *The Divided Self* (1960; repr. New York: Random House, 1970), 45.

6. TO LIVE TOGETHER

1. Sister Christian, "My Philadelphia Adventure with Shane Claiborne at the Simple Way," *A Daily Miracle*, August 5, 2013, www.chicagonow.com/daily-miracle/2013/08/philadelphia-adventure-shane-claiborne-the-simple-way/#image/1.

2. Sasha Adkins, "Plastics as Spiritual Crisis," in *Watershed Discipleship: Reinhabiting Bioregional Faith and Practice*, ed. Ched Myers (Eugene, Ore.: Cascade Books, 2016), 163.

3. Valerie Taliman, "Veterans Ask for Forgiveness and Healing in Standing Rock," *Indian Country Today*, December 7, 2016, www.indiancountrytoday.com/archive/veterans-ask-for-forgiveness-and-healing-in-standing-rock-k2fLUonhqEy6D-NjnhlJJw.

4. Paige Blankenbuehler, "Cashing In on Standing Rock," *High Country News*, April, 13, 2018, www.hcn.org/issues/50.6/tribal-affairs-cashing-in-on-standing-rock.

5. Peter Weiss, "Economic and Social Rights Come of Age," *Human Rights Brief* 7, no. 2 (Winter 2000), www.tni.org/es/node/7200.

6. Christalyn Concha, "Death, Life, Hope," talk given at Pecha Kucha Night, Taos Center for the Arts, Taos, N. Mex., January 12, 2017.

7. Elizabeth Bott Spillius, Jane Milton, Penelope Garvey, Cyril Couve, and Deborah Steiner, *The New Dictionary of Kleinian Thought* (Abingdon, U.K.: Routledge, 2011), 63.

8. Michael Feldman, "Splitting and Projective Identification," in *Doubt, Conviction and the Analytic Process: Selected Papers of Michael Feldman*, ed. Betty Joseph (Abingdon, U.K.: Routledge, 2009), 22.

9. Melanie Klein, "Notes on Some Schizoid Mechanisms," paper presented to the British Psycho-Analytical Society, December 4, 1946.

10. Robert A. Johnson, *Owning Your Own Shadow: Understanding the Dark Side of the Psyche* (San Francisco: HarperSanFrancisco, 1991).

7. IN THE GARDEN

1. This story was first reported by Zoe Greenberg for the Rewire Newsgroup, a pro-choice outlet. The assemblywoman later claimed she was partially misquoted, but confirmed that she told supporters about the rain in Texas (as reported by ABCNews7, Chicago).

2. Harry Williams, "Track 8: Harry Williams, Bishop Paiute Tribal Member," *There It Is—Take It!: Owens Valley and the Los Angeles Aqueduct, 1913–2013*, California Humanities audio program, 2013, www.thereitistakeit.org/portfolio-item/track-8.

3. Northern California Historical Records Survey Project, "Inventory of the County Archives of California," no. 27, Mono County (Bridgeport), San Francisco, 1940.

4. *Diario del capitán comandante Fernando de Rivera y Moncada*, ed. Ernest J. Burrus (Madrid, Spain: José Porrúa Turanzas, 1967).

5. R. E. Martin and D. B. Sapsis, "Fires and Agents of Biodiversity: Pyrodiversity Promotes Biodiversity," *Proceedings of the Symposium on Biodiversity of Northwestern California*, Santa Rosa, Calif., 1991.

6. Lauren Sommer, "Forest Service Tries a Different Approach on Whether to Let Fires Burn," *Morning Edition*, National Public Radio, January 5, 2017.

7. M. Kat Anderson, *Tending the Wild: Native American Knowledge and the Management of California's Natural Resources* (Berkeley: University of California Press, 2005).

8. Charles L. Camp and George C. Yount, "The Chronicles of George C. Yount: California Pioneer of 1826," *California Historical Society Quarterly* 2, no. 1 (April 1923): 3–66.

9. Ibid.

10. Ibid.

11. Joshua Paddison and the University of California, "Before 1768: Pre-Columbian California," essay for an exhibition curated by the University of California, 2011.

12. Anderson, *Tending the Wild*.

13. Ron Goode et al., "Summary Report from Tribal and Indigenous Communities Within California," California's Fourth Climate Change Assessment, September 28, 2018.

14. Tao Orion, *Beyond the War on Invasive Species* (White River Junction, Vt.: Chelsea Green, 2015), 87.

15. Ibid., 63.

16. Carl Rogers, *A Way of Being* (New York: Houghton Mifflin, 1980), 43.

17. Ibid., 118.

18. Ibid.

19. Ron W. Goode, "Tribal-Traditional Ecological Knowledge," memo, September 9, 2014, California Water Library, www.cawaterlibrary.net/document/tribal-traditional-ecological-knowledge-and-the-use-of-fire/.

8. RESTORING PARADISE

1. Jon Mooallem, "We Have Fire Everywhere: Escaping California's Deadliest Blaze," *New York Times Magazine*, August 4, 2019.

2. California Air Resources Board.

3. Esperanza Project & Matthew Trumm, "Restoring Paradise: Permaculture Meets Disaster Response," *Esperanza Project*, April 27, 2019, www.esperanzaproject.com/2019/sustainability/natural-building/restoring-paradise-permaculture-meets-disaster-response-2.

4. John D. Liu, "The Holy Grail of Restoration: Mending the Sinai Peninsula," *Kosmos Journal*, 2019, www.kosmosjournal.org/kj_article/the-holy-grail-of-restoration.

5. Ibid.

6. Andrew George, trans., *The Epic of Gilgamesh* (London: Penguin Books, 2016).

7. Robert Pogue Harrison, *Forests: The Shadow of Civilization* (Chicago: University of Chicago Press, 1993), 14.

8. Ingrid Sischy, "Good Intentions," *The New Yorker*, September 9, 1991, 92.

9. Susan Sontag, "Looking at War," *The New Yorker*, December 9, 2002, 94.

10. Millán M. Millán, "Extreme Hydrometeorological Events and Climate Change Predictions in Europe," *Journal of Hydrology* 518, Part B (October 10, 2014): 206–24.

11. Ibid.

12. John D. Liu, "Reversing Desertification—Restoring Massively Degraded Ecosystems," speech at the Global Earth Repair Conference, Fort Worden, Wash., May 3–5 2019, posted on YouTube, www.youtube.com/watch?v=pD-o8unEMh0.

13. From The Weather Makers website, www.theweathermakers.nl /?page_id=874.

14. Liu, "Reversing Desertification—Restoring Massively Degraded Ecosystems."

15. John Forbes, Alexander Tweedie, and John Conolly, eds., *Cyclopædia of Practical Medicine; Comprising Treatises on the Nature and Treatment of Diseases, Materia Medica and Therapeutics, Medical Jurisprudence etc.* (London: Sherwood, Gilbert and Piper, and Baldwin and Cradock, 1833).

16. United States Surgeon-General's Office, *The Medical and Surgical History of the War of the Rebellion (1861–65)* (Washington, D.C.: Government Printing Office, 1870–1888).

17. "Restoring China's Loess Plateau," World Bank, March 15, 2007, www.worldbank.org/en/news/feature/2007/03/15/restoring -chinas-loess-plateau.

18. Richard Blaustein, "Turning Desert to Fertile Farmland on the Loess Plateau," *Re.Think*, April 5, 2018, www.rethink.earth /turning-desert-to-fertile-farmland-on-the-loess-plateau.

19. Sheila Rule, "Drought Easing, Africa Has New Enemy: Locusts," *New York Times*, August 7, 1986.

20. "Ethiopia: Ato Gebremichael Gidey Berhe, Village Chief," Deutsche Gesellschaft für Internationale Zusammenarbeit, www.giz .de/en/worldwide/21906.html.

21. Ibid.

22. John D. Liu, "What If We Would Regreen the Sinai?," Green the Sinai, www.greenthesinai.com/home.

23. Jonathan Sanderman, Tomislav Hengl, and Gregory J. Fiske, "Soil Carbon Debt of 12,000 Years of Human Land Use," *Proceedings of the National Academy of Sciences of the United States of America*, September 5, 2017.

24. Ibid.

25. Ian Johnson, Nigel Dudley, and Sasha Alexander, "Global Land Outlook," United Nations Convention to Combat Desertification, 2017, knowledge.unccd.int/glo/part-one-big-picture.

26. World Economic Forum, "What If the World's Soil Runs Out?," *Time*, December 14, 2012, world.time.com/2012/12/14/what-if -the-worlds-soil-runs-out/.

27. Liu, "Holy Grail of Restoration."

28. James Hollis, *Creating a Life: Finding Your Individual Path* (Toronto, Canada: Inner City Books, 2001).

29. "Butte County Local Hazard Mitigation Plan Update," October 2019, www.buttecounty.net/Portals/19/LHMP/2019/LHMP UpdateExecSummaryTOC.pdf?ver=2019-11-13-121934-960.

30. Matt Fidler, "Permaculture and Restoring Land After the Camp Fire," *After Paradise*, North State Public Radio, March 21, 2019.

31. Thomas Milz, "In Brazil, Photographer Sebastiao Salgado Finds Hope in Reforestation," *Deutsche Welle*, October 20, 2019.

32. John Vidal, "Sebastião Salgado Focuses on Big Picture with Parable of Reforestation in Brazil," *The Guardian*, July 27, 2015.

ACKNOWLEDGMENTS

Being written about is no picnic. All portraits are partial. To those who've allowed me to tell pieces of their stories anyway, who've forgiven my misunderstandings and omissions, I am grateful. Finisia Medrano, Jesse, Kelsey, Michael, Seda, Matt Fitzgerald, Nicholas Tillett, Todd Wynward, Peg Bartlett, Tony, Mike, Tyler, Ched Myers, Elaine Enns, Fernando Moreira, Willem Larsen, Christalyn Concha, Ryno Herrera, the Simple Way community, Ron Goode, Joanna Clines, Matthew Trumm, John D. Liu, Ties van der Hoeven, the Salgados, and those who prefer to go unnamed.

To Peter Bauer: keeper of shared memory and inside jokes, translator of subculture and gripe. Thank you for the hours.

In addition to the above, an eclectic handful of people influenced my thinking during this writing, though not all are quoted directly. I've spent time with some, and corresponded with others; one or two may be surprised to find their names here: Daniel and Rennie Quinn, Patricia Whereat Phillips, M. Kat Anderson, Douglas Deur, Nancy Turner, Ron Goode, Robin Wall Kimmerer, R. D. Laing, Jane Peterson, Carl Rogers, C. G. Jung, Sigmund Freud, Tao Orion, Joy Degruy, David G. Lewis, Melanie Klein, Simone Weil, Daniel Shapiro, Aaron Johnson, and Daniel Siegel.

Thanks to the first editors of some passages: Karolina Waclawiak and Andi Winnette at *The Believer*, Ned Lannamann at the *Portland Mercury*, Katy Henriksen at *The Rumpus*, and Nikil Saval at *n+1*. Thanks to Charles D'Ambrosio, Rabbi Nate DeGroot, Kate Lebo, Alex Madison, Stephen Markley, Ian Miller, and Andy Young for helpful readings and encouragement, and to friends and family for moral support throughout. I'm particularly grateful to my mother, Kim Anderson, for her trust, belief, and many sacrifices on my behalf. Thanks to Artist Trust for much-needed financial support at the eleventh hour.

Many thanks to Stephanie Cabot, my brilliant agent, who cares deeply about our world. And to my editor, Jenna Johnson, who patiently excavated this book from the detritus of several meandering attempts. I am also grateful to Ellen Goodson Coughtrey at the Gernert Company, Lydia Zoells, and the whole team at FSG.

Thanks most of all to Josh, for the radiant attention you gave to every page. This one's for you, and for our Jude, the life that reached through.

INDEX

PERMISSIONS ACKNOWLEDGMENTS

A Note About the Author

Lisa Wells is a nonfiction writer and poet from Portland, Oregon. Her debut collection of poetry, *The Fix*, won the Iowa Poetry Prize. Her poems and essays have been published by *The New York Times*, *Harper's Magazine*, *Granta*, *The Believer*, *n+1*, and other publications. She lives in Seattle and is an editor at *The Volta* and at Letter Machine Editions.